DATE DUE

BRODART, CO.   Cat. No. 23-221-003

Red, White, and Drunk All Over

"MacLean is an exuberant guide to common and uncommon realms of the wine world. I found her enthusiasm not only for her subject, but also for the people who commit their lives to it, impossible to resist and thoroughly enjoyed this book."

—Michael Ruhlman, author of *The Soul of a Chef*, co-author of *The French Laundry Cookbook*

"Natalie MacLean is a voluptuary. Her reactions are deeply physical. But Natalie also has brains. So when she takes you on a journey to meet the most interesting people in the world of wine, be prepared to learn everything there is to know about wine, while gleefully abandoning your inhibitions."

—Louisa Thomas Hargrave, author of *The Vineyard: a memoir*

"Natalie MacLean imparts much knowledge and history of wine without ever preaching to us. Rather, we are drawn into a fascinating historical essay. Woven into the history we are also introduced to the debate-driven world of wine today. The whole package is punctuated with insights that are placed easily within the grasp of people interested in wine at any level. . . . All of this is delivered in a tone that is inviting and that betrays the passion and love that she has for her subject."

—Jamie Kennedy, chef and author of *Jamie Kennedy's Seasons*

"An engaging and very accessible guide to the world of wine."

—Naomi Duguid, co-author of *Mangoes & Curry Leaves* and others

"Natalie MacLean writes about wine with a sensuous obsession. Hopscotching the globe from wine regions to wineries to wine emporiums, interviewing everyone in the realm of wine from winemakers to purveyors to critics, *Red, White, and Drunk All Over* is an eclectic compendium about almost everything relating to wine. Never pedantic, but always erudite and eminently readable—and often laugh-out-loud funny—MacLean's book is a terrific introduction for the beginning wine connoisseur."

—Rex Pickett, author of *Sideways*

Red, White,
and
Drunk
All Over

A Wine-Soaked Journey
from Grape to Glass

Natalie MacLean

DOUBLEDAY CANADA

Doubleday Canada and colophon are trademarks.

Library and Archives Canada Cataloguing in Publication

MacLean, Natalie, 1966–
Red, white, and drunk all over : a wine-soaked journey from grape to
glass / Natalie MacLean.

ISBN-13: 978-0-385-66154-6
ISBN-10: 0-385-66154-1

1. Wine and wine making. 2. MacLean, Natalie, 1966—Travel.
I. Title.

TP548.M33 2006   641.2'2092   C2006-901460

Printed and bound in the USA

Published in Canada by
Doubleday Canada, a division of
Random House of Canada Limited

Visit Random House of Canada Limited's website: www.randomhouse.ca

BVG 10 9 8 7 6

For my mother, Ann, the ground in whose soil I have my roots; my husband, Andrew, the trellis to whom I cling; and my son, Rian, the eternal sunshine in my life.

CONTENTS

The Making of a Wine Lover

I REMEMBER THE night I tasted my first good wine. My future husband, Andrew, and I had just graduated from university and were enjoying our "wealth" relative to our student days. We dined out a lot and our favorite place was a small Italian restaurant around the corner from our apartment in Toronto.

The first time we went there, the owner, a tall, burly man with fierce dark eyes, asked us if we'd like to try the brunello. We thought at first it was a regional dish, but it turned out to be a red wine from central Italy. We were relieved not to have to tackle the wine list: neither of us knew much more about wine than which fluffy animals on the label we liked best.

When the owner opened the bottle tableside, the pop of the cork seemed to pierce something inside me and relieve a little pressure. He poured the brunello, a rich robe of mahogany, into two tumblers with none of the pretentious sniffing and approval ceremony. "*Chimó!*" he said, and bustled off.

As I raised the glass to my lips, I stopped. The aroma of the wine rushed out to meet me, and all the smells that I had ever known fell away. I didn't know how to describe it, but I knew how it made me feel.

I moistened my lips with the wine and drank it slowly, letting it coat my tongue and slide from one side of my mouth to the other. The brunello trickled down my throat and out along a thousand fault lines through my body, dissolving them.

My second glass tasted like a sigh at the end of a long day: a gathering in, and a letting go. I felt the fingers of alcoholic warmth relax the muscles at the back of my jaw and curl under my ears. The wine flushed warmth up into my cheeks, down through my shoulders, and across my thighs. My mind was as calm as a black ocean. The wine gently stirred the silt of memories on the bottom, helping me recall childhood moments of wordless abandon.

Andrew's eyes had softened and we talked with the wonder of unexpected abundance about our lives together, our career goals, our hope for a family. The pasta seemed unnecessary next to this wonderful wine. To paraphrase Robert Frost, our conversation glided on its own melting, as we moved from delight to wisdom. By the time we were on our second bottle, I started to feel so flammable that I wondered if I were violating the building's fire code.

When we finally got up to leave, we realized that the restaurant was empty. We said good-night to the owner and he slapped Andrew on the back as if he were choking on a bread stick. That was the first of many happy evenings there, and we drank that brunello for a year. A pilot light had been ignited inside me; over time it would grow into the flames of full-blown passion.

Today, I joke that I started drinking seriously when I met Andrew. (Andrew is good-natured about this because there's still some upside to having a wine writer for a wife.) However, my earliest experiences with wine should have driven me into the frothy embrace of beer forever. Growing up in Nova Scotia in the 1970s and '80s, I'd be given one undrinkable glass of wine to toast the New Year, and another at Easter—usually from the same box. During the rest of the year, my Scottish family knocked back beer and whisky.

My teen drinking began and ended at the same high school dance, behind the utility shed where all the illicit activities took place: I chugged half a bottle of syrupy sparkling wine. Not only did it taste wretched, but it also made me spend the next day in the vise grip of a searing, sugar-withdrawal headache. After this, there were family celebrations. At a cousin's wedding, I drank their homemade wine: Tanya and Ronny's *True Love Forever Chablis*. I hoped the marriage would age better than the wine.

In the years that have passed since we discovered that brunello, the taste of wine has helped me store many memories. I remember one particular bottle because of the weather. Andrew and I were snug inside a rented cabin as rain battered the roof, dripped down the chimney, and hissed on the fire. Thunder rolled overhead as the windows rattled. The wind whipped across the lake in angry gusts, as if hurling itself at our cabin. The smoky aromas of that Rhône Valley syrah wrapped around my head and filled my body. The storm outside made the calm pleasure of the wine deeper, more sensual. As long as my glass was full, I wanted it to rage for years. Even when I'm drinking alone, my mind will still clink with past toasts, glasses drained, fond farewells. Some wines will always taste like a lost argument or a long embrace. I think many of us have a secret cellar in our minds where we collect our empty bottles filled with memories.

As I developed a taste for wine, I wanted to find words to describe the way it lightened and lifted me. I had long admired the way Colette, Dorothy Parker, and M. F. K. Fisher wrote about food and drink. They fused mind and body with their narratives, and I reread my favorite passages until I was drunk on their prose.

While Andrew and I were still in the bloom of childless romance, we decided to take an evening course: wine appreciation.

Drinking at night was something we could handle after a long day's work, and perhaps I'd even learn how to describe those feelings. That course opened our eyes to the diversity of wine: all the wine-producing countries, the subregions, appellations, quality designations, and the thousands of wineries—some of which are centuries old. There are hundreds of grapes, blends, styles, and winemaking methods to learn about, not to mention the chemistry of aging wine, the art of matching it with food, and the history of its role in civilization. In fact, at first our eyes were wide open in fear—the range of the subject seemed so daunting. How would we ever master even a small part of it?

Our teacher—a jocular fellow with the relaxed air of a successful nightclub owner who still goes onstage just for fun—reassured us. He guided us gently through the material, so that we weren't too intimidated. His frank admission of his own inability to detect certain aromas put us at ease. He even broke out some champagne and potato chips, an inspired combination, to demonstrate that wine isn't just for fancy food and special occasions.

The class was a mixed bunch: the guy who had read the entire *Oxford Companion to Wine* (and who lived for the moment when the instructor asked for the definition of *fermentation*); the quiet fortysomething woman who hoped that there was more to life than chardonnay; the savvy young waiter who wanted to earn bigger tips by selling better wines; and an older couple who planned to buy a vineyard in their retirement.

My favorite part was the wine tasting itself. I kept a hopeful eye on the stash of wine bottles at the front of the room until our teacher opened them. Never had I encountered a subject that so thoroughly engaged both the mind and the senses. I realized that wine is as cerebral as it is sensual. In fact, drinking wine is a full-brain exercise—until it becomes a foggy-brained exercise. Eighty percent of wine's character is in its aroma; and smell is the only one of our senses that connects directly to the brain areas responsible for memory and emotion.

Wine descriptions, however, often have a faint scent of condescension over a robust layer of barnyard by-product. The adjectives seem to be the fruit of overripe imaginations: when I hear *muscular, tight,* or *rakish,* it's hard to tell whether the critic is talking about wine or Brad Pitt. *Legendary concentration* is what I need to figure out my income tax return, and *perfectly integrated* is how I'd describe my son's school. But *opulent* is indeed a legitimate wine descriptor—it often refers to the price.

Most of us in the class were initially at a loss for words until the quiet woman tentatively suggested that one wine reminded her of the Dallas airport. We chuckled; but surprisingly, our teacher was delighted. He explained that we were tasting riesling, which when well-aged tends to have the faint scent of petrol or jet fuel.

Now we were on a roll. Another woman said the chardonnay reminded her of her son's gerbil cage; the oak-aged wine evoked the wood shavings. The young waiter likened a gewürztraminer to his grandmother's Christmas ham. That puzzled us until our instructor asked how the ham was prepared. Turned out, it was made with lots of spices, just like the classic gewürztraminer aromas.

That introductory course was enough for Andrew, but I wanted to learn more. I completed the four-level sommelier certificate, which gave me a basic understanding of the industry. I was learning to love wine not only hedonistically, but also intelligently, as a product of the vine grower's science and the vintner's art. A wine lover would no more order a "glass of wine" in a resturant than a gourmet would request a "plate of food." Most of us want to know what ingredients are in the dish and how it's prepared. Similarly, the differences between wines made from grapes grown in neighboring vineyards are as great as the difference between a rare steak and one that's well done.

Despite this formal training, my real wine education has largely been through the people I've met and the places I've been. Most of the time, I learn something interesting not because I ask an intrepid question, but because I stumble on something accidentally. I'd love to say that I was born with an uncanny palate, but I was just born thirsty.

I was still insecure about wine even after I had finished the course, especially at my first formal wine tasting. As our guide droned on about ripeness units and rainfall levels, I nervously knocked back all the wine in front of me—I needed a couple of stiff ones just to be there. Then I looked around and realized that all the others had only sipped their first wine and they were all busy writing notes. To avoid the disapproving stares, I put my head down and started scribbling too—my grocery list.

I can laugh now, but I'll never forget that heat of embarrassment at still not knowing much about the nuances of wine. Fortunately, learning about wine today is a lot easier than it was thirty years ago. Magazines such as *Wine Spectator* didn't exist back then and neither did the consumer-friendly version of the Internet—which, more than any other tool, has exponentially increased my knowledge of wine. Not only can you find the most obscure wines and producers online, but you can also connect with other people via Web sites, chat rooms, blogs, and e-mail. I find these connections essential when I'm writing about a topic on which there isn't yet much published, or about a region that's too far away to visit before my story is due.

When M. F. K. Fisher was asked why she wrote about food rather than about more "serious" subjects, she replied that she was really writing about love and our hunger for it. When bread is broken and wine is drunk, there is a communion of more than our bodies. Writing about wine has allowed me to extend my hedonism and give it a sharper, more satisfying edge. Language and wine are two of the most pleasing things we consume: they animate us and become part of us. The English language is as wide and deep and layered as wine is. When I write about wine, I feel expansive, as though I'm standing in a field of words and I can stoop to pluck any of them. The world is configured exactly to my needs.

But I have to confess, much as I'm drawn to its nuances, I wouldn't be writing about wine if it weren't for the buzz. I love the way a glass of wine makes me feel—invigorated and animated, released from my natural shyness. After a couple of glasses, I'm mellow, soothed, contemplative. Perhaps because I trained as a dancer, I cannot forget the body. My mind has always been an extension of every muscle, every bone, every breath. It's only when I let myself down into my body that I can write about it.

I'm sure other wine writers feel the same way; and yet when I read about wine, I often get the odd impression that it has no alcohol in it. Perhaps this unnecessary seriousness about wine is a hangover from Prohibition; or maybe it's because we think that the body can't be part of anything intellectual.

Yet I'm not blind to the damage that excessive drinking can cause: my parents separated when I was three because my father was an alcoholic. My Celtic relatives, with their dark sense of humor, find it amusing that I choose to write about this subject. I do too. Sometimes I wonder whether I'm drawn to wine partly because of that dangerous side. At dinner parties, I drink faster than almost anyone else, including the men. (I know this because I watch everyone else's glasses a little too closely.) I need a drink to get through the arsenic hours between five P.M. and seven P.M. If I ever gave in completely to those impulses, I'd throw away everything I've worked for. My subject is addictive.

However, I believe I'm less likely to abuse something I know well and love.

The thought of making my part-time passion into a full-time career didn't occur to me until I hadn't slept soundly for about three weeks. In November 1998, shortly after our son, Rian, was born, I was on maternity leave from my job as a "Web evangelist" for a California-based computer company. One day, shopping at the local supermarket, I picked up the store's food magazine. It was beautifully illustrated and packed with recipes, but not a word about pairing them with wine. Desperate to reactivate my brain, I rushed home to call the editor with my idea for a story about where shoppers could find wine-matching information on the Internet. I figured that I knew just enough about both areas to say something. (But only in a sleep-deprived state could you believe that jumping from a career in high-tech marketing to writing about wine made any sort of sense.)

The editor asked if I had been published before, and I said yes, thinking of my high school newspaper and praying she wouldn't ask me to send samples. Luckily, she didn't. Instead, she gave me that assignment and several others to follow. I felt that a bolt had slid back and the door to my future life had opened. Six months later, when my maternity leave was over, I decided not to go back. I had already given my heart, mind, and liver to wine.

The desire to write about wine was irresistible; I couldn't believe that people would actually pay me to drink. Still, the field turned out to be hard to break into. That first assignment had been misleadingly easy to come by; rejection was far more often my fate. The established writers in the business had been penning their columns for twenty years or more, and they weren't about to step aside for a newcomer.

At one point, I called one of the most senior columnists for advice. He told me not to expect to earn a living from wine writing and to treat it as a hobby career to pursue on weekends. So I started selling stories about wine to small, local publications.

After three years of this, wanting more independence and a more direct connection with readers who shared my passion for wine, I took the plunge and launched my own Web site, www.nataliemaclean.com, and an e-newsletter. The comments and questions I got back from readers added to my own curiosity. I started to wonder about new issues: for instance, why are Burgundy's wines so sought after, and so costly? What makes them different from wines made in newer regions, such as California? Is it just a matter of climate and soil or does the vintner play a larger role? I had no idea.

Then there were all the other aspects of wine to consider, beyond just the making of it. What about buying it, tasting it, and matching it with food? I wanted to find out why we accord wine such high status, more than any other drink we consume. We rate it, we age it, and we often remember it years after we drink it. Why? This book is the result of my journeys through the wine world—from vineyard to wine shop, from restaurant to dining room—in search of the stories to help answer some of those questions.

Writing this book has deepened my belief that wine both brings us together and brings us closer to ourselves. In drinking it, we find camaraderie and consolation. Comfort me with cabernet.

Natalie MacLean
August 2006

ONE

The Good Earth

THE RIPPLES ON La Bouzaise River flash like blades in the cold morning light. Slate roofs and spires point to an expressionless gray sky. I'm in Beaune, a medieval city in the heart of Burgundy, surrounded by some of the most revered names among lovers of pinot noir: Romanée-Conti, Richebourg, La Tâche, Vougeot. Most people come to Burgundy for the fall harvest, when the hills roll like playful green dolphins. But I've come in February when winemakers have more time to talk about pinot noir—the world's most exhilarating and exasperating wine.

Burgundy's Côte d'Or, a thirty-mile necklace of a region just three hours southeast of Paris, is divided into the Côte de Nuits and the Côte de Beaune. It starts in Dijon to the north and falls in a graceful arc, like the curve between a woman's shoulders and hips, to the fortress of Beaune in the middle, continuing on to Chagny in the south. The Côte d'Or or "slope of gold" faces the east, which bathes the vines in the soft morning sunlight. The gentle early rays ripen the grapes more gradually than the hotter afternoon sun from the west.

But that's in the summer. As I drive out of the city in my small rented Renault, it all looks more like the Côte de Gray. Spindly white roads thread through the vineyards. Wisps of white smoke snake up from piles of burning dead vines, casting a pale haze over the landscape, like a Matisse drained of its color.

The villages whiz by me: Aloxe-Corton, Nuits-St-Georges, Ladoix. I feel I'm in what former French president François Mitterrand called *la France profonde*—"deep France," the real France. There are no grand châteaux here; only the occasional church steeple pierces the pastoral setting like a pin on a wine-making map. These places draw burgundy lovers back time and again, like golfers returning to overpriced greens for the perfect shot. Such drinkers are willing to lay down serious cash for a mind-bending, body-wrapping, soul-quenching experience no other wine gives.

I turn into the town of Vosne-Romanée in search of Domaine de la Romanée-Conti (often referred to as DRC), home to what many consider the greatest wine in the world. Devotees of this dream wine, simply called Romanée-Conti, love it for its haunting aromas of ancient earth and exotic spice. It's a pricey dream, though—on release, the New York wine retailer Sherry-Lehmann sold the 2002 Romanée-Conti for $2,275—per bottle.

I drive through the hamlet, which doesn't seem to have changed much in the past two hundred years. Small stone houses and shops still huddle around narrow doors. After criss-crossing the village for fifteen minutes in search of a grand entrance, I pull into the deserted post office. The clerk smiles, obviously having been through this before, and points the way I've just been six times. *"Une petite porte rouge,"* he says, and draws the shape of a small gate in the air.

I retrace my route and sure enough, in a narrow alley, I finally see it: the letters *RC* atop a modest red gate. If wine lovers could find this place, I'm sure they'd stand outside brushing their finger-tips along the door, as tourists do at the Eiffel Tower when it's closed for repair. Unlike North American wineries, which are usually open to the public, many in Burgundy, like this one, aren't. It's rumored that DRC has even refused appointments with celebrities and politicians chasing after a liquid badge.

I ring the intercom and a man who looks like Sean Connery's brother opens the gate. With pepper-gray hair and dark eyes, and wearing a tweed jacket, cap, and wool scarf, he seems to have just stepped off the cover of *Gentleman Gardener's Quarterly*. He's Aubert de Villaine, the vintner at Domaine de la Romanée-Conti.

"Ah, Madame MacLean, welcome," he says in a soft voice that makes women twenty years younger consider the many virtues of older men. He leads me up into the vineyards where, in a just a few months, the vines will burst into lime-green foliage, lined up like schoolchildren, all knobby knees and elbows. In the fall, they'll enter de Villaine's academy to learn the concentration of the press and the discipline of oak.

But today we lean against a howling wind that bows down the scarecrow vines. At this time of year, fingers seize up with arthritic cold and winemakers squint at the horizon, wondering if it will be a good vintage. It's also when the first critical cut is made in the life of the vine. A young man and woman are snipping off dead branches and throwing them into a fire in a wheelbarrow. This isn't just to keep warm, but also to destroy any plant diseases and pests. A delicious hickory-like aroma fills the air. Their fire, and others dotted across the slope, look like signals warning of an invasion by the barbarians.

As de Villaine chats with the pair, I watch their hands flit from vine to vine like hummingbirds, using electric scissors or secateurs attached to power packs on their backs. De Villaine explains that they cut one cane on the vine back to the second "eye," the notch where a bunch of grapes hung last fall; the other cane is cut back to the fourth or fifth eye, where this year's grapes will grow. The result is a reduction of the bunches per vine to just four or five—unlike Champagne, where eight to ten are common, and much less than some New World wineries that harvest as many as seventy-five. Severely restricting the vine's production focuses its nutrients into fewer grapes. The result is more complex wine—but also fewer, more expensive bottles.

What would it be like, I wonder, to cut the vine of such a great wine? Surely, it would be both spiritual and sensual. Finally, during a pause in the conversation, I pluck up the courage to ask de Villaine if I can trim one myself.

"No, absolutely not," he says firmly.

Oh no, I've offended him. How could I be so arrogant as to even suggest touching his vines? What if I'd accidentally snipped after the first eye, making a thousand-dollar mistake? I'm so embarrassed. But he turns to me with a smile and says, "I can't let you; it's too dangerous."

I'm relieved that the issue is just liability, not my insensitivity. De Villaine gestures toward the Romanée-Conti vineyard and we walk over to it—a mere 4.46 acres of land with a continental reputation. The wine made from this vineyard is one of six superb pinot noirs produced by the domaine: Romanée-Conti, La Tâche, Richebourg, Romanée-St-Vivant, Grands Echézeaux, and Echézeaux. The total production for all is only some eight thousand cases a year—and that also includes the output of a vineyard in Côte de Beaune that makes Montrachet, a chardonnay that is the estate's only white wine. (In Burgundy, all grand cru white wines are made from chardonnay, though a simple, rustic white wine is made from the grape aligoté.) That output pales next to Bordeaux's first-growth châteaux: Château Lafite-Rothschild, for example, usually produces more than twenty thousand cases a year. (A standard case has twelve bottles.)

No piece of land is more carefully monitored and tended than DRC's (except perhaps certain well-guarded plots in Colombia). Every nuance has been known for centuries, such as how the slope's rocks absorb sun during the day and then release it at night, for a slow maturation of the grapes. Or how in the winter, the hills provide shelter from frost.

The best wines are made from grapes grown in the middle of the slope. At the top of the hill, the soil is eroded by rainfall runoff; and at the bottom, where the runoff collects, the soil is too rich and wet. But along the center, the vines struggle for water and nutrients, thrusting their roots some sixty feet down into the soil and, in doing so, imbibing a spectrum of nutrients and minerals from its layers. Paradoxically, the vines that suffer most just trying to survive produce the most nuanced wines because they need to be more resourceful.

"You can see a lot of the history of this vineyard here, but there is a far greater history you cannot see," de Villaine explains. "It's buried below us, where the vine roots have worked the earth and created its structure. They draw their life from the soil, and in doing so they also educate it."

Making the vines compete with each other for nourishment concentrates the wine and adds complexity. The Romanée-Conti vineyard is densely planted: between 4,400 and 5,600 vines per acre, whereas some New World regions plant just 900. As a result, the DRC's wines are dense but not heavy.

"Great wines are made by a large population of vines, not by one clone or one vine," de Villaine says. "In good years, we make just four hundred cases of Romanée-Conti. Many people confuse concentration with alcoholic strength. Concentration is when all of the elements in a wine are in balance—fruit, alcohol, acidity, tannin, and so on—and give the impression of power."

Part of Burgundy's value comes from its geological history. During the Jurassic period, which began about 200 million years ago, this entire region was covered by a prehistoric sea. Then the tectonic plates shifted and the water drained away, exposing the earth, rich in the fossils of marine creatures. The fossils eventually turned to calcium and limestone, and the earth became one of the most complex tracts on the planet. It imparts a mineral character to the wine that gives it an unusual length and depth. This is what the French call *terroir*—that unique combination of soil, climate, elevation, and topography that gives a wine its character.

De Villaine says that most winemakers in Burgundy and elsewhere don't really understand their soils, subsoils, and microbial activity. This composition changes with every ten feet, he says. That's why the wine created from grapes grown right where we're standing is classified as only a humble village wine, while those grapes just above us produce grand cru wine. *Cru* refers to a vineyard. In English, it translates to "growth." A grand cru or "great growth" designation in Burgundy is assigned to just thirty-three top-quality vineyards (about 2 percent). Some 15 percent are classified as the second best, premier cru.

These vineyards have been in de Villaine's family since the 1860s, but their history dates back to 1100, when the Benedictine monks tended the vines behind monastery walls called *clos*. A blackened stone cross still stands at the edge of the Romanée-Conti vineyard. Behind it, the dead limbs of the vines stretch out on the trellises like small gray crosses, giving the vineyard a spectral feel. Other vineyards in the area were also run by the monks and nuns of various orders. This monastery environment is why Burgundian wine is often named after the original cloisters, such as Clos de Vougeot, Clos de Tart, or Clos de la Roche. Others are called *domaine,* an inclusive term that refers to both the winery and the vineyards. In secular Bordeaux, wines are usually named *château*, which refers more to the winery itself.

Eventually, wine from this vineyard became the house tipple of the Bourbon kings of France, including the Sun King, Louis XIV, whose doctor is said to have prescribed it as a palliative. In 1760, the Prince of Conti, Louis-François de Bourbon, cousin of Louis XV, decided to guarantee his supply by buying the vineyard for his own consumption and added his own name to the vineyard. (Madame de Pompadour, mistress of Louis XV, who also enjoyed the wine, was not pleased.) In 1776, Louis-François's son, the last Prince of Conti, improved the quality of the wine by insisting on severe pruning, picking only the ripest grapes, restricting yields, and strictly controlling the winemaking process.

At the end of the eighteenth century, the French revolution shattered the monastic calm. The revolutionary leaders seized the vineyards from the holy orders and redistributed them to the peasant patriots. The savvy prince knew how to bend with the wind. To escape persecution, he became an ordinary French citizen and rid the vineyard and wine of all traces of royalty, creating the austere bottle label, with its plain black lettering, that's still used today.

The revolution and its aftermath changed Burgundian vineyards in another way. Until then, Burgundy had operated under the ancient Roman law of primogeniture: the eldest son inherited the entire family estate. In 1804, Burgundy replaced it with the Napoleonic Code, meaning any inheritance was divided equally among all male offspring, regardless of age. Eventually, female children were included too.

The result, over two hundred years, was that the vineyards were divided among greater and greater numbers of descendants and became ever-smaller parcels of land. One of the most extreme cases is the 125-acre vineyard Clos de Vougeot, which now has more than eighty owners—some of whom make only half a dozen barrels of wine and all of whom are entitled to put the renowned vineyard name on the bottle.

Many owners of small plots sell their grapes or wine to *négociants*. *Négociants* buy grapes and wine from different vineyards throughout the region. They make wine from the grapes and sometimes from their own. They can blend this wine with wine from other districts in Burgundy and bottle it under their own label. Then they age the wine in their cellars and sell it. Burgundy's 113 *négociants* control some 52 percent of sales. This is mainly because all those small plots in various vineyards must be combined for any sort of efficiency or coherency.

All wines, whether bottled by a *négociant* or a producer, will note an *appellation d'origine contrôlée* (controlled name of origin) or AOC on the label. This is a geographically based name defined by French law, with stringent controls on most aspects of winemaking, including the grapes used, maximum yields, and permitted alcoholic strength. The Côte d'Or alone includes twenty-nine village appellations. The appellation system was created in the 1930s to guarantee wine origins and to prevent fraud.

A wine's appellation starts with the broadest and most basic category, such as Burgundy. As you move up the quality scale, the appellation gets more specific as to the place within the region, to the name of the village and the vineyard. The quality designation of the particular vineyard may also be noted, such as grand cru, premier cru, and so on, as well as the name of a producer or *négociant*. (By now, you may have joined me in bitterly resenting the appellation system.)

The only way to make any sense of this crazy-quilt region

is to come here and taste the wines, mapping the small villages along the contours of your own palate. Drinking the wine where it's made gives that extrasensory voltage. The land is all around us, in the glass in front of us, and then finally a part of us.

For me, fine burgundy displays the full range of what wine can be, including a complete contradiction: as light and ephemeral as Ariel, but with Caliban's savage sexual energy. Pinot noir has a feral caprice and dazzling aromas of black cherries, roses, cinnamon, clove, mushrooms, and fresh-turned earth. William Shakespeare described it as "a marvelous searching wine and it perfumes the blood ere one can say, 'What's this?'"

Even though pinot noir makes divine wine, it's also known as the heartbreak grape. The thin-skinned varietal is fragile, temperamental, and susceptible to rain, frost, and even, it seems, voices raised above a whisper in the vineyard. That's why the producers of pinot noir (many self-described "pathological optimists") love it: it demands every ounce of their winemaking artistry and science.

In the New World, pinot noir is sometimes brutally treated to extract maximum flavor to compete with bolder wines such as shiraz and cabernet sauvignon. Grapes are left to ripen to excess on the vines, the juice is fermented for an extended period and then heavily oaked. Wines made this way taste cooked, sweet, and heavy, qualities that prompt some to mock them as "vinicolas."

Trying to sort out the differences between Old World and New World wines, I ask de Villaine, "How is your pinot noir different from those made in Oregon or New Zealand?"

"*Pinot noir* is not a word you should use in Burgundy," he says enigmatically.

Now I'm confused—or have I stumbled onto some dark

truth, hidden for centuries? Is what we thought the world's greatest pinot noir really merlot or shiraz?

"We don't focus on the grape here," he explains. "Pinot noir is merely a translation of the soil. That grape was first selected thousands of years ago by the Romans because it gives the purest expression of what Burgundy means. Pinot noir is a sponge: it absorbs the influences of the soil, the weather, and the barrel. The fruit doesn't get in the way of the place."

In fact, the grapes here just barcly ripen in most years, which is why you don't really get the fruity taste you find in warmer regions such as California and Chile. Rather it is the taste of the soil and the weather that emerge from the glass. People here don't talk about grapes or put them on the label, because you're supposed to know that if it's red burgundy from the Côte d'Or, it's made from pinot noir, the only grape permitted by law. If it's white, it's usually chardonnay or aligoté.

In de Villaine's view, he and other vignerons are just the midwives for the wine, trying to deliver it out of the land without losing the land itself. "We try not to get in the way either," he says.

De Villaine's focus is on his vines: he has been farming organically for twenty years, long before it became the rage in North America. He has also experimented with biodynamic viticulture, based on a theory first propounded by the Austrian agronomist and philosopher Rudolf Steiner in the early 1900s. This approach, like organics, fosters a healthy balance in the soil and eschews artificial pesticides, herbicides, or fungicides. Where they differ is that biodynamic viticulture stresses the link between the cosmos and the plant's health. Four cosmic elements are believed to affect the vines: the earth element energizes the roots; light, the flowers; heat, the fruit; and water, the leaves. Where organic vintners might use compost to fertilize, biodynamic vintners use minute quantities of homeopathic-style preparations to invigorate the soil. As in homeopathic medicine, the idea is to encourage the body to heal itself rather than to just treat the symptoms.

For example, one preparation involves packing cow manure into a cow horn and burying it in the vineyard during the winter so that it undergoes a chemical transformation. In the spring, its contents are diluted with rainwater and sprayed over the vineyard to promote the growth of the plant's roots and stimulate the soil's microbial life. (One horn is used for every two and half acres.) The aim is to balance the "life energies" or natural rhythms of animals, plants, and minerals. However, since vintners can't have cows wandering through their vineyards, they depend on this mixture to contribute the life energy of the animal. Some criticize biodynamics as organic farming taken to mystical extremes, such as harvesting according to the configurations of the moon and stars.

De Villaine didn't find biodynamic viticulture produced any significant improvements in the wine. He believes in a more general organic approach of respecting nature. "The more science has progressed in the last twenty years, the more it tells us that people in times before us knew what to do," he says. "The monks could bring forth many different expressions from the wine. This doesn't mean I want to go back three centuries, but I do think we have to forget what most of modern technology gives us: power without direction. The bulldozer transforms the land in one day; fertilizers change the structure of the plant in one season."

Instead, he thinks that technology should serve tradition. "The new grape presses are so gentle that we can press the same careful way they used to do by hand, but better. And the sorting table is now a slow-moving conveyer belt that improves selection of the best grapes."

Of the thousands of decisions de Villaine makes, aided by technology or not, the hardest is still the most basic: when to pick the grapes. On October 8, 1991, for instance, most of the other Burgundian wineries had picked their fruit a week before. De Villaine held off day after day to allow the grapes for his Montrachet to achieve that final measure of maturity and ripeness. When he finally decided to harvest that morning, he and his crew were alone; the neighboring vineyards were empty, the rows of vines denuded of their fruit.

Then he looked to the south, and his heart sank as he saw dark, heavy storm clouds forming. Estimating the wind speed, he knew they had only half a day before the rains would be upon them—and ruin any grapes still on the vine by diluting their juice. He and his pickers worked feverishly all morning; but by noon, the clouds had rolled on top of the village of Chassagne, just a mile away. The pickers moved even faster through the vines, still trying to sort meticulously.

Just after noon, a northerly wind suddenly sprang up. The storm clouds divided and scattered east and west of the vineyard. De Villaine and his crew were left to finish their harvest dry-headed and dry-handed. Perhaps this divine intervention should come as no surprise given that monks had prayed over these vineyards for centuries.

After de Villaine finishes his story, we walk back to visit the cellars under the old limestone abbey. I've developed a permanent sniffle from visiting several such cold, damp labyrinths, giving me the appearance of a cocaine addict in search of a less addictive drug. The stone steps are worn down in the middle from centuries of footfalls. I follow him cautiously through the dim caves. Unconsciously, we lower our voices so as not to wake the sleeping wines.

De Villaine scans the barrel names, knitting his bushy

eyebrows together like a professor trying to find an old tome in his office library. "Ah, here we are," he says. He inserts a long glass tube called a wine thief into a barrel of the 2004 Grands Echézeaux and pours some wine into two glasses for us to taste.

At first, the gentle scent of rose petals flutters up. Then it changes into a mixture of earth, leather, and spice—the aroma of indulgence. I dissolve with pleasure into the wine, like a sugar cube with warm water poured over it. The only way to convey the intensity of flavor in my mouth would be to make the words on this page burst into flames.

I ask de Villaine how he'd describe it, but he just laughs. "Wine is poetry itself, not what we say about it," he teases me. (Still, I have to write something or I'm out of a job.)

We move on to taste several more of de Villaine's red wines, including the Richebourg, a blackhearted, brooding wine with a good balance of tannin, alcohol, and fruit; La Tâche with its exotic notes of licorice and a little more tannin; and finally the Romanée-Conti itself, showing the greatest promise, like a precocious preschooler.

Tannin is a chemical compound found in wood, fruit, and in the stems, skins, and seeds of grapes. Unlike the juice of white wines, that of red wines is fermented along with their skins and seeds, which gives them color and tannin. When you taste tannic wine, it's more of a feeling than a flavor, like the dry, furry tongue you get from drinking tea (which also has tannins) that's steeped for too long. Over time, tannin molecules chain together and fall to the bottom of the bottle as sediment—that sludgy stuff we leave in the bottle when we decant. It's not harmful, it just tastes bitter. Tannin helps red wine age and is considered the backbone that gives it structure, whereas for whites, it's the acidity. Structure is the framework for the wine's aromas and flavors, much as a poem, a play, or a novel is the framework for the words and their meaning.

At one point, de Villaine motions me over to a barrel and gestures for me to listen. I put my ear to an open bunghole and hear the gentle bubbling of malolactic fermentation, a process whereby lactic bacteria, which is naturally present in most wineries, convert harsh malic acids into softer lactic ones, giving both red and white wines a rounder, richer texture in the mouth. This conversion occurs after the alcoholic fermentation and is especially important for softening cool-climate reds that tend to have too much natural acidity. Some vintners, however, may prefer a crisp wine, especially for their whites, and therefore suppress malolactic fermentation with various methods, such as adding sulfur dioxide to the wine or keeping the cellar too cold for the process to take place.

DRC wines spend about eighteen months aging in new French oak barrels, made from the best trees in the forests of Nevers and Allier, several hundred miles away. A single barrel costs some $900, and de Villaine must buy two hundred to three hundred of them every year. (Other vintners may reuse their barrels, but he doesn't.) Still, he's judicious in his use of oak, considered by many winemakers to be the ketchup of the wine world, its strong flavor masking flaws or making up for a lack of character.

"You should feel oak, not smell it," he explains. "The wine should swallow the oak, digest it, not the other way around."

As we walk past a stack of dusty bottles, he mentions that they're on allocation, meaning that they're all sold before they're even finished, such is the demand for them. "This is the 2002 Romanée-St-Vivant," he says, evoking one of the names that always seems sold-out on upscale restaurant wine lists. "Would you like to taste one?"

"Oh, okay," I say, trying not to scream with rapture. The 2002 vintage is considered one of the best in Burgundy in the last ten years, effortlessly blending elegance and concentration, which de Villaine compares to transparency and density. Many wines, he says, are concentrated: they feel dense and heavy in the mouth, but have no elegance. Other wines are elegant: they taste almost transparent in their refinement, but they have no concentration. A great wine, he says, gathers together concentration and elegance.

I'm surprised to be charmed by a wine that doesn't have the palate-whacking power of big fruit and alcohol. Yet as I swirl it around, the aromas seem to pull me headfirst into the glass, as though I'm drawn by gravity through layers of timeworn soil—the earth's power to reclaim all that belongs to her.

"Would you like to see the historic cellar?" he asks. I nod vigorously, as though the joints holding my head have loosened. Dust-caked bottles line the shelves of the small room. Most don't even have labels on them, just small wooden plates with a chalk-written year. The oldest is 1918—"A good vintage," de Villaine muses as he runs his fingers along the shelves. Though when I ask him about it, he says, "I've never tasted the 1918, but very old wines, like this one, have lost all the body of the fruit. They gain a spirituality from their long meditation in the bottle. It is the spirit that speaks and no more the flesh.

"You stand over there now and turn around," he says, pulling out a bottle I can't see. "If you don't guess the vintage correctly, you don't leave the cellar." His smile is roguish, but slightly alarming. I start to feel like a character in Edgar Allan Poe's story "The Cask of Amontillado," lured into the cellar and then trapped there to die.

"I don't mind being locked in here." I laugh nervously. "But at least leave me a corkscrew."

He places the bottle beside a flickering candle on an upended barrel, uncorks it, and pours. "Smell before it escapes," he suggests. I close my eyes as the aroma envelops me, a silk drapery of scent brushing my cheeks and settling gently around my shoulders. Then it enters and saturates me with the expansive feeling I had as a child: I'd fill my lungs with air and float on my back in the bay. Sunlight kept my eyes closed; my legs and arms dangled just below the surface as one breath kept me afloat.

Now I am aroma-logged: my arms and legs hang heavy, but still the scent suspends me. My mind floats over a field of wild strawberries, then swoops through a forest carpeted with violets. At last, I emerge bathed in the soul of scent. It spirals down my DNA and awakens me from an aesthetic sleep.

There is a beautiful mystery in some wines that evaporates with the cold touch of analysis. But analyze it I must, or at least, guess the year. De Villaine gives me a couple of hints: it's La Tâche and that year had a lot of worrying rains at harvest.

"I'm sorry, but knowing the weather won't help me," I confess. "I haven't had a chance yet to memorize Burgundy's vintage charts for the past hundred years, so this will have to be a wild guess."

De Villaine looks at me expectantly, like the head of faculty waiting for me to defend my thesis. I can't imagine he pulled out the 1918, so I take a stab somewhere in the middle.

"It is from the 1950s?" I ask.

De Villaine raises his glass a little and nods, still waiting.

I decide to cut near the middle again: "Um, 1956?"

"Well done!" he cries with pleasure, clinking his glass against mine.

"Oh, it's nothing," I say with mock modesty. "Those late-September rains really gave it away."

The game finished, he smiles and smells the wine. His eyes close and his head tilts back on an invisible pillow.

"Ah, this wine is alive," he says, opening his eyes again. "It was brought up in the barrel, then imprisoned in the bottle where it could only wait and wait for this moment. It's terribly constraining, but a great wine must accept those constraints. When we release it from the bottle, the wine is like a prisoner who has been captive for thirty years." His eyes blink in the bright sunlight; he cannot believe his good fortune. "Or perhaps," he says, winking at me, "this wine is more like a young girl in a convent school, who now is grown into a woman."

I feel sorry for the wine: out of the bottle and down my gullet. What kind of release is that? Then I start to feel sorry for myself as I realize that after tasting this wine just once, I'm already missing it, needing it. And how can I spit out $100 worth of liquid on the cellar floor, even though "expectorating" is proper etiquette so as not to cloud your judgment when tasting? I do the decent thing and swallow.

De Villaine observes that tough years, such as 1956, can reveal the finest wines, even though critics often condemn the entire vintage. The best vignerons may drastically cut back on the production or they may "bleed" the juice from the tanks (a process known as *saignée*) to cut the ratio of juice to the flavor-imparting skins. So the generalizations in vintage charts can be misleading. In truly horrible years, many domaines don't make any wine at all, or if they do, they don't bottle any as their top wine. Instead, they declassify it under less-august labels or sell the wine in bulk anonymously to *négociants*, who in turn sell it under their own labels.

As we leave the cellar, I hear the muffled chime of the old church bells in the village. It reminds me of how eternal wine is, and also of how my visit here has flown by. By now I've lost all sense of professional distance, and I blabber to de Villaine what a thrill it has been to drink the world's best wine.

"We are not the best in the world, we are just trying to make good wine," he says gently.

The next day, I'm back in Vosne-Romanée, just five minutes down the road from DRC, to visit Lalou Bize-Leroy. Her family's *négociant* business, Maison Leroy, founded in 1868, was so successful that it allowed her father, Henri Leroy, to buy a 50 percent share in DRC in 1942 as well as precious distribution rights to sell the wines. She started working as a vigneronne with her father in 1955 when she was only twenty-three years old; and in 1974, she joined de Villaine as co-manager at DRC.

Bize-Leroy is known as La Tigresse for her sharp opinions, and her tenure at DRC was tempestuous. She bought the Charles Noëllat estate in 1988, whose Richebourg and Romanée-St-Vivant vineyards ran alongside those of DRC, and renamed it Domaine Leroy. It looked to some that she had set herself up as the main rival to DRC, and the other DRC shareholders dismissed her.

Today, Bize-Leroy still owns 25 percent of DRC, even though she's no longer involved in the winemaking. She also owns other vineyards scattered across Burgundy, including nine grands crus: Musigny, Clos de la Roche, Richebourg, Corton-Charlemagne, Corton-Renardes, Romanée-St-Vivant, Clos de Vougeot, Latricières-Chambertin, and Chambertin. Even though she lost the sales rights to DRC, her company is still known for the reserves in its cellars, which many compare fondly to the treasures in the Louvre. She believes that fine burgundy needs lengthy aging and only releases wines when she believes they're ready. Her prices are stratospheric, often higher than DRC's.

I'm more than *un peu* nervous about meeting a woman who seems to thrive on confrontation. My heart pounds as I drive past her iron gate and into a white gravel courtyard in front of a long, white house. Taking one deep breath to calm my nerves before ringing the bell, I hear small dogs yapping inside.

"Bonjour!" Bize-Leroy is all charm as she opens the door. I've read enough to know that her dogs (a black poodle named Ines and a mixed breed named Basile) are her babies and I should greet them warmly. I give them my best aren't-they-cute smile, even though I usually avoid anything on four legs. Ines growls back at me.

Bize-Leroy is a woman painted by a miniaturist, barely five feet tall, with fine features. You must look closely to catch a mischievously arched eyebrow; but there's no missing the caged ferocity in her eyes. While I didn't expect her to be in muddy overalls, I also didn't anticipate the chic haute couture: black designer pants and sweater with high-heeled, black boots. Her light brown hair is pulled back in a ponytail, accented with girlish bangs. Her fit, wiry body is a testament to her love of mountain climbing—in 2001, she climbed Mont Blanc. It's hard to believe she's seventy-three.

Her office, just off the kitchen, has only a simple wooden table stacked with neat piles of papers. On the wall are photographs of her at tastings. Ines sits at my feet, staring up at me unnervingly from under bushy black eyebrows; Basile curls up on a wide window ledge and watches us.

We start by trying to discuss her philosophy of winemaking, with an uneasy mix of franglais and hand gestures. She's a strong advocate of biodynamic viticulture, which she adopted in 1988. *"Très controversial!"* she declares, adding her mantra:

"Respectez la terre! Respectez la terre!" Just 2 percent of Burgundian vineyards are biodynamic. The approach is more labor-intensive and about 10 percent more costly than non-biodynamic viticulture. Yields are lower too because use of fertilizer in most forms is uncommon.

My conversation with Bize-Leroy goes in circles. *"Tiens!"* she says at last, with a Gallic shrug and a coquettish smile. She phones Frédéric Roemer, her sales manager, to come over and translate. He's in a vineyard some ten miles away; so as we wait, we talk in simple sentences and munch on organic potato chips.

Roemer, forty-two, has been working with Bize-Leroy for twelve years. He's as mild and quiet as she is fiery. As he translates for her, Bize-Leroy never takes her eyes off me, locking me in the magnetic field of her concentration.

We walk over to the winery, where she shows me the sorting room (its wall bears a large glass case with a circular zodiac made of colored stones). At harvest time the workers pick through the grapes here, throwing out any less than perfectly ripe. In the fermentation room, Bize-Leroy explains that the large wood vats infuse the wine with the circular energy of the cosmos. I nod in agreement, which seems the safest thing to do. The fruit from the sorting table goes into the vats for a slow fermentation to gently extract color and flavor from the grapes. The stems are left on to add tannin, which allows it to hold together for more than thirty years of aging in good vintages.

The crust that forms on top of the fermenting wine is pushed down regularly—not by machine, as many other wineries do, but by the traditional method with the feet. Breaking up and submerging the cap of skins helps them impart more flavor and color to the wine. This process is gentle and ideal for good wine, but it's also labor-intensive and costly. For the more modern method, wine is pumped from the bottom of the tank to the top to circulate it.

"I love them all," she says, lightly touching one of the vats.

On the floor, springy, ten-inch insulation absorbs noise to protect this sensitive, temperamental wine. The dogs break the holy hush, yipping, running, and bouncing over each other like black, hairy soccer balls. As we go down to her cellars, we accidentally trip a security alarm that goes off like an air-raid siren. The dogs bark crazily with excitement. It's about five adrenaline-pumped minutes before Roemer shuts it off.

In the dead calm that follows, Bize-Leroy shows me where her wines are aged in new oak for about eighteen months before being bottled unfiltered. No mechanical pumping is used, and the wine is racked twice: it's gently siphoned from one barrel to another through a hose to clarify it as the sediment that has settled to the bottom is left behind. This also gently aerates the wine, which brings out more of its sensory properties, such as color and tannin.

"I hate technology, it produces fake wines," she says with the same disgust my sixth-grade teacher had for dangling participles. "If chablis tastes like chardonnay, then it's no good!" (*Chardonnay* joins *pinot noir* on my mental list of words not to use in Burgundy.)

All these techniques are part of her "noninterventionist" philosophy of winemaking, which strives for minimum handling so as not to strip away wine's natural character. She claims the biodynamic preparations increase the vineyard's life force and, as a result, strengthen the plants' vitality to naturally fight disease and pests. However, mixtures such as stinging-nettle tea and cow's dung buried during the equinox sound less like viticulture than stage directions for *Macbeth*'s witches.

The trouble with nonintervention and biodynamics, though, is that it leaves your vineyards vulnerable to insect infestations, rot, and other plant diseases, especially in the early years of adopting these approaches.

"I don't want to eat poison, and neither do my vines. They were like drug addicts in withdrawal," she says sadly, her hands with their paper-thin, almost translucent skin quivering. "I suffered with them. But we survived together. Every year is a new war, but the vines are strong now.

"Many vintners start with biodynamics but they don't stick with it long enough," she says as we walk back to her office. She pauses for me to copy down each word. "The earth responds slowly. You must go to the end of what you think: having an idea is not enough."

Bize-Leroy does indeed carry through on what she thinks. In 1993, when Burgundy suffered a virulent attack of mildew, she didn't relent and use chemicals. As a result, she produced about 125 gallons per acre, less than half her normal production.

A vine's roots are its brains, she says—the vital link between plant and soil. Not relying on chemicals encourages the vines to gradually thrust their roots deeper into the soil. Treated this way, vines are healthier and more resistant to diseases and pests. Old vines, in particular, produce less fruit that is more concentrated as they age. Some of hers are eighty-five years old, compared to an average life span of twenty-five to forty years. "They're on their last legs, but they make magnificent wine," she says fondly.

Such is her empathy with the vines that she also allows their tops to grow tall. Other vintners prune back the leafy canopy to partially expose the grapes to the sun. But Bize-Leroy believes it's traumatic to cut the heads and that her system allows more leaves to use photosynthesis to transform sunlight into additional nourishment for the grapes. As a result, in summer her vineyards look like an overgrown garden with sprawling leafy tops—unlike the manicured, waist-high plants in most vineyards. Still, she's not certain it's the best method nor is there conclusive evidence about biodynamics itself. It seems to be more of a religion whose devotees accept certain tenets on faith and are zealous to convert others.

"Are you ready to love the vines and the soil? Are you ready to work hard?" she exhorts me like a vinous Tony Robbins at a motivational conference.

"Yes, I'm ready to love the soil! Yes, I'll work hard!" I want to respond as we walk back to her kitchen. The chicken she's cooking for lunch (I discover I'm expected to stay) seems to be burning in the oven. My eyes well with tears from the smoke and it's all I can do not to cough.

She looks around with a troubled gaze, but it's not about lunch. "Where are Basile and Ines?" she asks Roemer. He looks around and then hurries out the front door. Then as the smoke continues to stream from the oven, she pours her 2001 Corton-Charlemagne, a gorgeous chardonnay with concentrated mineral depth and spicy pear notes. I eagerly agree to a second glass.

"Colors change at different vibrations, why can't the quality of wine?" she asks, tilting her head coyly. I'm feeling the vibration but it's more to do with how much I'm drinking. When my wine is gone, I sniff the empty glass pathetically. I want to lick it, but draw a wobbly line of decorum.

Roemer and the dogs return, all of them panting from their little romp down the road. He pulls the sizzling chicken out of the oven, and to my relief it doesn't seem badly burned. We sit down in her dining room, which now doubles as her bedroom. When her husband, Marcel, died of cancer in 2004, she moved down here, afraid to be alone upstairs. The pair had been together since 1958, a devoted couple, with a shared passion for skiing, mountain climbing, fine art, and making wine.

"When he died, this vine died," she says, pointing to a gray stick still planted in a pot on the windowsill. *"Il était un homme de lumière,"* she whispers, turning away. In the picture on the wall, he does indeed look like a man of light, with his warm smile.

The chicken is actually delicious and we keep sipping on the wine. Roemer clears the dishes, and Ines curls up in a chair and snores like a chain saw. Bize-Leroy's clasped fingers in her lap move over each other like pale silkworms. We settle into that sleepy, sated part of the meal when people sit back in their chairs and look up thoughtfully. Maybe it's the French love of abstraction that makes me ponder the challenge in defining a wine with *terroir*—one that expresses the place where it's made—but words fail miserably. Like biodynamics itself, it reveals itself only when you taste it.

"Wine is an inspiration of the cosmos," Bize-Leroy says, offering me her 2003 Nuits-St-Georges. Fine red burgundy is said to enter the mouth like a peacock's tail: narrowly at first, then fanning out unexpectedly across the palate, with flashy aromas of raspberries, leather, sandalwood, smoke, burning autumn leaves, and earthy truffles. This particular one wants to play coy with me before filling my pleasure center. The wine's suppleness feels as though unseen hands pull a velvet dress over my head and down over my breasts and hips, until the hem brushes my thighs. By now, my tasting notes have become contented purring noises.

Bize-Leroy asks me what I think of it. I know what my

hawkeyed teacher wants to hear, but straight-up sycophancy is worthless. She's a connoisseur of flattery. Instead, playing for time, I ask how long her wine should be cellared. I know that burgundy is usually ready to drink earlier than bordeaux, having less tannin to smooth out. But should that be five years, ten, twenty?

Her face darkens. "Who knows?" she snaps. "Certainly, the critics don't. How can they predict when to drink my wine, when even I can't? They're making it up. *C'est terrible!* And their descriptions—filled with every silly berry on the planet!" We both shake our heads grimly over the stupidity of wine writers.

"They should write about how they feel, what's going on inside them when they drink wine," she says. "That would be much more helpful and interesting—and more truthful."

And with that, my visit is over. I thank her for lunch, shake hands with Roemer, and am tempted to give Ines a nudge before I take my leave of one grande dame of the Côte d'Or. This afternoon, I'm off to visit another: Anne-Claude Leflaive of Domaine Leflaive in Puligny-Montrachet.

Leflaive is a strong contrast to Bize-Leroy. For one thing, she's more famous for her chardonnay than for her pinot. For another, she's as cheery as Bize-Leroy is intense. The fifty-seven-year-old *vigneronne* greets me in front of her office, wearing a bright blue jacket with a rainbow-colored scarf, her silver hair contrasting with her merry blue eyes.

Still, Leflaive is just as passionate about biodynamics as Bize-Leroy. She adopted biodynamics some fifteen years ago because she was concerned about the food her three daughters were eating. As well, like many vintners, she had problems with soil erosion and imbalances. "My soil was like the Sahara Desert: it had lost its richness and complexity," she explains. "Using fertilizers meant the vines didn't have to send down their roots deeper to find nutrients and produce fruit for a true *terroir* wine."

So in 1990, after thirty years of chemical dependency in the vineyard, she started experimenting with the new approach. In one plot of land she kept using chemicals; in another, she adopted organic methods; and in a third, she had a biodynamic consultant help her. After seven years, she and her vignerons held a blind tasting; they all agreed that the biodynamic approach produced the best wines. So she converted all her vineyards.

I'm impressed by this pragmatic approach, which seems more grounded, less cosmic than Bize-Leroy. Leflaive says it has paid off. Conditions that hit other winemakers hard, such as the extreme heat of 2003, affected her vines much less. The drought cut most vintners' crops in half since irrigation is illegal in Burgundy. But her vines' roots were so far down into the earth that they were able to tap deep reserves of water and maintain a balanced acidity in the grapes. "My vines have their own resilience," she explains. "They rely on their own immune system to fight disease."

Leflaive believes that even budget wine producers can adopt certain measures. "It can work anywhere people want it to work," she says. "It just makes good sense; it's not a matter of marketing—we don't even put *biodynamic* on the label."

She drives me out to see her vineyards along an old Roman dirt road lined with knee-high limestone walls. In 1902, Leflaive's grandfather bought the vineyard in Puligny-Montrachet. Today, she makes some of the most famous grand cru white wines in the region from her fifty-six-acre estate: Le Montrachet, Chevalier-Montrachet, Bâtard-Montrachet, and Bienvenues-Bâtard-Montrachet, as well as several outstanding premier crus.

Over one wall, we see the fields of neighbors who use chemicals. We pull over to take a closer look. The earth between the vines is covered with tractor marks under a dusting of snow, compressed as though one of those evil *Star Wars* machines has rolled through. The blackened vine stumps look like victims in a burn unit, sitting up on their hard, white hospital beds, reaching with outstretched spindly arms for morphine. By contrast, Leflaive's hand-tilled soil is a vibrant mahogany color and smells like a forest floor: fresh, mushroomy, alive. The earth wraps like a lavish pashmina shawl around contented dark gray vines.

"The first time you use four grams of quartz on the vineyard, you think it's crazy," she says, referring to a mixture of quartz and rainwater that is supposed to enhance a plant's ability to assimilate light and warmth. "But then you start to see the difference in the health of the vines. We observe nature more closely now. Instead of us trying to control the vineyard, we acknowledge that nature controls it—and us."

She says the chemical companies try to make farmers dependent on expensive fertilizers and pesticides to control more and more of the process. Other companies are marketing genetically modified yeasts, which Leflaive is worried will get into her natural fermentation. When wine was first made thousands of years ago, wild, airborne yeast would fall into the open vats of grape juice. The voracious single-celled organism would devour the sugars as food to reproduce.

Today, many winemakers use cultivated strains of yeast, such as Saccharomyces, that can control the speed of fermentation and impart certain flavors to the wine. They also die off after the main fermentation is complete, whereas a wild strain of yeast called Brettanomyces, if present, can hang on, surviving on trace sugars in the grape juice. As a result, the wine fault known as brett creates a pungent barnyard smell, with mousy aromas. Brett can be slowed or eliminated with sulfur dioxide, though fans claim that just a hint of it is a desirable part of the character of Old World pinot. But it masks the fruit flavors and other nuances of the wine, and I consider it a fault from microbial spoilage.

As the Saccharomyces yeast eats the sugar, it gives off alcohol and carbon dioxide as by-products. After about ten days, when all the sugar is consumed, a dry and fully fermented wine is created. Leflaive and others favor natural yeasts as they can produce a wine with a wider range of flavors, while others prefer strains that control fermentation and give predictable fruit flavors.

With all the uncertainties of viticulture, Leflaive says, "I'm happiest when the last grape has been cut and everything is in the cellars." She takes me down to her cellars. As we pass each dark tunnel and room, I'm like a well-trained rat in a science maze experiment, looking for an upended barrel with a bottle on top of it. At last we get to it: four open bottles and several wineglasses. She pours me her 2002 Clavoillon, a premier cru. It's a wonderfully spicy chardonnay, with aromas of ripe green apples—and a beautiful example of Montrachet. Now I understand what Alexandre Dumas meant when he said of the famous white burgundies that many believe are the apotheosis of chardonnay: "Montrachet should be drunk kneeling, with one's head bared."

There's also something at the back of the wine—like a note held while the mouth music plays on. It's the mineral taste of the earth where the vines grow. More a texture than a flavor, it counterbalances the wine's fruitiness. This minerality gives the wine a density and concentration that's quite different from the power and heat of high alcohol. It's like the contrast between the garish rouge of thick makeup and the natural rosy glow from good diet and exercise. This vivid quality is difficult for many North Americans to detect because we're so used to wine with up-front fruit that we're unfamiliar with the taste and texture of clay, chalk, limestone, and earth. Some people can more easily identify it in various mineral waters than they can in wine.

Next we taste her 2002 Les Folatieres, another exuberant premier cru chardonnay with aromas of nutmeg, crème brûlée, and toast. It rolls to the back of my mouth like an incoming tide of pleasure, growing and growing until I'm flooded with its scent. If the Anything But Chardonnay (ABC) crowd could taste this wine, they'd change their minds quicker than you can say Wolf Blass.

It too has that mineral character and a balanced acidity that protects it against oxygen. Many white wines lose their freshness after being open for a day, even if recorked. I ask Leflaive how long this wine would last.

"These bottles have already been open for four days," she tells me. I'm stunned. The wine tastes as though it's just been opened. From now on, maybe I'll carry a lump of quartz in my pocket.

I bid adieu to Madame Leflaive and drive away pondering the mysteries of burgundy. I can do without the discussions of the cosmos; but all this talk of minerality and *terroir* makes surprising sense when you're actually drinking the wines.

Realistically, though, most of us will never become experts on burgundy in our lifetimes, and for a good reason: it's too darn expensive. Never mind being able to afford the grands crus, even the cheaper ones have hefty price tags. The adage is that a burgundy costs $500: $450 for all the mediocre bottles you try before finding a good one for $50. Or as food writer

A. J. Liebling put it more elegantly, "Burgundy is a lovely thing when you can get anybody to buy it for you."

Perhaps wine lovers wouldn't mind the high prices so much if they could at least be confident of the quality. But overcropping—an all-too-common practice of allowing the vines to produce too many grapes—has resulted in fruit low in nutrients. These create thin wines that are often given a boost by adding sugar to the fermenting wine to increase its alcohol—a practice called chaptalization, which is legal in the region and often necessary in this cool climate where the grapes don't fully ripen. Like all viticultural practices, though, it can be used excessively to mask flaws. Of course, the wineries I visited weren't overcropping.

The most affordable and easiest way to discover the wines of Burgundy is to buy from reputable *négociants*. The best merchants are restoring wine lovers' faith in burgundy by making consistently good wines at less outrageous prices. They're the closest thing burgundy has to brand names: Bouchard Père & Fils, Joseph Faiveley, Louis Jadot, and Louis Latour. Even Domaine Leroy makes a basic red for about $25.

To check out one of the most progressive and quality-driven of Burgundian *négociants*, I head back to Beaune to meet Frédéric Drouhin. He manages Maison Joseph Drouhin, the merchant house founded in 1880 by his great-grandfather. Back in the 1920s and 1930s, Maison Drouhin became one of the first *négociants* to buy its own vineyards, including a particularly good plot in Clos de Vougeot and most of Beaune Clos des Mouches. Today the company makes wine both from its own ninety acres of vineyards and from grapes bought from local growers.

It's not averse to expanding its holdings in other regions and even other countries. In 1979, at a blind tasting of Old World and New World pinots in Paris, Burgundy's best were un-expectedly beaten by a colonial upstart: Eyrie pinot noir from Oregon. *Naturellement*, this could not be permitted, so showing fine French resistance, Frédéric's father, Robert Drouhin, hosted the same tasting on his own turf in Beaune. This time, his entry (a 1959 Drouhin Chambolle-Musigny) placed first; but only by two tenths of a point over the second-place wine— Eyrie again. With uncommon openness to the potential of the New World, Drouhin bought 225 acres in Oregon's Willamette Valley, where his winery produces lovely pinots.

The business is very much a family one. Frédéric's sister Véronique is the winemaker for the Oregon property. Brother Philippe manages the vineyards in Burgundy, and Laurent is the U.S. sales manager. As we descend into his family cellars, Frédéric, a suave thirty-seven-year-old with auburn hair and a quick smile, says, "My sister and I used to roller-skate and play hide-and-seek down here." It's a cheerful image that helps dispel the eerie cryptlike feeling of the place, where bottles have lain undisturbed for decades. Beaune is an ancient city, first inhabited by a Gallic tribe, the Eduens, and then built as a fortress by the Romans. It still has circular stone walls, and its cobblestone streets conceal a labyrinth of subterranean caves holding millions of bottles. The powerful dukes of Burgundy made their home here until 1477, when they lost the Battle of Nancy to the king of France, Louis XI, and Burgundy became a French province.

Battles have long been fought overhead from where we're standing. During World War II, Frédéric's grandfather Maurice Drouhin was a member of the French Resistance. Before the invading Nazis arrived in Beaune, he walled up the cellar and made the new masonry look old. (Robert helped by setting down small spiders in front of the wall so that it would be convincingly cobwebbed.) Maurice was betrayed to the Nazis, but escaped through the cellars. Even though the Germans had blocked all the known exits, the savvy vigneron had built a concealed one especially for escape. He hid for three months until the Germans left—not even his family knew where he was.

The nuns at the Hôtel Dieu, a hospital built in the heart of the city in 1443, had taken him in. After the war, he showed his gratitude every year by donating the wine made from some five acres of his vineyards to the hospital's fund-raising auction, continuing the centuries-long tradition of many local *vignerons*. Today the hospital is a museum, still supported by the annual wine auction, which also helps to set the prices for the new harvest each year: the bids don't dictate the prices but act as a general gauge for the vintage.

Frédéric tells me more of this history as we walk through the shadowy caves. Some of the oldest holdings go back as far as the mid-nineteenth century.

"What is the value of this bottle from 1856?" I ask.

"What is the value of emotion?" Drouhin counters. "What's the value of all that has happened to France since 1856? The wars, the monuments, the art, the people? All the people who made this wine—including my grandfather—are now dead."

Drouhin likes to philosophize rather than give a direct answer. It's the same when I ask how much he produces: "Not enough. The demand for our wines exceeds the supply." He makes wine from many Burgundian vineyards, in lots of seventy-five cases to eighteen thousand. His company is the fourth-largest *négociant* in the region.

He smiles as he gestures at several caches of old bottles. "I don't tell my importers about these stocks," he says. "We want the next generation of wine drinkers to know what a wine tastes like at ten, twenty, and thirty years old.

"The more you know about wine, the more you love burgundy: it gives you the most pleasure," he says. "We are not scientists; we are farmers. There is no recipe for making wine and there is no formula for sensuality."

He turns more serious and pragmatic when talking about Burgundy's place in the wine world of the twenty-first century. "Twenty years ago, we only thought of Bordeaux and the Rhône Valley as competition," he says. "Now there's California, Oregon, Australia, New Zealand, Chile, and South Africa—and their wines that are much easier to understand and drink. The younger generation of winemakers here is more aware of modern tastes, but our customers are getting old."

Burgundy does indeed need revitalization. Even Drouhin seems to disdain words like *marketing* and *trendy*—unlike the New World vintners, who embrace them. A couple of New Zealanders have already set up a wine shop in Beaune to sell their pinot noir, surely the vinous equivalent of marketing oranges in Florida. It saddens me that all but the rarest wines here are falling out of fashion to the more robust wines of California, Australia, Chile, and other regions. Perhaps the vintners' renewed focus on Burgundy's precious soils will resonate with the next generation of wine lovers. Looking back through my notes, the descriptions seem futile: only the wine splotches and a few mud smears evoke the aching pleasure that is Burgundy. The challenge is conveying that message and ensuring that the region's distinctiveness is never supplanted by a bolder, homogenous style. That would be tragic—like selling the Louvre to Disneyland Paris.

Harvesting Dreams

As I STAND at the top of Rattlesnake Hill, a steep five-hundred-foot slope in the heart of California's Sonoma Valley, I try to imagine the view as Edoardo Seghesio would have seen it in 1902, the year he opened his winery here. At the bottom of the hill, its crumbling stone wall is a silent reminder of a century flown by. Beside it are several large redwood vats, a couple of wagons, a tractor, some chicken pens, and the old Seghesio home. But the vines Edoardo planted flourish with new life, their leaves fluttering in the light September breeze like marching bands wearing floppy, green-tasseled hats.

The surrounding mountains hold up the sky on either side of the valley, and the silver sleeve of the Russian River meanders out to the southern edge. Running through the middle, where the highway is now, would have been the rail line, with a half dozen tiny wineries dotted along it. Standing next to me, her thick brown curly hair pushed back by Chanel sunglasses, is Edoardo's granddaughter, Camille Seghesio. At 37, she's the export sales director of Seghesio Family Vineyards and one of nine family members now running the winery.

"Grandpa taught us: never sell the land, the land makes it all possible," Camille says, as she shields her intense brown eyes against the sun. "Control the land, control your destiny."

That fierce self-sufficiency, which she inherited from her fore-fathers, is what has made the Seghesios among the state's most successful small winemakers. While they may be building on a history that is centuries younger than Burgundy's, it is just as integral to their current success and dreams for the future.

In 1886, Edoardo, then a young man of twenty-five, left his native Piedmont in northern Italy to make the grueling month-long journey by ship to America. The family has never forgotten that important arrival: one of their wine labels today bears the image of Edoardo's passport stamp from Ellis Island. After crossing the country by train, he arrived in Sonoma, seventy miles north of San Francisco.

There he joined a thriving community of expatriate Italian winemakers that eventually included families such as Gallo, Parducci, Pedroncelli, Martinelli, Rafanelli, and Foppiano. Edoardo went to work at the Italian Swiss Colony, a cooperative of grape growers that produced bulk wine. Under a typical arrangement, he wasn't paid regularly during his first three years. He boarded for free; and then, at the end of that period, he was paid for his work in one lump sum—which he put aside, building toward his dream of starting his own winery.

By the time Edoardo was thirty-two he felt ready to marry and start a family. He told Angelo Vasconi, his boss, that he was going back to his homeland to find a bride. Vasconi told him not to bother: his pretty niece Angela was already in Sonoma and would make Edoardo a lovely wife. The year before, Angela had left her own hometown in Italy at the age of fourteen because there wasn't enough to eat in her large family. Although it was a practical match that saved time and money, the young couple actually fell in love.

The Seghesio story resonated deeply with me because that immigrant yearning to own a piece of land is part of my own family's history. My great-great-great-great-grandfather, Lachlan MacLean, left Scotland in 1817, during the Highland Clearances, when British landowners evicted the Scots from the land. Lachlan journeyed with his family to Nova Scotia, where he joined other Scots in building new homes and lives.

Many members of our family, including me, have since moved away to find work and to buy our own plots of earth. But most of us feel drawn back to that land, where the craggy coastline plunges a granite fist into the ocean and the pine-covered mountains cup small glens like green-gloved hands. It's a place so hauntingly beautiful that Andrew and I take our son there on vacations so that Rian can catch up with his past.

Similarly, for many families here in Sonoma, the past surrounds them. It's even in the ground itself: the zinfandel grape made its own voyage to the New World. Just as Australia has shiraz, Argentina has malbec, and South Africa has pinotage, California has zinfandel to call its own. Its story is as American as the rags-to-riches characters in an E. L. Doctorow novel. The vine stock is believed to have traveled here with early immigrant winemakers—those thousands of men and women, like Edoardo, who left their homelands for the New World.

For years, zinfandel was considered a bastard child with no known European lineage and not counted among the classic grapes such as chardonnay and cabernet. The early Italian winemakers were particularly fond of zin because it reminded them of their homeland wines. In the 1970s, it was thought to have come from Italy, since it was determined to be the same variety as the Italian grape primitivo. However, in the 1990s, Carole Meredith, then a professor of viticulture at the University of California at Davis, an institution considered a world leader in viticulture and enology research, proved otherwise. She worked with colleagues at the University of Zagreb to confirm that zinfandel is also the same variety as the Croatian grape crljenak kastelanski, from which it probably originated. They were aided in their research by advances in decoding vine DNA—akin to the human genetic techniques now used to identify criminals and establish paternity. Other researchers at the California university are now working on a genetic map of the grape, much like the larger map of the human genome.

Regardless of its origins, zinfandel thrived in California's soils. Today, it accounts for 80 percent of what the Seghesios produce. The family, like zinfandel itself, had to work its way from the ground up. Edoardo's first goal was to buy land so that he could be certain of his family always having enough to eat. In 1895, he bought a two-room house with fifty-six acres of land beside a one-room train station in the Alexander Valley from the Colony. (He paid $200 an acre for it; today it's worth $70,000 an acre.) He planted sustenance crops in the richest soils; the vines had to be planted in what was left, which was gravel and clay loam—ideal for producing good wine. Just as in Burgundy, the vines had to reach far down into the earth for nutrients and thus picked up nuances and complexity.

Initially, Edoardo sold all his grapes back to the Colony, which in turn made the wine and sold it. After several years of saving, he had enough money to build his own winery to make wine, which he then sold to the cooperative at a higher profit. However, he also kept selling grapes since he grew more than he could vinify. He and Angela did all the winemaking manually, using a hand-cranked crusher on the grapes and then carting their wine to the Colony. As the years passed, the couple prospered; they bought more land, added more rooms to the house, made more wine, acquired more customers, and had six children.

Angela gradually took over the business side of the operation, negotiating most of the grape contracts with buyers, who now came from farther afield. She had a shrewd eye for customers: her method was to sit on the veranda and watch the passengers disembark at the station. The train made only two other stops up the line at the stations of Barbera and Asti before returning to San Francisco, so she assumed that if a man in a suit got off, he had probably come from the city to buy grapes. Angela would then kill a chicken to make the broth for a heady homemade risotto: business was always done over a meal.

In 1919, Edoardo bought shares in the business of his former employer, the Italian Swiss Colony. At that time, it was producing some 4 million gallons of wine from fifteen hundred acres of vineyards. His timing couldn't have been worse: just months later, the government in Washington enacted Prohibition, which limited winemaking to two hundred gallons per family. Anything more had to be sold as sacramental wine. A few wily growers sold "must," the dried, compressed grape material in brick form—warning that the brick should never come into contact with yeast, or wine might inadvertently result. Of course, most of those buying the bricks were home winemakers.

About a year after Prohibition became law, Edoardo closed his winery and sold his stock in the Italian Swiss Colony. Many producers went out of business. Before Prohibition, California had 713 wineries, and afterward just 40. The Seghesios survived by farming their own land. With the repeal of Prohibition in 1933, they started making wine again. But there was grief for the family the following year when Edoardo, then seventy-three, died. Angela took over running the business herself until 1941, when she turned it over to her three sons: Frank, Art, and Peter. In 1949, the family expanded the business, buying another local winery at a bankruptcy sale.

While Edoardo and Angela had learned the wine business on the job, the next generation studied the subject in university. In 1940, Peter, Camille's father, graduated from the enology program at UC Davis. He then apprenticed at Beaulieu Winery with Andre Tchelistcheff, who would become Napa's most famous winemaker in the 1960s. Before Peter could use his skills in the family business, he was drafted into the infantry in World War II. While he was fighting in Italy, his siblings set aside his share of the earnings from the winery. When he returned home in 1945, he was so touched that they had done this that despite having considered a career in the military, he joined the family business.

Peter sold Seghesio wine in bulk for other wineries to bottle under their own labels: Gallo, Petris, Paul Masson, Italian Swiss Colony, and Roma were all customers. The practice was common and continues today, with many wineries buying grapes and fermented juice because they don't produce enough wine from their own vineyards.

By the 1960s, the Seghesios owned four hundred acres of land and produced a quarter of all the grapes in Sonoma. But in the late 1970s, sales of bulk wines plummeted as consumer tastes became more refined. So the family decided to create its own label. By that time, the next generation had come to the fore: Pete Jr., who had graduated from the viticulture program at California State University at Fresno, was managing domestic sales, and his cousin Ted (Art's grandson), who'd attended the UC Davis program, made the wine. They bottled their first vintage of 100 percent red zinfandel in 1983.

Like the Seghesios, many California vintners tried to make good zinfandel in the 1980s, but the wine's history made it a tough sell. Consumers shunned it because it was traditionally blended with other varieties in lackluster wines. Even the new

unblended styles varied so widely that the wine had no particular profile. In fact, zinfandel has been called the world's most
misunderstood grape. Until recently, many wine enthusiasts
thought it could only produce pink syrup—not realizing that
it was also capable of being made into a dense, opulent, struc-
tured red wine.

The saving grace of zinfandel (and its curse) was white zin.
In the 1970s, Bob Trinchero of Sutter Home decided to bottle
and sell the runoff juice from pressing red zin. Customers
complained that the resulting wine was too dry, so he sweetened it—and then could barely keep up with demand. Other
wineries jumped on the bandwagon, but Sutter Home still leads
the market: in 2004, it produced almost a fifth of all the white
zin, some 20 million cases, sold in the United States.

Despite its popularity, though, connoisseurs view white zin
as an industrial Kool-Aid and "accessible"—a descriptive kiss
of death to them. Still, 35 percent of all U.S. wine consumers
drink white zinfandel, according to a 2005 Scarborough
Research study. Some drinkers think of it as a transitional tipple
that bridges the taste gap between soda pop and dry table
wines—including red zinfandel. Whatever the experts' disdain
for the pink stuff, people buy it and its popularity has helped
to save many old vineyards from being ripped up and replanted
with more fashionable grapes. With more than fifty-one thousand acres planted today, zinfandel is third, after cabernet and
merlot, among red grapes in California.

In 1991, the boom in white zin motivated a small group of
aficionados to establish Zinfandel Advocates and Producers
(ZAP), an organization dedicated to restoring red zinfandel to
its rightful status as America's heritage grape. ZAP's informal
motto became "The first obligation of wine is to be red." It's
now one of the largest consumer-based wine advocacy groups

in the world, with some six thousand purple-card-carrying members, a quarter of whom live outside California. (A support group for a grape—it could only happen in America.)

When Camille and I come back down from Rattlesnake Hill, she introduces me to her mother, Rachel Ann, the last link to the second generation of the family. She looks every inch the strong matriarch that Angela must have been, with glittering eyes and skin that seems lit from within. We follow her into the small, white building beside their home: the old Chianti train station has become a small family museum.

Inside, on a bed covered with a white quilt, is the baby dress that Angela knitted for her fifth child, who was just seven days old when he died. Angela's big wooden pasta board leans against one wall; the trunk she brought from Italy sits against another; and the original creased deeds to the land lie on a small table. The walls are covered in yellowing photographs of stern, weathered men and women holding serious babies in lacy bonnets.

Rachel Ann smiles as she talks about her early years with Pete Sr., who died in 2004. "He would be so proud," she says, her voice wobbling. "The young people made the new winery."

In 1994, the new generation had to settle some tax issues that forced them to reevaluate the business. Pete and Ted realized that the winery couldn't make a profit producing low-end generic wine, even though many winemakers were doing just that since zinfandel seems to crop faster than ragweed. Yields of ten to twelve tons per acre weren't uncommon. Cabernet, by contrast, yields only five to eight tons. Zinfandel also ripens earlier than cabernet because the grapes are larger and their higher ratio of skin to flesh means they're not as tannic. This means that zinfandel can be drunk young, which gave vintners a quick cash return.

The cousins took the opposite approach, making the business small and exclusive. They cut production drastically, from 150,000 cases to 35,000, and chopped vineyard yields from some ten tons an acre to just two by "green harvesting." With this technique, used by vintners willing to sacrifice quantity for quality, slow-ripening bunches are pulled off the vines in the summer and thrown away. This forces the vines to concentrate their nutrients in the remaining grapes and also allows for better air flow among the clusters to dry the moisture that can cause rot. The leaves are also pruned so that the sun can ripen the grapes more evenly. Pete calls his technique sun-flecting: he looks for a certain ratio of sun-dappled shadow on the ground behind the vines.

The new strategy initially caused some friction with the older generation: it was hard for them to move away from their traditional bulk-wine mind-set of more is better. Pete Sr. couldn't bear to watch all that fruit being "wasted" and would leave town when it was time for crop thinning. (Even with low yields, it still takes eight hundred to a thousand grapes to make one bottle of wine.)

The Seghesios knew that cutting yields wasn't enough; they had to specialize. What Pete and Ted realized was that they had something special: eighty acres of old zinfandel vines, some of which Edoardo had planted in 1896. The average age of the family's vines is ninety years. "They're still here today because those early Italian winemakers were just too stubborn to pull them out," Camille says affectionately.

In fact, the densest concentration of old vines in all the United States is in Sonoma's Dry Creek Valley, where the Seghesios have several vineyards. Zinfandel is grown throughout California, and in thirteen other states, but its home is here. Napa may claim cabernet and Carneros pinot noir, but the best zinfandel thrives here because of its proximity to the Pacific

Ocean, with its ideal climate of warm days to ripen the grape sugars and of cool nights to preserve acidity and fruit flavors. The combination slows down and evens out maturation and makes for greater intensity and complexity in the wine. Slow maturation versus a quick ripening is like the difference between lifting weights over a long period and bulking up quickly on steroids.

Zinfandel is one of the few vines deliberately grown well past its prime. The twisted, arthritic-looking plants are often featured in photographs: in coffee-table books, in gauzy wine lifestyle ads, and on bottle labels. Many zinfandel bottles carry designations such as gnarly vines, knotty vines, century vines, and ancient vines.

Zin has a longer lease on life than most vines. Bordeaux vineyards, for example, are replanted every twenty-five to forty-five years (although there are some old vines in that region too). Zin vines, like people, become less productive but more interesting with age. It takes about fifty years for them to develop the deep flavors that make superior wine. With severe pruning, young vines can be forced to mimic the color and power of old vines; but not their nuanced concentration—much like smart young doctoral graduates still needing the wisdom of life experience. At around thirty years old the vines calm down, Pete says, and you can see a real shift in the way they produce fruit that imparts character to the wine. However, many in the industry believe that old vines don't necessarily guarantee a better end product: it's not age that matters most, but superior planting sites.

Only a few hundred acres of old zin vines are left in California. James Wolpert, chair of the viticulture and enology department at UC Davis, established the Zinfandel Heritage Vineyard in the early 1990s as a vinous bridge to the past. He and his colleagues drove around California in search of lost vines—often taking cuttings just ahead of the bulldozer. They gathered about ninety cuttings, some more than a century old, on these "old zin safaris" and replanted them. This Noah's ark of vines will be cultivated for the benefit of future winemakers, preserving the diversity of zinfandel.

It's this increasing rarity of old vines, and consequently the diminishing yields, that is driving up the cost of good zin. In fact, the hardest thing to swallow about zinfandel today is often its price. Once considered more affordable than most reds, zin is now becoming more fashionable and hence more expensive.

When Pete and Ted decided to focus on old zinfandel, they took it a step further by making several single-vineyard wines. Low-yield zinfandel actually gives one of the purest expressions of *terroir*—the reason that producers often designate the vineyard on the label. Rosenblum, for example, produces seventeen different zins, some in batches of only seventy-five cases. The downside is that winemakers are much more vulnerable to bad years because they can't compensate by blending with grapes from another vineyard or region where the weather was better. Tomorrow I'll learn firsthand just how closely zinfandel is tied to the land and weather here.

Even though it's mid-September, it's a bone-damp four degrees Celsius at seven A.M. the next day when I meet Pete, forty-one, at the winery. He has black hair, peppered with gray at the sides, and steely blue eyes. Pete is now the CEO and very much a hands-on executive. Once the grapes ripen from green to red (a transformation called veraison) around the third week of August, he's out in the vineyards every day to taste them and decide when to pick. Right now, as he tells his assistant vineyard manager, Laura Villarreal, only two plots are showing any progress on ripening. She's to drive out in her own truck to sample those grapes to see if they're ready to be harvested.

"From veraison, there should be about forty-five days to harvest," he tells me as we bounce in his pickup along a rutted road beside one of the vineyards. Continents of fog lift slowly off the vines. "We're not even close. We need a week of ninety-degree weather, but all we've got is fog. If we don't get some daytime heat soon, the cold nights pull the sugar from the grapes back into the vines and the moisture will make the grapes rot."

Zinfandel teeters on the edge of palatability—there are so many ways to ruin it. If the grapes aren't fully ripe when harvested, the wine can taste green and vegetal; or it can jump to the other end of the spectrum if the grapes are too ripe, and the wine has a porty, burnt-prune taste. Deciding when to pick is tricky because there can be extreme differences in the maturation of the individual grapes in a bunch. One cluster can have unripe green pellets alongside shriveled raisins. If winemakers wait for the slowpokes to ripen, even more grapes will turn to raisins, and the alcohol level of the resulting wine can soar to 18 percent or so. Wine alcohol that high can stop fermentation by killing off the yeast. It's also of a cortex-marinating strength that burns the palate and obliterates the fruit flavors.

To fix the problem, some winemakers remove the excess alcohol with a machine called a spinning cone. But this makes the wine uneven. The effect is like liposuction: the skin is never as smooth afterward as if the person hadn't gained weight in the first place. Another even less publicized approach in the industry is adding "Jesus units," a reference to the miracle at the wedding of Cana, where Jesus is said to have changed water into wine. This technique dilutes the wine with water and, in doing so, lowers alcohol by volume and "creates" more wine, or at least more liquid. The result is a jammy but thin wine with no structure or ability to age.

Even constant heat can be problematic for zin. The grape sugars may soar but the tannins in the skins don't mature, so they taste bitter like green tea instead of rounding out to a smoother texture. The seeds have a harsh taste and don't part easily from the grape flesh when crushed. And if the grapes are too ripe, without enough protective acidity, the juice is more vulnerable to bacterial attack during fermentation.

The ideal is when all the grape elements—sugar, skins, tannins, acids—are mature and the resulting wine has balance and structure. This only happens after a long, slow ripening, during weeks of warm days and cool nights—and frayed nerves for winemakers, who must wait out the fall in the hope that the grapes achieve sufficient ripeness before the wet weather sets in.

The best zinfandel is still usually high in alcohol (13–14 percent) and isn't hailed for its elegance among red wines. The dense fruit and opulent texture can make syrup seem runny by comparison. Many zins embody Ravenswood winery's faux-Latin motto: *nullum vinum flaccidum*—"no wimpy wines." As one vintner observed, aging zin in French oak is like putting perfume on John Wayne.

The names California vintners give to their zinfandels go for weight over grace: The Monster, Wild Thing, Monga Zin, and Blockheadia. Others take a more comic approach with names like Commander Zinskey, ZinMan, and Zebra Zin. Bonny Doon's Cardinal Zin has a wine label by satirist Ralph Steadman that features a church prelate in full scarlet regalia spitting out the wine. (The back label links the wine with "the seven deadly zins" and suggests pairing it with game and other wild animals—including sloth.)

Great zinfandel has just the right balance of concentration, structure, and fruit flavors. The aromas vary from red berries (from the cooler region of Dry Creek Valley) to blackberries (from the warmer Alexander Valley). The Seghesio zinfandels I taste have a mouthwatering range of berry aromas: blackberry, blueberry, boysenberry, as well as more rustic, woodsy aromas of brambly briar and spicy white pepper.

With the Seghesios, new focus on premium wine in the mid-1990s, they hired two consultants: Phil Freese, a viticulture expert, helps Pete with vineyard management decisions, and Alberto Antonini, a viniculture expert, works with Ted in the winery. Both men have worked with leading wineries: Freese with California cult wines such as Opus One, the joint venture between Robert Mondavi and Baron Philippe de Rothschild; and Antonini with Italian stars Marchese Piero Antinori for his wine Tignanello and Angelo Gaja on his eponymous wine, Gaja.

As I follow Pete through one of the vineyards, he's talking with Freese on his Blackberry, using the speakerphone so that I can listen. "Don't worry, the grapes are just ripening slowly and that's a good thing. All we can do is wait—and, Pete, don't drink any more caffeine until the harvest is over!" Freese laughs.

Another change Freese brought in was drip irrigation. The family used to dry-farm without watering the vines because they believed doing so would allow the roots to stay lazily close to the surface rather than reaching far down into the earth for water and nutrients. Freese says that it's like buying fire engines: "You hope you don't have to use them, but when that's what you need, there is no substitute." This is especially true when it comes to the oldest vines experiencing extreme late-season stress: a slight drip helps the grapes to stay on the vines longer, and this extended "hang time" means more complex flavors. They also wouldn't survive otherwise.

As the morning wears on and the temperature rises, we arrive at the oldest vineyard—Pete's favorite. These zinfandel vines were planted on a robust rootstock that doesn't need much water. And unlike other rootstocks, this one resisted the insect phylloxera, which destroyed many other California vineyards in the 1990s, as it had the European vineyards in the late 1800s.

It's time for me to exercise more than my ability to listen— I'm going to help collect grapes to be taken back to the winery and tested for ripeness. As Pete hands me two pails for the grapes, he says with just a corner of a smile, "If you carry both, it's more balanced." He cuts off bunches and drops them into the pails. As we walk through the rows, the baked jagged clay collapses beneath my sandals like meringue, sending puffs of dust up between my toes. Pete stops to inspect some of the bunches and I put down the pails for a moment to turn my face up to the autumn sun and inhale the sweet vine breath.

These old vines are planted haphazardly rather than in rows, as though they wandered off and forgot where the winery is. That's because machine harvesting wasn't available in 1896. They're also head-pruned, meaning that they're clipped with shears like hedges. In fact, with no trellis wires supporting these five-foot-tall, chunky vines, they look more like small trees. I feel as if I'm in the enchanted forest from *The Wizard of Oz*: their long branches trail on the ground.

Although these zinfandel vines are old, Pete tells me the wines are best drunk young, within five years of their vintage. After that, their fruit flavors soften. In ten years or so, they become like bordeaux—still lovely but without their vibrant fruit character. According to a *Wine Spectator* tasting of thirty-seven zinfandels, ranging from seven to ten years old, the wines didn't evolve to a more complex character, like bordeaux and burgundy. But neither did they fall apart and become thin and insipid. They simply held their own.

Other winemakers believe that zinfandel can age for years with distinction. "Since zinfandel is such a fruit-driven wine, people love drinking it within the first five years," says Joel Peterson, winemaker at Ravenswood. "But if you look at the statistics, this is true of all wines. The exceptional zinfandels, those that have good balance, good color, and are made with some age in mind, tend to do very well for fifteen to twenty years."

Perhaps I've spent too much time in vineyards, but these vines remind me of some of my older, hard-drinking relatives. They're gnarly and difficult to control, but radiate the weathered wisdom of many years. I want to straighten out their tangled, leafy branches, the way I ran my fingers through my grandfather's windblown hair when I was a child.

For the Seghesio family, a strong zinfandel tradition has aged well over several generations. "There's something about making wine from your own land," Pete says. This year, he and his seven-year-old son will farm a couple of acres together so that his son can start to feel just how deep those roots go.

California's oldest vineyards may be in Sonoma and Napa, but newer wine regions have emerged south of San Francisco. The weather, grapes, soils, and approaches there are radically different; and no one embodies these differences more than Randall Grahm. The fifty-four-year-old puckish president of Bonny Doon Vineyards defies categories; he's a man best described by what he's not. And he's not like most wine producers in California and the New World, who have, he believes, lost sight of what great wine is: not a confection of the laboratory, but a subtle expression of the soil from which it sprang. He describes himself as "a champion of ugly-duckling grapes whose existence is threatened by the dominant chardo-centric paradigm."

In fact, Grahm approaches winemaking like performance art: he has posed in a purple silk cape and mask as the Rhône Ranger for the cover of *Wine Spectator* magazine and hosted a funeral service for traditional cork. But no one can dismiss him as simply a bad boy or a nutcase because his influence on the American wine industry is as wide as it is deep. He has helped to transform it by introducing less fashionable grapes, experimental winemaking techniques, unconventional marketing, and levity in a business that often takes itself too seriously.

I asked Grahm if I could work with him for a couple of days during the harvest. When he agreed, I realized that there was no way to prepare to meet this former philosophy student who has had an asteroid named after him, does cryptic crosswords to relax, and admits to being "only mildly sociopathic." All I could do was brush up on my Socrates while listening to Alice Cooper.

Bonny Doon is an hour's drive south of San Francisco in the ocean-hugging college town of Santa Cruz. The winery, which sells some 360,000 cases a year, is on a quiet back street. But the building itself seems to trumpet its presence: a bright red corrugated-metal barn with giant cartoon children painted on the sides.

The two-story doors are open on this warm September morning; the heady smell of fermenting grapes billows out from the shady cool inside. Grahm, in a denim shirt and khaki pants, stands by a gleaming thirty-two-hundred-gallon stainless steel fermentation tank, tasting wine from a small glass. Beside him is Alison Crowe, twenty-eight, his associate winemaker.

"Welcome to our Lees Hotel," Grahm greets me in a voice that sounds as though he's been gargling with stones from his vineyard. When he says lees, he's referring to the dead yeast cells, grape seeds, and skins that give the wine its color, flavor, and body. These eventually settle to the bottom of the tank as fine sediment. "Lees check in, but they don't check out," he adds.

Grahm has a weakness for wordplay: the gait of his thought leaves me mentally thumbing through Bartlett's *Familiar Quotations* to decode his mixed metaphors. With his long, impish face, he could be Gene Wilder's brother. But there's also something of an eighteenth-century portrait about him— the kind of eyes that follow you wherever you go. Strands of renegade gray hair have come loose from a ponytail to frame his weathered face. He looks like a wild desert man, aflame with ideas.

The wet floor around us is strewn with gray, python-sized hoses slithering thirstily up to the tanks. The smell of sulfur and yeast prickles my nose; the whirring tanks circulating the skins and juice to enhance the wine's color and flavor make it hard to hear. At any other time of the year, a winery is an orderly place of quiet symmetry. But the harvest reveals its pulsing libido, a sticky, chaotic lust for life.

Crowe gives me a tasting glass; Grahm, grinning, hands me the spit bucket. We do the morning "tank walk," an essential part of the harvest routine: checking how the newly picked grapes are fermenting in the tanks. We also taste the ones that have been aging in barrels for a year. Although young, they're surprisingly well-balanced, with good fruit character and structure.

"French wines rock—they have soul," Grahm declares over the din, as we taste his syrah. "New World wines are all a façade."

"Even yours?" I ask.

"Ours are . . . genuine plywood veneer," he says. Crowe rolls her eyes with an affectionate smile and crooks two fingers in quotation marks. She's accustomed to Grahm's sound bites for the media, having worked for Bonny Doon for four years. She joined after graduating from UC Davis, where Grahm himself trained.

His passion for wine was first ignited after graduating in 1974 from the University of California at Santa Cruz, where he studied literature and philosophy. He moved to Los Angeles and worked at a wine shop in Beverly Hills. There he washed the floors and tasted an "ungodly number of transcendental French wines." This Dionysian-Damascus experience convinced him to enroll in the UC Davis program. In 1981, two years after graduating, he bought Bonny Doon Vineyards with a loan from his family.

"This zinfandel is a high-needs child," Grahm says of the wine we're now tasting. He suggests to Crowe that they increase the tank temperature to speed up fermentation and extract more color from the skins. "If that doesn't work, we're stuffed."

As we taste, Grahm describes yeast as "a fast-food slut" because it devours all the sugar in the grape juice as it ferments the wine. We also talk about tartaric acid, which stabilizes the acidity and the color of wine. Vintners try to remove any excess of this acid by deliberately chilling the wine before bottling to create tartrates, which look like crystal deposits, and then removing them. Otherwise, this process can happen in the bottle and the crystals settle on the inside of the glass or the cork. Tartrates, more common in white wines with high acidity, don't harm the wines' taste or aroma, but they can look like tiny glass shards, which alarms some consumers. They're nicknamed wine diamonds.

All this technical talk is leavened as we walk past one tank bearing a sign with the face of an alien in a circle, with a slash through it. Through the open door to Grahm's office, I see a disco glitter ball hanging from the ceiling.

When Grahm first started in the business, he planted pinot noir, but quickly learned that those red grapes grow best in a cool climate. California's warmth, by contrast, was better suited to the grapes that thrive in the Rhône Valley of southern France: syrah, grenache, mourvèdre, cinsault, carignane, roussanne, marsanne, and viognier. The inland side of the Californian coastal mountain range, which runs some sixty miles south of San Francisco, mimics the furnacelike heat of the Rhône Valley. Long hot days ripen the grapes; but cool nights add balancing acidity and structure to the wines. Andre Tchelistcheff described the region as "a jewel of ecological elements." The Santa Cruz Mountains, known as the golden chain, were designated an American Viticultural Area in 1981 and soon became known as the Rhône Zone.

Although other pioneers (such as Jim Clendenen of Au Bon Climat, Bob Lindquist of Qupé, and Gary Eberle of Eberle Winery) were also planting these grapes, no one did more to popularize them than Grahm. His publicity antics led the trade to dub him The Rhône Ranger, and in 1992 Arizona's Lowell Observatory named an asteroid the Rhôneranger. (Ted Bowell, an astronomer there, was a big fan of Grahm's wines.)

In 1984, Grahm bottled his first wine, a red blend in the style of Châteauneuf-du-Pape. He called it Le Cigare Volant, a mocking tribute to the Rhône town's ordinance passed in 1954 at the peak of the Cold War. It forbade flying saucers (or "flying cigars" as the French call them) from landing in the vineyards. The bottle's sepia label has the traditional French aesthetic, but also features a spacecraft hovering over a vineyard, zapping it with a *Star Trek*-style beam.

Grahm named his second tribute to Rhône wines Old Telegram, a literal translation of one of the valley's great wineries, Domaine du Vieux Télégraphe. The domaine is itself named after the telegraph relay towers that dotted the vineyard a century ago. Grahm's label looks like a 1950s Western Union telegram.

As we walk through the winery, I spy more of his bottled wines. Their bright labels with splashes of color contrast with the grays, blacks, and browns of the building. Their names— from A Clockwork Orange Muscat to a Critique of Pure Riesling—and their illustrations are an extension of Grahm's whimsical mind. His French syrah is Domaine des Blagueurs, "estate of the jokers," and his tasting notes describe the wine as having a "Parisian brothel fragrance." Its label features a Ralph Steadman illustration of a playing card, the joker. One can only imagine the label for a new premium wine he's thinking of naming Succotash after the Southern corn dish because he likes the idea of "really rich people in fancy restaurants ordering an expensive bottle with such a homely name.

"We don't have a particularly wine-savvy culture in this country, so a lot of people buy wine based on the label," he says. "We try to design our labels taking some cues from the wine itself."

Despite Grahm's humor and good wine, it was still a challenge to sell his wine in the early 1980s. Back then, Americans were just learning to like domestic cabernet and chardonnay, and to buy them by name. Even in the Old World, the Rhône Valley was always overshadowed by Bordeaux and Burgundy. The challenge was to inform drinkers about the wide range of Rhône wine flavors and their ability to pair well with many dishes.

In those days, the California wine industry was experiencing explosive growth, but most of the attention was focused on Napa Valley. There vintners such as Robert Mondavi, Joseph Phelps, and Jacob Beringer were making good wines. Grahm, though, considered himself "anti-Napa," the opposite of the "Axis of Cabernet-Chardonnay." He also declared his vineyards a "merlot-free zone," because merlot is "boring cubed." In his view, it's delusional to pay too much attention to the market-place. "The market is fickle, it doesn't know what it wants," he says. "Your best bet is to create something that makes sense to you and then explain to other people what you've done."

The Rhône region got its first big break in the 1980s, when the powerful U.S. wine critic Robert Parker started giving the French wines high scores. That endorsement also helped their New World counterparts. Today, syrah is the fastest-growing, most popular Rhône wine in America—thanks to the Australian invasion of the shiraz, the same grape with a slightly different name. It's made in a ripe, round style that's less austere than the French version.

But Grahm isn't a fan. He describes Australian shiraz as a caricature of syrah: "It's a thoroughly corrupted grape; it's got too much of everything. It is not what syrah is about. Syrah is a very refined grape, not a powerhouse wine. It's a finesse wine, and that's not a style that's particularly encouraged in Australia. If it's from the antipodes, the label is probably yellow and involves a marsupial.

"I'm an Old World guy trapped in a New World life," he laments.

To be successful today, Grahm says, wine must be "optically opaque, alcoholic, tannic, and woody as hell—it's vinous Viagrafication." Despite this sensory onslaught, he opines, "It might be nice if the tannins were strong but on some level soft—sort of like George Clooney or Harrison Ford."

He believes that winemakers do have a choice: "Either follow your own vision of producing a wine that the world needs—a wine of originality and distinctiveness—or else just create the illusion of distinctiveness by amping up the volume. If you're in Burgundy, distinctiveness arises from the soil. In the New World, the dilemma is how to legitimize your efforts without relying on the usual suspects: concentration, big fruit, new wood, the *Wine Spec*, and Parker."

Grahm blames wine critics for giving high scores to such steroid wines, thereby creating a buying frenzy and influencing the future styles vintners choose to make. "It's much easier to wave around a sign that says '94' than to articulate how you're different," Grahm says. Referring to the *Wine Spectator*'s influential critic James Laube, Grahm quips, "I'd rather have a frontal lobotomy than a Laube in front of me."

He's fond of quoting economist Thorstein Veblen's theory that any pursuit filled with jargon is largely make-believe. He himself has created a "Doon dialect" in winery newsletters that read like Geoffrey Chaucer on LSD, flitting from "The Man for La Garnacha" to "The Love Song of J. Alfred Rootstock." But he doesn't criticize all wine writers; he has deep respect for Kermit Lynch, the California wine importer and author of *Adventures on the Wine Route*. "In his writing, he always evoked the place where the wine was made," Grahm says. "He didn't chase after the glamorous wines and he was willing to get dirty to understand wine."

Now that I've spent most of the morning listening to Grahm and Crowe discuss volatile acidity, pH, sugar, and nitrogen, I'm about to get my own hands dirty. Crowe introduces me to Matt Kenneally, twenty-seven, a visiting "cellar rat" from Australia who's working at Bonny Doon during his country's winter season. He gives me a pair of knee-high black rubber boots and leads me over to a pile of those python hoses. "Let's staaart with recking some woin, shell we?" he says in a muscular Aussie accent. He puts a heavy nozzle in my hands and walks away.

He's ten feet off before I realize that I'm supposed to follow him while hauling this hundred-pound sucker.

With much unwriterly grunting and wheezing, I finally catch up with him in front of an empty giant wooden vat. "We're gonna reck the woin over theah into this vet. It'll be loawds of fun," Kenneally says with a Tom Sawyer grin. After the first vat is emptied, we wash it with water using a garden hose, then hook the big hose up between the two vats. Kenneally adjusts ten or so valves and then hits a switch to start the transfer. Racking may be done several times before a wine is bottled, depending on the amount of sediment and how much air it needs. It may also be clarified using substances such as egg white or bentonite, a type of clay. Both of these are highly absorptive so they bind to excess proteins, tannins, and pigments in the wine and then settle at the bottom.

We spend the rest of the afternoon checking wine vats, including an inspection from a narrow, second-story metal walkway that gives me vertigo. Kenneally uses a hydraulic pulley to take off the giant lids, then records the evaporation levels and the readings on various dials. From above, the big tubs look like witches' cauldrons of bubbling, frothy purple soup. He whistles a happy little tune as I slog behind him hauling hoses. I'm surprised that someone hasn't yet published a book called *The Total Winery Workout: Develop Harvest Abs, Grape-Crushing Thighs, and Buns of Stainless Steel.* At last, I have become one with my subject. I feel like a human grape: sticky, purple, and completely crushed.

At six the next morning, it's already a hot, heavy day. Silver streaks pierce sunburned pink clouds over Monterey Bay, which sparkles like crushed diamonds. I'm picked up at my hotel by twenty-nine-year-old Nicole Walsh, a tall, athletic brunette who is Grahm's vineyard manager and works with his forty or so grape growers. (Grahm describes himself as a "promiscuous grape buyer—in the words of Brian Wilson, 'I get around.'")

I climb into Walsh's rusty Chevy Silverado, which has several large plastic pails in the back, along with a surfboard. "Good morning!" she says, like someone who thinks that six A.M. is a good time to be awake. I mumble a reply from behind a shaky cup of black tea.

As we drive down the coast, straight rows of green-stitched vines fly by us on both sides of the road. Strips of aluminum foil, tied to the vineyard rows to frighten hungry birds, flash a thousand tiny mirrored Morse codes. Autumn dyes on the trees smear together as we speed past.

I'm still struggling to put together two consecutive syllables, but Walsh is already voluble. "Randall is such an exception to most vintners," she says. "He's always out there trying new things; he doesn't wait until it's safe. Last year, we tried whole-cluster fermentation for the riesling: we kept the bunches of grapes together and didn't destem them. Hadn't been done before. Randall said, 'Why not?' so we did, and it produced wonderful wine. Not all his ideas work, and I get nervous when he comes up with something in the middle of the harvest; but often it's worth trying."

When she's not telling me about Grahm, Walsh is on her cell phone scheduling plots to be picked, booking cold-storage space, discussing lab results, and checking weather forecasts. After an hour of this, we arrive at Chequera Vineyard, owned by Chris Couture (who looks like John Denver).

Grahm agrees with the Seghesios' assertion that the best wine is made from the grapes you own. He says it was a strategic error not to have bought vineyards in Bonny Doon's early days. Now, with land prices so high, it's not financially feasible to do so. Therefore, he and Walsh work closely with their grape growers, with whom they have long-term contracts.

Couture and Walsh walk through the vineyard, eating grapes, spitting out the seeds, and discussing when different rows will be picked. I follow with Juan Rendon, the vineyard manager, a Mexican who has worked with Couture for fourteen years. After Couture and Rendon leave us, Walsh kneels and digs her fingers into the soil. "Smell this," she says. I squat down beside her and put my nose to the handful. The rich dirt has a voluptuous savory-sweet aroma. I have a strange craving to eat it. I can almost feel the ground beneath me seething with microorganisms groping in the dark. The vine roots extend their gnarled fingers blindly down into the soil whispering reproduce, reproduce, reproduce.

Grahm believes that good grapes, and hence complex wines, only grow when there's a healthy and diverse population of microflora competing with the vine roots for nutrients. "You also need to limit the yields and bonsai the vines," he says, referring to a method of training them close to the ground so the sap doesn't have as far to travel to the fruit. But since this technique doesn't permit mechanical harvesting, it's expensive. It also creates the beautiful chaos of these unruly-looking vines.

"Okay, we're going to pick now," Walsh says, standing up and handing me a pail and a small pair of shears.

"All this?" I ask, looking at the twenty-acre spread in alarm.

"No!" she says, laughing. "We're just going to pick for a while to see how the grapes are ripening. Why don't you start down there?" She points to about thirty rows away, at the bottom of the sharply sloping vineyard. "Walk a few paces, then snip off a bunch. Try to vary what you take: some bunches that are shaded, others that are in direct sun, some low down, others at the top. We want to measure the average ripeness."

At first, I feel like a hero returning to a hometown parade: leafy, green vines reach down in front of me on either side, like well-wishers wanting to shake my hand. The wire trellis is for crowd control. But after three hours, the streets are deserted and I'm alone. It's backbreaking work, carrying an ever-heavier pail, bending down to get the low-hanging fruit, scrambling up and down the forty-five-degree graveled rows that give the vines excellent drainage but no traction for me. At a distance, I can see Walsh's head bobbing up from the vines and then disappearing down into them again, like a flying fish in an ocean of green kelp.

Up in the marine-blue sky, blackbirds circle like words trying to arrange themselves into a sentence. They're the bane of grape growers, since they also consider the crop a delicacy. Couture has tried various methods of scaring them off, all ineffectual. He even installed an automatic cannon to fire blanks into the air. But after the first few shots, the birds got used to the sound and took to settling on the cannon, finding it a comfortable roost.

The ancient repetition of vineyard work is meditative: plant, prune, pick, prune. No wonder early cultivators of this art were the Christian brothers, both originally in France and later here in California. Yet the work is also intellectual: my mind soars freely while my body is engaged. However, the work destroys my former notion of vineyard life, which was full of gentle breezes and white verandas. The sun, now directly overhead, is an angry white and beats down on me in a personal way. The stones under my feet fume their stored heat. I envy the spiders that can crawl to the shady underside of leaves. Even my thoughts are bubbling hot—they'll have to cool and congeal into experience later. I look down at the remnants of my manicured nails. Sweat plasters my hair to my forehead and my bangs fall into my eyes, but this problem is easily solved with the shears. (Now I understand why monks favored the bowl cut.)

Every half hour or so, I head back to Walsh's truck and we plunge our hands into the pails to squish the grapes like ink-stained laundry. Manic flies, their diaphanous wings glowing like cobalt-stained glass in the sun, take suicide dives into the sweet mess.

"I want to check the pH levels we're getting from the lab," Walsh says, taking out something that looks like a small telescope. She splashes grape juice on it and the refractometer measures the Brix (sweetness) in the grapes. "Wow, 23.5 Brix and the weather is supposed to be ninety-five degrees all week," she observes, looking through its end. "We'd better pick Monday."

Getting the timing right is essential for harvest. Pick too early in the season, and the grapes may not be ripe; too late, and excess sugar converts into a clobbering alcohol without any balancing acidity. And no matter how careful you are, nature can always throw in a rainstorm that bloats the grapes and dilutes the wine.

Still, many New World vintners deliberately pick late in the season. Grahm criticizes these "high-impact wines" as boringly overripe. "As primates, we prefer ripe fruit, whether it's bananas or grapes. It's just human nature," he says. "But these wines are like baby food for grown-ups—puréed things with butter and cream in them." He feels that highly alcoholic wines overwhelm subtle food, just as the new trend to fusion cooking overwhelms nuanced wines. He disapproves of both: "In the New World, wine and food are in two simultaneous monologues—a dysfunctional pairing."

In fact, New World wines have become increasingly alcoholic

in the last five years. Where 10–12 percent alcohol by volume used to be the norm, modern blockbuster reds, such as shiraz and cabernet, often weigh in at 15 percent. Not only do these wines assault the palate, but they make their presence known only when you get up from the dinner table and discover that your legs have turned to jelly.

It's a welcome moment for me when Walsh announces that we're done here. But our day is far from over: we cover another hundred miles throughout the afternoon, visiting several more vineyards scattered along the coastal range, picking more grapes at each. I could open a small winery with the ones that we throw out after every testing.

As we drive back along the glittering gold coast in the late afternoon, Walsh suddenly sniffs the air and says, "Green peppers." I wonder if she's thinking of dinner—I certainly am. But after a few minutes, we round a corner to see a produce truck pulled off at the side of the road, its load of green peppers spilled mostly in the ditch. I'm impressed by her keen sense of smell, an essential skill in this line of work.

Our final call of the day is the crushing facility at the Monterey Wine Company, a warehouse that processes some nine thousand tons of grapes every fall for Grahm and other winemakers. Making wine is a capital-intensive business, so shared facilities are common.

A rich, sweet smell, like raspberry pie, wafts through the air as we walk between rows of giant steel tanks. A truck loaded with grapes rumbles in and is weighed. As Walsh talks with the manager about the crush, I watch the truck slowly tipping its load over sideways into one of these big steel drums. A massive body of grapes falls out, and then dark red juice gushes out behind like blood. Inside the thundering drum, a large rotor screw separates the grapes from their stems, which are spit out through a pipe—as though even the machine finds them too bitter. (They'll later be processed into compost.) The de-stemmed grapes are pumped into large presses, where the juice is gently squeezed from the skins. Finally the juice is siphoned into tanks, where it can start fermenting. Once fermented, the wine is trucked back to Bonny Doon. (Grahm also ferments some of his wines at his Santa Cruz winery.)

After an hour of this, we emerge from the warehouse blinking in the extravagant light of a California evening, the kind of honey-gold rays that pour through the window in a Vermeer painting. As we drive back, the sun is starting to back off from its heated argument and violet tones unfurl over the vineyards. The dark-ening fields of grapes are now ghostly line drawings, shadows sketched in a hurry, to be painted into oils tomorrow morning.

I feel a stinging sensation in my blistered fingertips; my muscles quiver in a song of fatigue. Still, I sense that if I just drop into bed after dinner, I'll seize up. So a few hours after Walsh drops me off, I drive my rental car out to a vineyard. The moon-illumined vines seem strangely alive, swaying in lime-sequined gowns. There's magic in work that goes on around the clock: walking among the vines at dawn, picking grapes through the day, monitoring the fermenting grapes during the night. I breathe in sweet-scented darkness and exhale the vineyard calm. When I've finally released the day's tension, I head back to my hotel.

The next day I meet with Grahm one more time. After planting Rhône grapes, he tried Italian varieties. Like the Seghesios, he found them difficult to cultivate. His best effort so far is a blend of thirteen Italian and Rhône grapes called Ca'del Solo Big House. The grapes are grown in Soledad, Monterey County, near one of California's state prisons—a.k.a. The Big House. (The name is also a play on "house wine," but translates into Italian as "house of solitude.") The label features a cartoon picture of an escaping inmate and the comment that the vines are planted "just beyond the searchlight's reach of the state penitentiary." It also warns that this wine might "incite a crime of passion." Both the red and white versions are popular, and they're priced in the $10–$15 range.

Grahm now makes more than fifty different wines and admits he's "never met a grape I didn't want to crush." As a result, his vineyard is a menagerie of obscure grapes such as scheurebe, treixadura, loureiro, and alvarinho. He's most interested in those that produce wine with a "hidden zing."

Some critics take Grahm to task for this lack of focus: they say he plants too many grapes rather than perfecting a few, as Paul Draper has done with zinfandel and Steve Kistler with chardonnay. But while the rest of the state suffers periodic gluts of the big-name grapes, Grahm is sitting pretty with his ugly ducklings. His sales have increased at least 10 percent every year for the past five.

Still, he admits that he hasn't produced any great wines yet. "New World wines, including mine, are trivial, they're banal," he says. The reason, he believes, is that California lacks any real *terroir*. "True *terroir* wines are leaner and more subtle and they allow mineral flavors to seep through. I suspect we might have *terroir* in California, but I don't know where."

Grahm believes that mineral character doesn't just define *terroir* wines, it also gives them their long life because they have protective acidity. "If you drink New World wine that's been open for a day, it's dead, it's oxidized," he points out. "Not so with Old World wines, like German riesling or Burgundian pinot noir. They have depth and soul, and lots of life left in them. They are gathered into themselves and complete, like the work of James Joyce."

The secret to the high standards of French wine—burgundy and bordeaux—Grahm believes, is geology. Bordeaux, five hours southwest of Paris, is influenced by the Garonne River, which runs down from the Pyrénées Mountains on the border of France and Spain and brings in complex layers of clay and gravel over a limestone base. Although infertile for most crops, the land is ideal for wine grapes: the gravel gives excellent drainage, forcing the vine roots to thrust deep down into the rock for water and nutrients, thus absorbing many nuances that contribute to more complex wines.

For me, great bordeaux is a mansion of a wine, solid and imposing in structure, with stately finishes and designs. At first, it seems locked shut, but as the years pass, long corridors of aromas open up and I discover secret rooms that reveal new dimensions. It is a wine that you can drink again and again as a way of understanding how you've changed over time. I can still remember my first glass of one of the region's finest wines, Château Latour: the taste of furious passion. Rich aromas of cassis, smoke, and leather curled around me. Then it finished like a dagger, cutting across my mind to divide my life into what I had drunk before Latour and after Latour.

Frustrated with his vineyards' lack of minerality, Grahm tried adding chips of shale, granite, cobblestone, and black slate to several batches of his 2001 Le Cigare Volant as the red grape skins macerated (steeped) in the juice. He jokingly attributed this Rock Quartet idea to "drugs, basically." He found such a marked difference in the wine's mineral nuances that he seriously considered importing stones from France for the next vintage—until federal wine regulators told him that he couldn't do so because it didn't fall under the rubric of "standard wine-making." (They were also worried about potential traces of elements such as lead and arsenic getting into the wine.)

Despite his scientific training, Grahm believes that wine can't be much improved by winemaking tricks. Instead, he says, the new revolution will be in the vineyard. He has even contemplated planting vines in the shape of a helix rather than straight rows because it's more "agriculturally and cosmically sound." He adds gleefully, "The California Department of Agriculture would completely freak out, and that would be very satisfying."

In a more serious vein, he's trying to reverse-engineer the genetic complexity because he's concerned that there just isn't enough genetic variety left in American grape clones, many of which have been grafted from the same nursery rootstock for generations. His ambition is to collect samples and reestablish a large population of genetically different vines.

Grahm prefers to kick and splash away from the mainstream, whether it's grapes, winemaking, packaging, or promotion. After all, he observes, "California started with monks in monasteries, away from the commercial world—we need to return to that cloistered thinking."

And yet Grahm is very much a man of this world, intent on playing to the very market he claims to mistrust. His concern is that people don't take him seriously because he plays the fool—a Lear in Falstaff's clothing. "At my funeral, I don't want people to say, 'Wow, he was a great marketer.'"

Behind Grahm's publicity stunts and circus tricks is some great wine that's getting better every year. "I do take this seriously," he tells me, in an uncharacteristically earnest voice, his blue-flame eyes piercing over his tinted glasses. "It's not just my livelihood; it's my life's work. I'd like a good long run at it. And maybe when I'm done, more winemakers will believe that you can take risks and survive—even thrive."

THREE

The Merry Widows of Mousse

THE CHAMPAGNE REGION of France is Renoir country, where the impressionist spent his summers for twenty-five years—rendering vibrant images of the local trails, the forests with their gnarled trees, the Roman bridge at Loches-sur-Ource. In the fall, on a sun-jeweled afternoon, the leaves of the vineyards flame into crimson red, russet orange, and flaxen gold.

Of course, it's not art that makes this region famous, it's the luxury bubbly. Most people have heard of champagne, the wine, but few know much about Champagne, the region, just ninety miles northeast of Paris. This makes champagne unlike most other wines of France, which emphasize the patchwork of vineyards where the grapes are grown as a selling point. But in Champagne, famous winery names such as Veuve Clicquot, Moët & Chandon, and Bollinger eclipse the nuances of the area itself. I wanted to find out why.

Grapes for champagne are grown in four districts: the Marne Valley, which dips gracefully between two other areas, Reims Mountain to the north and Côte des Blancs in the south. Côte des Bar, a fourth district, lies to the southeast. The chalk soil, bone-white like summer snow, may have originated the region's name: in Celtic, *kann pann* means "white country." (The Romans called the open land *campania*.) The chalk, a thousand feet deep in places, is so porous that it absorbs up to 40 percent of its own volume in water, then releases it again in dry times, naturally irrigating the vines. The chalk also absorbs heat from the sun and at night warms and helps to ripen the grapes. That's critical here in France's most northern wine region, just above Burgundy, where the average annual temperature is only ten degrees Celsius.

Champagne possesses just 3 percent of France's total vineyard acreage and produces only 12 percent of all sparkling wine worldwide. The region is almost completely planted, with 81,500 acres of the total 84,000 acres of vineyard land already cultivated. That's why just two and a half acres of vineyard land can command as much as $1.2 million. More than fifteen thousand small growers own 90 percent of the vineyards; the large champagne houses own the rest. Most of the growers sell their grapes to these houses. Every year, one hundred thousand people pick enough fruit to make an average of 300 million bottles. The wine may be pricey, but it isn't scarce: as with diamonds, the producers have cultivated its image of rarity.

The region sells almost every drop it produces. Some of the larger houses, such as Moët & Chandon, have started buying up smaller producers to acquire their vines. Every year, the Champagne authorities discuss extending the region's boundaries so that more vineyards may be planted. Not everyone is in favor of this idea, particularly those whose families have spent centuries building up Champagne's reputation and prices. Even if there were agreement on expanding the area, authorities believe it would still take another ten years to assess soil and weather conditions in order to define those new boundaries precisely.

Champagne's twin cities, Reims and Épernay, sit on either side of a mountain, connected by a necklace of stone villages built by the Romans in the fourth century. As my taxi flies through the streets of Reims, we pass its thirteenth-century Gothic cathedral, soaring 265 feet up into the sky. The stained-glass windows depict wine themes from the Bible such as the miracle at Cana, the chalice of wine turned into blood at the Last Supper, St. Vincent (patron saint of the wine growers), and St. John the Baptist (the patron saint of the cellar). As the rays of sapphire, ruby, and amber light stream through, visitors just inside the entrance look up with gemstone faces, like the figures from the panes.

The city has an odd mix of blackened stone buildings and flamboyant art déco architecture. Ever since the Middle Ages, Champagne—centrally located in Europe—has been at the crossroads of both war and trade. In the fifth century, Attila the Hun, one of Central Asia's most feared barbarians, passed through on his way to sack Paris. Reims wasn't sheltered from the Hundred Years' War in the fourteenth century, nor Épernay from the Thirty Years' War in the seventeenth. In the First World War, there were two Battles of the Marne, and of the fifteen thousand houses in Reims, only sixty remained standing after extensive bombing. The city was rebuilt throughout the 1920s in a style to lift the spirits of its inhabitants, with bright colors, floral figures, mosaics, and wrought iron. During the Second World War, Hitler's troops camped there for four years.

The resilience of the locals was evident in an early wine-marketing tactic: being first onto the battlefield to toast the victor with champagne. That ability to reinvent and rebuild is a big part of the region's success. Still, as with many culinary luxuries, the product itself is so labor-intensive and costly that you wonder how anyone could ever have thought of it in the first place. It sounds like something that laid-off marketing executives would dream up in a skills retraining workshop:

"First, we'll find one of the coldest climates on earth for growing grapes; and then we'll plant red ones, even though we want to make white wine. We'll be completely dependent on top-quality grapes but we won't actually own any vineyards— we'll just have fun negotiating every year with the grape growers. Then, when it's time to make the wine, we'll do it not once but twice: we'll ferment it in the fall and again in the spring.

"Over the winter, we'll stand the bottles nearly upside down in massive racks and give them a quick turn every day for about eight weeks until all the goopy dead-yeast stuff slides into the neck. Then we'll freeze the top and let that stuff fly out. We'll add some sweetened wine, then recork it and wait for it to age somewhere between three and twenty-five years. To do all this, we'll sink a small fortune into equipment, even though we won't see any return for fifteen years or so. Voilà! Champagne in three hundred easy steps!"

This sounded so bizarre to me that I decided to sort out the making of champagne by visiting one of the leading producers, Veuve Clicquot. The winery is one of many that were run in the nineteenth and early twentieth centuries by young women who had lost their winemaker husbands to war or illness. Instead of stepping aside in favor of a male relative, selling the business, or remarrying to hand over the reins to a new husband, these celebrated *veuves*, or widows, took control and produced some of the most prestigious wines in the world.

In an era when few women were in business at all, these women headed what were, for the time, some of France's largest companies. Most of them used bold, unconventional strategies that would today be called direct-marketing campaigns and export to unproven markets. Most of them more than doubled production during their tenure.

Barbe-Nicole Clicquot Ponsardin, of Veuve Clicquot, was probably the most famous of this group. Her husband died of a fever in 1805 when she was only twenty-seven, leaving her with the business and a six-year-old daughter. She wasn't one for endless weeping and wringing of hands: only weeks after the funeral, she continued to coordinate shipments of wine to Russia—an extraordinary feat, given the uncertainty of trade during the Napoleonic wars. Her shipments got through and her champagne became so popular in Russia that Pushkin, Gogol, and Chekhov all wrote about it. When the fortunes of war swung the other way in 1814, Russian soldiers invaded her hometown of Reims and raided her cellars. "Let them drink," she is rumored to have said. "They'll pay for it later."

Women still run Veuve Clicquot. In 2001, Cécile Bonnefond was named president and chief executive officer. Mireille Guiliano, currently the president of the U.S. division, is also author of the best-selling book *French Women Don't Get Fat*, which of course allows for wine in a reasonable diet.

Today in Reims, I'm meeting winemaker Frédéric Panaïotis. His grandparents owned vineyards in Champagne to make wine for their own consumption. But it wasn't until Christmas 1984—when his uncle brought home a coveted burgundy, the 1976 Richebourg from Gros—that Panaïotis was turned on to wine.

"It stunned me. That's when I knew I wanted to make wine myself," he says, after we've been introduced. He's an attractive forty-one-year-old with dark, serious eyes. After some pleasantries, he takes me to the winery's laboratory tasting room, a surprisingly clinical environment, with bright fluorescent lights and gleaming chrome equipment.

Panaïotis graduated from the prestigious Institut National Agronomique Paris-Grignon and the École Supérieure d'Oenologie de l'Agro Montpellier, as well as training at the Comité Interprofessionnel du Vin de Champagne, the regional wine trade association. He apprenticed with winemakers in France and California before joining Veuve Clicquot in 1994.

His current job takes him on frequent road trips around the world to market the brand and conduct tastings—it helps that he's fluent in French, English, Spanish, Italian, and Japanese.

Most importantly, he works with Jacques Péters, the cellar master (*chef de cave*), to blend the wines. In Champagne, the difference between a winemaker and cellar master is that the latter is responsible for more than just winemaking: he also is the preserver of the house style and is usually the spokesperson for the winery. He is much like a restaurant's executive chef rather than a line cook—he develops the menu and has a large team supporting him. Blending is one of his most important tasks. The Champenois have made a virtue of their harsh climate by focusing on blended rather than vintage-dated wines. Blended, nonvintage wines may come from different grapes, vineyards, and years. Vintage-dated wines may also be a blend of different grapes and vineyards but must all come from the same year. On average, only three years in ten have the necessary warmth to make vintage-dated champagne; four years will be average, and winemakers count on three to be too cold, wet, or otherwise poor for grape growing.

Although consumers are conditioned to believe that wines with a date are better than ones without and pay twice as much for them, the champagne makers themselves are actually most proud of their nonvintage, blended wines. These challenge the vintner's ability to produce a consistent and complex house style—and to make a good wine even in a bad year. Some think that vintage wines are actually easier because they're only made in good years. The key to maintaining the signature house blend isn't a simple formula but rather the taste memory of the *chef de cave*. Veuve Clicquot invites back three previous cellar masters to consult on the final blend—the eldest is 101.

"We taste the wines for what they will become, not for what

they are now," Panaïotis explains. "It's like cooking with spices. Each year is different, so you swirl a bit and taste and see how that affects the blend. Then you mix in some other wines."

In Champagne, producers are required by law to reserve at least 20 percent of the wine from those years that are declared to be vintage years to blend with wine in future years. These older wines add depth, character, and consistency, and they soften the tart, young flavors of the new wine. That's why you don't really need to age nonvintage champagne: it's already been done for you. (Most champagne is consumed within a week or two after its purchase because so much of it is bought in the last quarter of the year for the holidays.) Blending is the reason for champagne's overall high quality, and it makes the product easier for buyers to understand: memorizing grapes and vintage charts isn't necessary. Just remember the brand names you like. Perhaps that's why the top five houses, Moët, Veuve Clicquot, Perrier-Jouët, Mumm, and Piper-Heidsieck, account for 71 percent of all champagne imported into the United States, according to the research company Impact.

That same consistency makes champagne less interesting for some wine lovers, especially those who thrive on the small or obscure. Less than a third of Champagne's fifteen thousand growers make their own bubbly rather than selling all their grapes to the large houses. It's a daunting prospect for these mostly small, family-owned firms, though, given the investment required to buy equipment and to age the stock.

Nevertheless, much like single-malt scotch and microbrew beers, these smaller, single-vineyard bubblies are becoming popular with drinkers who find value in specificity and hand-craftsmanship. Some of the best are Egly-Ouriet, Chartogne-Taillet, René Geoffroy, Jean Milan, and Maison Cazals.

Even the larger houses are beginning to experiment with the

novelty of making single-vineyard, single-grape champagnes. In 2001, Moët & Chandon started producing three of these, called Les Vignes de Saran, Les Champs de Romont, and Les Sarments d'Aÿ—known collectively as La Trilogie des Grands Crus (and sold as a three-pack set). Only four thousand sets are produced, and each fetches a price of about $350. More robust than the typically medium-bodied Moët house style, these wines showcase the individuality of each vineyard and *terroir*.

In 2005, Mumm launched a nonvintage grand cru made from five vineyards around the villages of Avize, Cramant, Bouzy, Aÿ, and Verzenay. Mumm's cellar master, Dominique Demarville, worked with British star chef Gordon Ramsay at his eponymous London restaurant to pair the wine with a five-course menu. Each dish highlighted the character of one vineyard in the blend.

For a closer look at that specificity, I turn away from the big champagne names and head for the tiny winery Maison Cazals. It produces just seventy-five hundred cases a year, which are sold mainly in France. The place is now run by Delphine Cazals, whose winemaker father, Claude Cazals, died in 1996. Cazals, a porcelain-skinned thirty-seven-year-old with deep blue eyes, shows me around her clos, the modest low-walled fields on the hills behind her house where she grows her grapes. She uses pheromones instead of insecticides to protect them and tries to minimize other chemicals. It's a wonderful inheritance, but she has one regret: "I took over the winery without ever having had the chance to work with my father."

Back at the house, she opens a bottle of her 1995 Cuvée Vive. "We forget that champagne is wine, not a fashion accessory," she points out. "This wine evolves; it has aromas. Smell this." I put my nose deep into the glass and inhale aromas of freshly baked bread, hazelnuts, and some scents that take me back to my Maritime childhood: long-stemmed lilies in the garden and the spray of the Atlantic on a blustery day.

"It is deeply pleasing to create something beautiful," she says softly. "This bottle from the 1995 vintage—it was the last wine my father ever made."

Whether champagne is vineyard-specific such as Cazals or a blend, most of it is white wine made from red grapes. Two of the region's three grapes are red: pinot noir and pinot meunier. Pinot meunier, found mostly along the rich floor of the Marne Valley and in Aube, is considered a simple workhorse grape, giving the wine a fruity, perfumed roundness and early maturity. Pinot noir, grown mostly on the slopes of Reims Mountain, contributes aromas of cherries, berries, and other red fruit; it also gives the wine structure, length, and body. The third grape is white, chardonnay from the south-facing Côte des Blancs; it offers aromas of daisies, white peaches, and lemon, as well as a creamy texture, mineral depth, and elegant finesse. With all these grapes, the challenge is to get sufficient ripeness and maturity in the skins themselves, and the right amount of acidity, color, and other compounds that give wine its taste and structure.

Most champagne is a blended wine from all three grapes, but *blanc de blancs* (white from whites) is made exclusively from chardonnay and has the lightest and most sprightly style among bubblies. One of the most prestigious is Salon, which has made wine just thirty-seven years since its launch more than a hundred years ago. In these declared vintages, it produces only some five thousand cases from chardonnay grown around the village of Le Mesnil-sur-Oger. It gains its incredible nuances from aging in the bottle on the lees for at least ten years—the minimum required by law for vintage champagne is only three.

A number of champagne houses don't use chardonnay exclusively, preferring simply to make it the dominant grape in the blend. These produce light styles, such as Perrier-Jouët and Taittinger. Some houses allow their wines to undergo malolactic fermentation, which creates a creamier wine such as Pommery. Others, such as Lanson, do not do a malolactic fermentation and therefore create a crisper, more vibrant style. Still others make pinot noir the signature grape in the blend for a more robust style, such as Bollinger, Krug, Louis Roederer, and Veuve Clicquot. Champagne made from just pinot noir and/or pinot meunier, such as Duval-Leroy, Nicolas Feuillatte, and Veuve Devaux, are called *blanc de noirs* (white from blacks) and have even deeper fruit and nut flavors.

Speed is critical when you're trying to make white wine from red grapes: the color in the red grape skins will stain the clear juice of the fruit itself if left in contact with it too long. This is also why machine harvesting, which is cheaper and faster than picking by hand, is illegal, because it would break the grape skins and color the juice of the wine. Growers can't truck grapes over such a wide region fast enough, so dozens of "press houses" close to the vineyards press the grapes in whole bunches just after they're picked, and the extracted juice is driven the next day to the winery to ferment.

Of course, sometimes winemakers actually want that staining when they're creating pink champagne—a rosé style that makes up less than 5 percent of all production. Personally, I love the naughty color of rosé bubbly and its sexy short-dress raspberry aroma. It conjures up the decadence of a weekday afternoon picnic beside the Seine, eating caviar with the caped musketeer D'Artagnan.

Rosé champagne has a reputation as an inferior wine because some of the first wines many people drank were saccharine, pink fizz such as Cold Duck, just one step up from soda pop. Good rosé is actually dry, crisp, and full-bodied. Its aromas of strawberries and raspberries pair well with duck, game, and salmon. Lovers of red wines often prefer rosé and *blanc de noirs* over *blanc de blancs* champagnes.

Rosé is also slightly more expensive than its white siblings because making it is even more labor-intensive and time-consuming. The most common method in Champagne is to blend nonsparkling red wine into the champagne. The other approach is more difficult because it involves carefully limiting contact between the red skin and the juice to create the coveted pale salmon color known as *oeil-de-perdrix* or partridge eye. Wine made this way has a more delicate flavor, whereas rosé made by blending in red wine has deeper, more robust red fruit aromas. The main challenge with either approach is to create the same color year after year even though the blend of grapes changes.

Regardless of the wine style, grapes in Champagne are classified according to a strict scale of quality, just as in Burgundy. Of its 243 villages, just 17 are designated grand cru, the finest grapes. Premier cru wines come from 44 villages, and the remaining villages are in less favored areas. Although prices used to be based on these designations, today grape growers charge what the market will bear. As most houses actually own less than 20 percent of the grapes they need to make the wine, the Comité Interprofessionnel du Vin de Champagne (CIVC) requires that all the producers develop a reserve of wine in good harvests. This protects both the growers and the makers. In years of shortage, it prevents prices from going through the roof; while in abundant years, it ensures that the prices don't plummet.

Of course, some years are better for one grape or vineyard than the others, so winemakers adjust the blend accordingly to create a consistent profile. The Champenois liken this task to creating the harmonies of an orchestra rather than individual notes of a violin solo. At Veuve Clicquot, winemakers taste about three hundred reserve wines and five hundred base wines for their blends. Panaïotis allows me to sample several of their young, unblended base wines: he lines up five glasses of cloudy white wine, ranging in color from almost white to golden straw. Tasting them, I get a rare peek at one of the components of great champagne. It's like walking into the Chanel dressmaking shop and looking at the threads, buttons, and fabrics before they're assembled.

It's also a tasting tour of the region, like running my tongue over the essence of each vineyard. It's odd not being able to actually see the difference between the pinot noir and chardonnay; only the taste and texture reveal which is which.

Veuve Clicquot's top wine or *tête de cuvée*, La Grande Dame, is made from eight grand cru vineyards that were originally owned by the widow herself. Other *têtes de cuvée*, such as Krug Grande Cuvée, may blend as many as sixty wines and ten vintages, some as old as fifteen years. (Devoted fans are called Krugistes.)

Several years ago, I attended a tasting of Krug champagne hosted by the charming executive chairman, Rémi Krug. "Champagne is a created wine, not just a wine given by climate and soil," he explained. "What consumers should want to know about their champagne is who made it. That is far more important than where it comes from, or even when." Blending, in his view, doesn't destroy individuality, rather, it creates a style.

It's believed that the art of blending different grapes from different vineyards was originally perfected by the seventeenth-century Benedictine monk Dom Pérignon—the namesake of Moët & Chandon's *tête de cuvée*. As with most origin stories, accounts vary widely. One tells of a frustrated man trying unsuccessfully to get the bubbles out of this "mad wine"; another speaks of him tasting his new creation and exclaiming, "I am drinking the stars!" Some don't believe he invented champagne at all, but rather that the English were making it two decades before the French. Regardless of its origins, the monk is believed to have learned how to clarify the wines so that his were more brilliant than most; to have used stronger bottles, made of thicker British glass; and to have stoppered his bottles with Spanish cork, supposedly brought to his abbey by pilgrims or traders.

Modern champagne is assembled in large tanks that contain the juice from pressing along with yeast to ferment for the first time. Then the fermented wine is poured into bottles along with a small amount of sugary, yeasty liquid (*liqueur de tirage*) and sealed with a metal crown cap—a temporary stopper that will be removed later on. A second fermentation, which lasts about a month, converts the *liqueur de tirage* into alcohol. Normally, when a still wine is fermented in a tank, the carbon dioxide created evaporates. But trapped in the bottle, it dissolves into the wine, giving champagne its effervescence.

Once the yeast has finished its work, it dies and falls to the bottom of the bottle as the lees. The yeast's own enzymes break down in a process called autolysis, which releases various compounds into the wine that give it a toasty, yeasty character. It takes time to complete, which is why there are minimum aging periods for nonvintage and vintage champagne.

The lees also create an unsightly sludge that clouds the wine at the slightest disturbance. Since this diminishes its visual appeal, Madame Clicquot developed the technique called *remuage* or riddling to remove sediment. She drilled holes into her kitchen table and inserted the bottles neck-down. Each day, she and her assistants gave the bottles a small, quick twist. This slight movement dislodged the sediment, which gradually collected in the bottle necks, where it could more easily be removed using a process called disgorging.

Today, when bottles are disgorged, the necks are dipped in

icy brine to flash-freeze the lees. The temporary metal cap is removed and the frozen plug of yeast flies out and is discarded. Once that sediment-gunk is out, the bottles are topped up and resealed quickly with their traditional chubby mushroom corks.

Eventually, Madame switched to upright racks, which took up less space in the cellar. (And presumably, she grew tired of having to chop vegetables on her lap.) But her technique was so effective that the entire Champagne region soon adopted it. A good riddler can give that eighth-of-an-inch turn to about fifty thousand bottles a day.

Ninety-five percent of champagne bottles are now riddled by machine: each bottle is turned multiple times over eight days rather than the eight weeks it takes by hand. Riddling can happen anytime, but is usually done a few months before the bottle is disgorged. The 5 percent still turned by hand are usually either magnums that don't fit the standard slots or prestige bottles such as Dom Pérignon, La Grande Dame, and Cristal. The latter is the *tête de cuvée* made by the House of Louis Roederer, which is where I visit after saying good-bye to Frédéric Panaïotis.

One of the most profitable of all family-owned champagne houses, Roederer is also one of the few that actually grows more than half of the grapes for its own wine. Cristal is made from the best grapes from the vineyards and aged in the bottle on the lees for five years. Even in a good year, the winery only makes sixty-five thousand six-bottle cases; in bad years, it produces none. That happened three times during the 1990s and in both 2001 and 2003.

The director of public relations, Martine Lorson, an elegantly coiffed woman in her early fifties, first gives me a quick history lesson. The house was founded in 1765 by Étienne Dubois, then passed through several owners before Louis Roederer inherited it in 1833 at the age of twenty-four and named it after himself. He built a successful operation, focusing on exporting his wines to Russia, the United States, and the U.K.

In 1932, his grandson Léon Olry-Roederer and his wife, Camille, inherited the winery. Léon lived only two years longer: he died in 1934, leaving Camille to run the champagne house while overseas markets were weak because of the Great Depression and the aftermath of Prohibition. Camille Roederer quickly became another of France's famous widows. A newcomer to the Champagne region, and considered an interloper, she knew practically nothing about making wine. Still, she had an excellent instinct for business; while land prices were low in the 1930s, she bought more vineyards. Today, Roederer owns five hundred acres, which provide 66 percent of the winery's grapes. Camille ran the company for forty-two years until 1975, when her grandson Jean-Claude Rouzaud took over.

Lorson tells me this as we walk down to the cellars where Cristal is aged; the magnums are neck-down in the racks. The bottoms of the bottles glow in the dimly lit caves like the honeycomb of monster bees. Many of them have long, yellowish trails of yeast along the inside of the glass.

"May I try to riddle one?" I ask Lorson hesitantly, fearing to ruin a $500 bottle of bubbly.

She nods encouragingly.

I wrap my hand firmly around a bottle and twist it with what I imagine is a riddler's touch. Then I watch in horror as a cloud of yeast mushrooms upward like a tiny atomic explosion and spreads across the bottle.

Lorson laughs at my appalled expression; she pulls out the bottle and sets it on top of the rack. "Don't worry!" she says cheerfully. "Our riddler is always fixing these."

"Perhaps you could launch a label called Cristal Cloudy?" I

suggest. "It would be ideal for divorces, sentencing days, and other moments when life looks dim."

She laughs again. Roederer certainly doesn't need advice from me or anyone else when it comes to marketing Cristal, the favorite of emperors and rap stars alike. The champagne was created in 1876 for Czar Alexander II of Russia. Back then, Roederer sold a quarter of its production to Russia, most of it to the imperial court. When the emperor realized that he was drinking the same bubbles as everyone else, he was as mortified as if he had worn the same ermine cape twice.

So he asked Louis Roederer to make him an exclusive champagne from the best grapes. The bottle had to be distinctive too, so that everyone could see that Alex had the good stuff. The original bottles were made from lead crystal, hence the name of the new brand. Eventually, they were scaled back to clear glass, which cost less and didn't break as easily.

The new bottles lacked the traditional bottom indentation, or punt, so that would-be assassins couldn't conceal a weapon underneath. It didn't help though: the emperor was murdered in 1881. His son, Nicholas II, kept right on quaffing Cristal. In 1917, when the Bolsheviks didn't see the product as essential to the Communist revolution, it was bad news for Roederer: not only did it lose 75 percent of its business in one shot, but the house also got stiffed for the Russian court's considerable tab.

Fast-forward a century or so and it's now the kings of hip-hop, among others, who drink Cristal. In rapper Jay-Z's video "I Just Wanna Love U," he proposes trading his Cristal for extreme intimacy with a young woman. He also brandishes the drink on an expensive yacht in "Big Pimpin'"—just the kind of "livin' large atmospherics" that brand managers love. Cristal's bling-bling packaging (the clear bottle and gold foil) is also easy to identify even across a crowded bar. In fact, the rapper

seems to have become the unofficial pitchman for the brand.
(So many rap videos feature Cristal that Dr. Evil, the archrival
of Austin Powers, did a hilarious parody of them in the Mike
Myers movie *Goldmember*.)

"The way that Jay-Z drinks Cristal isn't quite the way champagne is best enjoyed," Lorson tells me with the tact of a Swiss
diplomat. "He hasn't sold one extra bottle for us."

Far from rapper territory, and back up from the cellars,
Lorson and I now sit in an elegant drawing room. Its soaring
ceiling, burgundy velvet, and gold brocade give the feeling of
period graciousness—retro bling. I stare thirstily at the bottle
of 1995 Cristal that she unwraps from its ultraviolet-
light-resistant, yellow cellophane paper.

"I'm so glad you've come to visit," she says, smiling. "We
don't get to drink Cristal often." Cristal is on allocation, every
bottle is sold before it's shipped.

I sink into a high-backed leather chair as she pours the
golden pearls into two flutes. Champagne seems to bring out
the most ridiculous of drinking vessels, such as the fad for
drinking it from women's shoes. (That tradition started with
French courtesans in the seventeenth century and kept going
until the 1920s, when the Paris demimonde sipped from slip-
pers at Maxim's restaurant.) Legend has it that the original
wide-brimmed coupe glasses were based on the shape of Marie
Antoinette's breast. But they're more decorative than useful
since their wide surface allows sparkling wine to go flat quickly.

There's a bearable lightness of being to champagne, which
comes not just from its low alcohol and zippy acidity but also
from the rain-cloud density of the drink. It's one of the few
wines on which I've never been drunk: perhaps my body just
knows it's undignified to get over-refreshed in champagne's
presence. As Madame de Pompadour, mistress of Louis XV,

once remarked, "It's the only wine that leaves a woman more beautiful after drinking it." Personally, I think the bubbles and acidity act as an early-warning system: my palate tires of them before I drink too much.

Champagne may be a celebratory drink, but it's also an intimate ritual that transports you into a private world. There's an adagio of the senses: the sweating cold bottle, the glinting stemware, the frothy pour, the small wrist action of raising the glass, the ocean-spritz on your face, the mouth-filling flavor. As I raise the glass to my lips, I breathe in both earth and sky. Gorgeous aromas of pastry-wrapped pears, baked apples, brioche, honey, and spice burst like beads in my mouth. Long after I've swallowed, I can still feel ghostly bubbles tickling the roof of my mouth.

When our glasses are empty, I pull myself up out of the chair with great reluctance and say good-bye to Lorson. Now I'm off to Bollinger, which, like Roederer, was run by a feisty widow and later received popular cultural endorsement that it never sought. Since 1953, when Ian Fleming wrote *Moonraker*, Bollinger has been famous as the favorite tipple of James Bond.

Bollinger is headquartered in Aÿ, a tiny village near Épernay. For thirty years, from 1941 to 1971, Elizabeth Law de Lauriston-Boubers, known as Madame Jacques, or Lily, ran it, doubling sales to more than a million bottles. Her first taste of champagne wasn't until 1923, at her engagement party to Jacques Bollinger, the third generation of the family to make the wine.

When the Nazis invaded France in 1940, they took champagne from many of the producers. Despite Allied bombing to oust the Germans, a depleted labor pool, and shortages of electricity, water, and gas, Madame Bollinger was usually in the vineyards by six A.M., often riding her bicycle up and down the vineyard rows. At night, with her château commandeered by the Germans, she slept in the cellars. On August 22, 1944, General Patton's Third Army arrived just in time to stop the retreating Germans from dynamiting the Bollinger estate.

After the war, Madame Jacques continued her ground-breaking work. In 1969, to mark her seventieth birthday, she introduced a new wine, Vieilles Vignes Françaises (Old French Vines)—the first champagne made entirely from pinot noir grapes. In 1976, the French government awarded her the Ordre National du Mérite, given to those who distinguish themselves in their field.

At the winery, I meet the public relations manager, Christian Dennis, who takes me to see the old pinot noir vines. They're the only ones remaining in Champagne that were planted before the root louse phylloxera destroyed most of the vineyards in France in the late nineteenth century. I feel as though I'm walking through a critical care unit and ought to be wearing a mask. These spindly vines are so vulnerable that they're planted in a walled vineyard not much bigger than a small garden.

Their carefully tilled soil looks a lot different from that of some of the vineyards I had noticed on the drive out here. Several had a few fluttering pieces of plastic in the ground—scraps of a bad memory for the Champenois. After the industrial revolution, farms became increasingly mechanized, and manure to fertilize the vines became harder to find and more expensive. So vintners started using garbage from Parisian households, which in those early days was mostly organic compost. But as the disposable culture gained momentum and people cooked less, more and more inorganic material was mixed in with the fertilizer. It wasn't so much an ecological problem as an aesthetic one: Should the vineyards of the world's luxury wine double as a dump? In 1997, the practice was stopped.

On our way back to the winery, we look into the cooperage: Bollinger is one of the few houses that still repairs its own barrels. The place looks like an eighteenth-century smithy, with iron tools and hooks hanging on the walls, small wooden rims and slats piled on the floor, and an anvil resting in the center of the room.

Whereas most champagne is fermented in stainless steel tanks, Bollinger vintage wine is fermented in old oak barrels, which gives the champagne a deep aroma of hazelnuts and roasted walnuts. The technique works particularly well for the gorgeous Bollinger R.D. bubbly. (R.D. stands for "recently disgorged" and indicates a champagne that's aged much longer than most in the bottle; rather than just spending three years resting on its yeasty lees, R.D. can spend as many as thirty or more.) Oak fermenting exposes the wine ever so slightly to air to better cope with the extended aging in the bottle and gives the wine longevity. When I taste it later, its creamy layers unfold to the back of my palate like an unfurled bolt of satin, while the strands of bubbles edge along the sides of my mouth like lace.

Next we visit the bottling area, where we watch cellar worker Franck Bompais stand at what looks like a metal voting booth, opening and disgorging bottles. As with riddling, large bottles such as magnums don't fit the standard machine slots and are still done by hand. He smiles and asks me if I'd like to try it. I hesitate, worried that I'll spray the wine all over him and myself, but then decide to go for it. He hands me a large industrial apron and I roll up my sleeves.

Bompais positions my hands as though I'm holding a golf club: one hand on the middle of the bottle, the other around the neck. I press the bottle end against my body at liver level. We do a few dry runs, with me practicing flicking the cap off, jerking the bottle up, and then snapping my thumb over the top to stop the foamy fluid. Each time he corrects my hands. A champagne bottle holds air at roughly the pressure of the tires on a city bus: ninety pounds per square inch. It's a bit like holding your thumb over a hole in a dam.

Then it's time to actually try it. My heart pounds and I'm pushing the bottle so hard against myself that I've probably developed a circular bruise. I flick off the cap and there's a deafening shot, like the sound of a revolver going off. I cringe and accidentally angle the bottle toward Bompais. The yeasty plug flies over his shoulder and the following wine sprays all over him.

Belatedly, I jerk the bottle up and put my thumb over the top to preserve the remaining half of its contents. When the yeasty plug doesn't come out fully, it's called a blue bottle. (And when too much wine comes out afterward, it's called a bad effort by a visiting wine writer—although the remaining wine in the bottle is returned to the tanks.)

"If you keep practicing, I'm sure you'll get it," Bompais says good-naturedly, drying himself off with a towel.

"If I keep practicing, I'll damage your bottom line," I say contritely.

If I had done it right, the disgorged bottle would only have lost about an ounce or two of wine. The shortfall would then be topped up with a "dosage" and recorked. The dosage is a mixture of wine and sugar syrup, and it determines the final sweetness of the bubbly. (Because of the high acidity in most champagne, the sweetness isn't perceptible in the taste.) The houses all have their own dosage recipes and guard them fiercely.

Today, the average for the brut, or dry, nonvintage wines (which comprise around 85 percent of all champagne) is eleven to twelve grams of liqueur. That's to appeal to modern tastes. Before 1850, most drinkers preferred their champagne sweet and drank it at the end of the meal with dessert. Wines range from very dry to sweet styles: extra brut, brut, extra dry, sec and demi-sec, and doux. The especially tart extra brut has no dosage added at all.

Another grande dame, Louise Pommery, was one of the first to create dry champagne. During her travels in England, Madame Pommery noticed that the British liked dry wines, such as mature bordeaux and burgundy. So she decided to make a champagne with these tipplers in mind and produced a *brut*, which means brutal, rough, or unrefined, which was how the French described British taste.

The idea caught on, according to Patrick Forbes in his book *Champagne: The Wine, the Land and the People*. Several houses made dry bubblies from the ripe 1857 vintage and shipped them to London in 1874. "Whether he was in the sweet camp or the dry one rapidly became a matter of considerable interest to a man's friends," Forbes observed. "Supporters of dry champagne dubbed the sweet variety 'gooseberry juice' or 'chorus girl's mixture.'"

While the British have retained their taste for dry champagne, many Europeans and North Americans like theirs a touch sweeter. (That's even though they may say they prefer dry—as the wine industry adage about consumer taste goes, "Talk dry, drink sweet.") As Rémi Krug sagely points out, the dosage represents the "complete philosophy of the whole product. If you take one stone out of the wall, the building will collapse. If you don't do the dosage, customers will say the wine is harsh. If you do it right, they won't notice."

Back at Bollinger, the bottles Bompais successfully disgorged are recorked and restacked, along with those that have been done by machine. The stacks are as many as twenty bottles high and rest on nothing but thin strips of wood. The six-year-old still lurking in me yearns to test their stability by pulling out a bottle from the bottom. (Fortunately, my inner adult keeps my hands in my pockets.) Unlike other wineries, which store their reserve wines for future blending in casks, Bollinger's are kept in magnums to preserve their fresh character. (A lower air-wine ratio means slower aging.) The house produces 2 million bottles a year.

Now comes the waiting game: by law, the ordinary, non-vintage wine must age for at least fifteen months; vintage champagne, three years. Dom Pérignon ages slowly according to winemaker Richard Geoffroy. The wine doesn't start to develop its intensity until some six to eight years of bottle aging. Then it enters a second stage, after twelve to sixteen years, when it develops more richness. Finally, after twenty-five years or more, the champagne's full signature is expressed: a creamy texture and toasty, nutty brioche aromas.

This used to be a dangerous period: the internal pressure created by the second fermentation regularly resulted in bottles exploding before the modern era of strong glass. Cellar workers wore Hannibal Lecter–style masks to protect their faces from flying bottle shards. That was the original reason for the punt in the bottom of the bottle: it increased the surface area of the glass, helping it to resist the pressure. Today, the punt isn't really required, but bottles still echo the tradition. In 1844, producers added the wire muzzle over the cork as a further measure of security. Even so, one bottle in a thousand still explodes.

Bollinger and other producers say that what makes champagne unique is the subtle blend of the base wines, but most of us think of those long golden-silvery streams of bubbles. That sparkling fizz is the essence of celebration, so I make a point of visiting Gérard Liger-Belair, an associate professor at the University of Reims, who studies the effervescence in champagne. I'm expecting the "bubble professor" to be a bearded and bespectacled elderly man, but in fact Liger-Belair is a small, wiry thirty-five-year-old. His office, like that of most professors, is filled with books on his specialty: *Universal Foam, Hydrodynamics, A Biography of Water.* Unlike other offices, though, his shelves are lined with bottles, both full and empty.

"I've always been interested in fluid and drops," he says, his eyes shining with enthusiasm. "I came to Champagne to discover the chemistry behind the wine. Bubbles are as mysterious and ephemeral as clouds or waves breaking on a beach—part of the beautiful, fleeting events happening all around us."

In his darkened office, he sets a champagne flute carefully on a small platform in front of a high-speed camera lens and tightens the clamps on either side. Then he opens a bottle of nonvintage brut and pours the wine into the glass. He flicks on the powerful camera light, revealing a metropolis of activity. Clusters of bubbles, looking as big as grapes under the magnification, rise and collapse. We drive around this galaxy of bubbles with the help of his powerful telescopic camera. I feel as though we're actually inside the champagne. It reminds me of my son's Magic School Bus books, where a zany teacher takes the kids on a ride through the body's circulatory system or inside a baking cake.

A bottle of champagne, he explains, contains some 250 million bubbles. That works out to about 50 million in a flute. Even if the wine tastes flat, there are still likely about 3 million bubbles left in a glass. The more bubbles there are, the more aroma molecules are carried up to the surface of the wine— and the more flavor is released in your mouth by those million tiny explosions of liquid fireworks.

It's a myth, he tells me, that bubbles are created from imperfections in the glass. Actually, microscopic flecks of dust are the real nucleation points. But asking for your champagne in a dirty glass just doesn't sound right. (A soapy glass will kill the bubbles because the fatty molecules thin the bubble membrane and burst it—lipstick and peanuts have the same effect.) The secret to preserving the bubbles is to keep the champagne chilled. Carbon dioxide remains dissolved longer in a cold liquid.

Big bubbles in sparkling wine have long been considered unrefined and ugly. The French call them *les yeux de crapaud* or toad's eyes. Producers of cheap bubbly from other regions mechanically inject carbon dioxide into the wine rather than allowing bubbles to form naturally in the bottle during fermentation. (In Champagne this method is illegal.) The opposite myth is that tiny bubbles mean better champagne: it's more delicate and refined. The truth is that older champagne has smaller bubbles just because it's lost some of its carbon dioxide over time. It only tastes better because its aromas have matured.

One motivation for all this research is the desire to develop an edge over ever-improving sparkling wine from other regions in France and around the world. These wines are often made from the same grapes as champagne and by the same methods. The best French sparkling wines come from cool-climate areas such as Burgundy, where they're known as crémants de Bourgogne. Sparkling vouvrays, made from the chenin blanc grape in the Loire Valley, have less fizz, but are still elegant and refreshing. Crémant d'Alsace is a blend of traditional champagne grapes and Alsatian grapes such as pinot gris, pinot blanc, and riesling. Depending on the blend, these wines can range from tart and citrusy to a steely, minerally sparkler.

Most other European countries now make some kind of

sparkling wine. Italy, for instance, produces several styles. One of the most popular, prosecco, is a dry, crisp wine, with a vibrantly floral and citrus character. About a third of proseccos are called *frizzante*; they have a lighter mousse than most, which are described as *spumante*, or fully sparkling. The second type of Italian sparkler, asti, has long been considered a syrupy concoction, but modern versions are much more balanced and refreshing.

Spanish sparkling wine, or cava (meaning cellar), offers some of the best values. Cavas are made with the traditional champagne method, but using three white Spanish grapes: macabeo, parellada, and xarel-lo. (Increasingly, though, chardonnay is in the blend too.) By law, cavas must be aged in the bottle on the lees at least nine months, eighteen months for the reservas, and thirty months for the gran reservas. Cavas tend to taste less yeasty and more earthy than champagne. However, they can still be refreshing.

Nearly all German sparkling wine is known as sekt and it's mostly made from a variety of white grapes. The sparklers known as deutscher sekt are considered better quality. German sparklers, which have a zesty mineral character, are usually either dry (*trocken*) or medium dry (*halbtrocken*).

Although many wine lovers may not think of Britain as a winemaking nation, in fact there are no fewer than four hundred vineyards in England and Wales. Of these, some fifty make sparkling wine from the classic grapes in areas where the soil and climate are similar to those of Champagne, mostly in the warmer southern counties of the country.

In the New World, sparklers tend to be more fruit driven. Those producers may not yet match champagne's premium brands, but their best bottles can easily stand up to the non-vintage champagne. In fact, many of the better Californian

wineries that produce sparklers are owned by the great cham-
pagne houses: Domaine Chandon (Moët & Chandon),
Domaine Carneros (Taittinger), and Roederer Estate
(Roederer).

In Canada, the cool climate produces sparkling wine as well
as sparkling icewine. For the latter, the effervescence of the
wine tempers the icewine's sweetness, making it wonderful
during dinner or after. In Australia, regions such as Tasmania,
Yarra Valley, and Pipers River produce fresh, delicious sparklers,
including the unique Aussie red sparkling shiraz.

More than any other region, though, Champagne accords
great importance to aging. To understand why, I visit the
Pommery winery, famous for its eleven miles of underground
cellars. Beneath the whole Champagne region is a massive
labyrinth of caves. Some of the main arteries are wider than
the streets above. More than three hundred miles of underground galleries, one of the largest cellar networks in the world,
hold more than a billion bottles.

These caves—as much a marvel to wine lovers as the pyra-
mids in Egypt are to historians—have been designated a
historic monument. In the third and fourth centuries, the
Romans excavated the chalk to build homes and roads. They
dug vertical pits, with thirty-foot shafts that widened as they
went down. Later, after the Romans left, the Champenois
connected the pits horizontally for their cellars. Pommery alone
has 120 of them holding some 20 million bottles.

The gloriously gaudy Pommery building in Reims is an
architectural hodgepodge of towers, domes, and spires, all
blazing with orange, red, yellow, and blue. It's a modified
Elizabethan neo-Gothic style, chosen by Madame Pommery
in tribute to the British. In 1886, after her dry champagne
became one of the top exports to the U.K., she used the profits

to build the grand Pommery estate, over which she presided for thirty years.

Life wasn't always easy for her. In 1858, her husband, a wool trader, died suddenly. At age thirty-nine, she was left a widow with two young children just two years after he had invested in the champagne business. Madame developed Pommery from a small winery into one of the world's most respected champagne houses, buying some of the best vineyards in the region and creating a new style of champagne.

My guide, Marianne Barbier, shows me down into the cellars, down 116 steps (I count), descending a hundred feet underground. Echoes whisper out of distant caves. They sound like voices of lost souls in a circle of hell, but more likely it's just the chatter of some of the eighty thousand tourists who visit the winery every year.

Surprisingly, the air doesn't smell stale like a basement. It's earth-fresh and humid, reminding me of mushroom risotto. In fact, mushroom mold hangs from the biscuit-pale ceiling and peels off the walls like old bandages. That's actually a good sign in a wine cave because it shows the proper humidity (thanks to that spongelike chalk). The temperature too is constant and a perfect ten degrees Celsius, ideal to allow the slow evolution of the wine without the corks drying out.

In this netherworld, all sounds except our footsteps are gradually absorbed by the blanket of quiet around us. The caves are darkly meditative, as though you're walking through the passages of your own thought. Madame Pommery had a whimsical approach to mapping out the cellar: every time she launched her champagne into a new city, she named one of the underground "streets" after it. We walk past avenues named Buenos Aires, Liverpool, Montreal, and other cosmopolitan centers.

During the wars, the caves belonging to Pommery and other

winemakers became refuges, housing sleeping quarters, hospitals, schools, churches, and even a theater. This is the underground Reims, the city's shadowy mirror image.

"Even during the bombing, they continued to pick the grapes because they had to earn a living," Barbier tells me. "The men had gone off to war, so it was the women and children who'd crawl out between the vines—many of them died." She points to a pile of bottles from the early 1940s. "The blood of France is in this wine."

We walk back past some of the black wrought-iron gates down here that guard stashes of sleeping bottles. Young champagne is almost a different wine from when it is mature. In its youth, it's bursting with zesty fruit; in old age, mellow toastiness.

Those 116 steps seem like a lot more on the way up, especially when I realize that they're the equivalent of ten flights of stairs. By the time we've returned to the top, I'm panting as though I've done three hours on a StairMaster. Back at the surface, the timelessness of the caves is dispelled as a tourist looks at his watch, and I'm reminded of more recent developments.

Pommery, like many other houses, has sought to keep champagne's image current, especially to the new generation of drinkers. In 1999, it launched a bubbly called POP (Product of Pommery), a sweeter, less-alcoholic version of its nonvintage champagne. The drink comes in a cobalt-blue bottle, a quarter of the standard size, and it pours about a glass and a half of wine. A straw that comes with the bottle was inspired by those parched, reedy models who were sipping their drinks backstage so as not to smudge their lipstick.

This "toy champagne" was created for the twenty-five-to thirty-year-olds who weren't drinking a lot of champers, even though they were social sippers in fashionable clubs. POP is easy to take out onto the dance floor. Pommery even hired Italian designer Maurizio Galante to create tiny "down jackets" for its minibottles (as adorable as Barbie outfits) to keep them chilled.

Several other houses followed the trend to making champagne more hip for the younger market. Piper-Heidsieck and Moët both launched minis. Veuve Clicquot came out with four half-bottles in a stylized paint can that conveniently converts to an ice bucket.

These baby bubbles also aimed to make champagne a more casual, everyday drink. In a way, the success of champagne has worked against it: most people only think of it for special occasions and large gatherings. They don't want to open an expensive bottle that will go flat if they don't finish it. (There are some special stoppers that claim to preserve most of the effervescence in leftover bubbly. Personally, I've thought the drink would be enticing the next day, but then again, I've never opened a bottle of champagne I didn't finish.)

Other producers took advantage of packaging different ways. For its 1988 Noble Cuvée, Champagne Lanson commissioned fashion designer Paco Rabanne to create silver-mesh drapery for the bottles that looked like the chain mail worn by medieval knights. Lanson even launched its design during Fashion Week, throwing parties for Rabanne, the bottle, and his new clothing collection. Female models wore head-to-thigh chain mail with champagne caps, and male models donned metal tunics and leather. In 1999, Piper-Heidsieck released its Special Cuvée Champagne, dressed in red pleather, lace-up corsets designed by Jean-Paul Gaultier, the man who created Madonna's famous corset with cone-shaped "headlights." The dominatrix style was also launched during Fashion Week.

In fact, many champagne houses have partnered with fashion

designers. The Hermès boutique in Paris serves Louis Roederer champagne at its receptions. And it's no coincidence that Louis Vuitton, the famous luggage designer, now owns several champagne brands. The company built its empire on conspicuous consumption including the eponymous luggage, TAG Heuer watches, Givenchy perfume, Christian Dior designer wear, Thomas Pink shirts—and the houses of Moët & Chandon, Veuve Clicquot, Krug, Ruinart, Mercier, and Canard-Duchene. In fact, the full corporate name is now Louis Vuitton Moët Hennessy.

Even Perrier-Jouët, famous for its Belle Époque white flower bottle (Fleur de Champagne), in 1998 launched gold-and-green versions with Beverly Hills handbag designer Kathrine Baumann. The bag is twenty-four-karat-gold-plated and hand-jeweled in Swarovski crystal and sells for a cool $2,687. They even come with $375 pillboxes to hold the champagne corks.

How, I muse, do the Champenois manage to maintain such an image of exclusivity when they produce some 300 million bottles a year? Even prestige bottlings, such as Moët & Chandon's Dom Pérignon, are reported to be made in relatively vast quantities of several million bottles a year.

Part of it, of course, is that champagne is so powerfully entrenched as a hallmark of society and celebration. But turning people on to champagne isn't as easy as persuading them to buy a different brand of breakfast cereal. "Our consumers are a relatively small group, so they'd only be ten percent of the audience if we advertised on television," Frédéric Heidsieck, the director of export sales at Louis Roederer, tells me later during an interview. "This isn't a simple mass-produced food product that's easy to communicate.

"The culture is so strong here and the weight of our history so heavy that marketing must really be creative now," Heidsieck says. Today, the association of champagne with top sporting events is a classic one. Mumm Cordon Rouge sponsors both the Formula One and Grand Prix races, where winners douse themselves with the champagne. Veuve Clicquot sponsors the Polo Gold Cup in the U.K. Winston Churchill's favorite, Pol Roger, has sponsored its placement aboard the *Sir Winston Tall Ship* and named its *tête de cuvée* Cuvée Sir Winston Churchill. Churchill himself once said of champagne, "In victory, we deserve it; in defeat, we need it." (Notably, the *Titanic* was one of the few ships not to be christened with champagne.)

Piper-Heidsieck, supposedly the bubbles in which Marilyn Monroe liked to bathe, is more into arts than sports: it sponsors the Cannes Film Festival as well as other film events. Louis Roederer sponsors classical-music events, Taittinger hosts a cooking prize, Pol Roger sponsors the Oxford versus Cambridge University Blind Tasting Competition, and Veuve Clicquot hosts France's Businesswoman of the Year award.

So why, I ask Heidsieck, haven't other wine regions been as successful in their marketing? Sure, many countries offer prestige bottlings, but no other area seems to have convinced us so thoroughly that every bottle they produce is a top-quality luxury. Granted, there are many contributing factors: consistent quality from blending, high standards, easy-to-remember brands, and pricing that is reasonable for the luxury segment.

"The champagne concept is fragile," says Heidsieck. "It can be ruined with deep discounting in supermarkets." The Champenois fight against having their product cheapened by price or position in British supermarkets and North American warehouse stores. It's a tough battle when Dom Pérignon is in the same aisle as Downy fabric softener.

In North America, in spite of its wide applicability to any celebration, champagne is considered a seasonal product. It's often referred to as a poinsettia wine because most North American sales are in the fourth quarter of the year. But in France and elsewhere, any time of the day is good for champagne. It's one of the few wines one can consume before noon without getting hauled off to Alcoholics Anonymous: no Mother's Day brunch would be complete without a round of champagne-and-orange-juice mimosas. In England, this cocktail is known as Bucks Fizz, invented in the 1920s at the exclusive Bucks Club, in London's tony Mayfair neighborhood. The club's founder, Captain Herbert Buckmaster, was golfing in France when he tried the cocktail made of champagne, peach juice, and a third mystery ingredient, which is a closely guarded secret. Buckmaster asked his own barman to make it, substituting orange juice for peach. The combination of peach juice and bubbly was the basis of one of Ernest Hemingway's favorite tipples, the Bellini, created for him at Harry's Bar in Venice using Italian prosecco.

In the middle of the afternoon, bubbly calls to mind sun-dappled lawns and picnic baskets full of smoked salmon. As the formidable Madame Bollinger said, "I drink champagne when I am happy, and when I am sad. Sometimes I drink it when I'm alone. When I have company, I consider it obligatory. I trifle with it if I'm not hungry and drink it when I am. Otherwise I never touch it—unless I am thirsty."

One of the challenges in marketing champagne is protecting the name itself, preventing it from devolving into a generic term for all sparkling wine. Champagne makers struggle to preserve their brand, just as the makers of Kleenex and Xerox must fight to keep their trademarks from becoming everyday terms for tissue and photocopying. Wine is a product of place, of local soil and climate. Simply using the same grapes and methods elsewhere doesn't create the same wine. Winemakers in Champagne must follow strict quality guidelines that makers of bubbly in other places don't have to. The danger is genuine: the makers of chablis, the lovely steely chardonnay made in the north of Burgundy, weren't as zealous in protecting their name. Now its reputation has suffered in North America, where even cheap white wine in boxes is labeled "chablis."

The Champenois must be vigilant and keep an eye out for infringements around the world. The CIVC even employs a team of lawyers to pursue cases and take malefactors to court if necessary. Usually, the infringers back down when confronted and change their product names. Interloper products seeking the image (and price) of luxury have included a German pear liqueur named Champagner Bratberne, a Norwegian lemon soda called Champagnes Brus, and even yogurt, chocolate sauce, sunglasses, a hotel, computers, jewelry, skin-care products, soap, and naturally lots of brands of bubble bath. In 1993, even the haute couture house Yves Saint Laurent lost the right to sell its Champagne fragrance. The French court found that the perfume name had "an attractive effect borrowed from the prestigious Champagne appellation."

One of the more complex cases involved the tiny Swiss village of Champagne, in the foothills of the Jura Mountains. The village (population 657) has made still white wine from the chasselas grape for more than a thousand years—long before the French started making champagne. The place produces only twenty-five thousand cases a year, worth some $1 million. (That's less than 1 percent of Champagne's production.) But in 2004, under a Swiss-EU agricultural agreement, Switzerland had to renounce its right to name the wine after the village.

Incensed, the villagers took their case to the European court, arguing that for one thing their wine could never be confused with bubbly. "For me, Champagne is not a brand name, it's the name of our village," said former mayor Albert Banderet, who spearheaded the case. "Our rights have been trampled in the interests of big business and French imperialism." While the court case is pending, the winemakers have agreed to name their product Libre Champ, loosely translating to "free the champagne." Production has gone up by five thousand cases since the dispute began because of the publicity.

At Veuve Clicquot, the display case of counterfeit wines showcases several that are extremely well done; it's almost impossible to tell they're fake. Others, such as the Veuve Clicquot golf balls or ginger ale, are easier to spot. Not only is the name Veuve Clicquot trademarked, so is the brand's signature color of egg-yolk yellow-gold. So if you're thinking of labeling your own hooch, stay away from 137C on the Pantone chart—it's taken.

Other countries have adopted their own nomenclature, dropping not only the name *champagne* but also *méthode champenoise*, the traditional method for making champagne. New terms now include *méthode traditionelle* (France), *metodo classico* (Italy), and *méthode cap classique* (South Africa). Today, most countries have even agreed not to import any non-Champagne wines that call themselves champagne or even have *méthode champenoise* on the label.

To firmly entrench champagne as a brand name and not a generic one for all bubbly with North American consumers, the CIVC has been running an advertising campaign for several years in magazines such as *Saveur, Wine Spectator, Vanity Fair*, the *New Yorker*, and the *Economist*. The humorous ads feature big question marks next to silly questions misplacing American products: Gulf Shrimp from Nebraska? Washington Apples from Nevada? Monterey Jack from Alaska? The campaign explains why misappropriating geographic names for food and wine products both misleads consumers and cheats producers.

Still, the product walks a fine line between insisting on special status and trying to make it an everyday drink. As Rémi Krug points out, "You can still listen to *Don Giovanni* in jeans."

No doubt the Champenois will find a way to cleverly position their product as both a celebratory tipple and a drink to brighten up ordinary meals. The success of their marketing efforts have made bubbly one of the few wines that consumers buy without relying heavily on critics' ratings. (That's helped, of course, by the fact that most are nonvintage wines, which makes them difficult to score since scores are usually tied to a particular year.) Champagne really belongs in the Food and Wine Marketing Hall of Fame, right up there with single-malt scotch and Cuban cigars.

"Champagne stands for love, success, smiles, all the positive moments in life," Frédéric Heidsieck tells me. "It's an international concept for events like welcoming diplomats, toasting weddings, sealing deals, and celebrating firsts: new baby, new boat, new champion, new king."

For some, the allure of champagne is the image of luxury and celebration; for others, it's one of life's greatest sensory delights. For me, it's the Champagne behind the champagne, a region as old as the Roman conquests, as deep as the chalk fissures, as artful as the riddler's hands, and as eternal as the taste itself.

FOUR

Purple Prose with a Bite

THEY CALLED IT a tempest in a wineglass: two of the world's most respected wine writers facing off against one another over one bottle of wine. Of course, there's nothing unusual about critics disagreeing, even vehemently. But this time, the debate degenerated into a rumble over the definition of wine itself—and the integrity of the critics.

In the American corner was Robert Parker, whose wine scores carry so much weight that they move the market. From Britain was author Jancis Robinson, Master of Wine and columnist for the *Financial Times* of London. Both have written more than a dozen books and both have been experts on wine for more than twenty-five years. The power of these writers reflects the overwhelming choice and confusion consumers face when they buy wine. There are more than a million wine producers worldwide, most quite small. No other industry has such a wide range of brands and prices, from boxed plonk for $10 at the liquor store to cult bottles for several thousand dollars at auction. Without a critic's tasting note and score, most consumers have to guess if they'll like the wine just by looking at the label.

At issue was a red wine from Bordeaux: the 2003 Château Pavie made by the controversial businessman Gérard Perse. In

the 1990s, Perse, who had made his millions by founding a
Paris grocery chain, bought several prestigious properties
around the medieval town of Saint-Emilion: Château
Monbousquet, Château Pavie Decesse, Château La Clusière,
and Château Pavie. He also invested millions in his new estates
and in their winemaking facilities. (Though one traditionalist
grumbled that his floodlighting of Château Pavie at night
looked "like Disneyland.") Bordeaux has fifty-seven appellations, but the five best known for their wines are Graves,
Sauternes, and Médoc on the left bank of the Gironde estuary,
and Saint-Emilion and Pomerol on the right. Perse was part
of a small group of nontraditional winemakers on the right
bank, some of whom were called *garagistes* because their
production was so small it could fit into a home garage. Others,
like Perse, had revitalized larger, existing wineries. Pavie, for
example, produces about one hundred thousand bottles a year.

These winemakers cut their yields dramatically and picked
late in the season to get extra ripeness from the grapes. (In fact,
many vintners considered 2003 hotter than the past fourteen
vintages, which exaggerated this ripeness.) They used winemaking approaches unconventional for the region, such as letting
fermentation and maceration go on for about thirty days
compared to the average twenty days to extract more color and
flavor from the skins. Some used micro-oxygenation, a technique that pumps tiny amounts of oxygen into the wine as it
ferments in the tank. The extra oxygen accelerates aging, which
normally happens slowly in the barrel. As a result, the wine feels
rounder and more full-bodied in the mouth earlier in its life.

Others went so far as to finish fermentation in new oak
barrels rather than the customary stainless steel vats—and some
even did it twice, transferring the maturing wine from one
extra-toasted barrel to a second one to extract the maximum

amount of those sweet, smoky aromas. (They called this 200 percent new oak.) Many of these wines weren't made from particularly exalted land or grapes, but their style was an extraordinary departure from what was typical in Bordeaux, usually a paragon of balance and elegance: they were rich, robust, deeply colored, and high in alcohol.

Some of these wines—Pavie, Le Dôme, Gracia, Valandraud—were strikingly similar to the cult cabernets of California, such as Screaming Eagle, Bryant Family Vineyard, Colgin Cellars, Harlan Estate, and Staglin Family Vineyard. In fact, traditional winemakers on the left bank criticized them for being more Californian than Bordelais. What really got up the noses of the establishment, though, was that these arrivistes had no track record—and worse, didn't price their wines according to the conventional pecking order. For French aristocrats, this was as deplorable as if their only daughter had eloped with a Las Vegas blackjack dealer.

The traditional order in Bordeaux had been established in 1855: to prepare for the Universal Exhibition in Paris, Napoléon III asked the Bordeaux wine brokers to rank the top châteaux. They classified the red wine, which is 88 percent of what the region produces. Sixty-one châteaux were put into five tiers. The top-ranked wines, called first growths, included Lafite-Rothschild, Latour, Margaux, and Haut-Brion. In 1973, Château Mouton-Rothschild was elevated from second growth to first, the only change to the original classification.

The classified wines all came from the left bank—they were thought to be more serious, with greater aging potential than those on the right bank. All Bordeaux wines are blends of grapes: the whites are made from sauvignon blanc, semillon, and muscadelle; and the reds from cabernet sauvignon, cabernet franc, merlot, petit verdot, and malbec. However, left-bank wines use more cabernet sauvignon in their blend, a tannic grape that gives the wine structure and the ability to age for decades. Right-bank wines use more merlot, a less tannic grape that creates a plusher, softer texture that allows the wine to be consumed earlier (though these can also be aged to distinction).

The 1855 classification was based largely on price, which at the time was the best indicator of quality. The top-ranked wines are still generally the most expensive today, though in the intervening century and a half, many of the châteaux have changed ownership. A new owner, for better or worse, can affect vineyard practices, quality, and even the exact boundaries of the vineyard.

Yet the garage wines sold for stratospheric prices, often higher than for the established first growths. Newly released bottles of Valandraud started at $250. The French may have been outraged, but New World buyers weren't. New York retailer Sherry-Lehmann sold the 2003 Château Pavie for $190 a bottle in 2006.

In his newsletter the *Wine Advocate*, Parker described the 2003 Pavie as "off-the-chart" and created by perfectionists. "It is a wine of sublime richness, minerality, delineation, and nobleness," he enthused. "Inky/purple to the rim, it offers up provocative aromas of minerals, black and red fruits, balsamic vinegar, licorice, and smoke. It traverses the palate with extraordinary richness as well as remarkable freshness and definition . . . A brilliant effort, it, along with Ausone and Pétrus, is one of the three greatest offerings of the right bank in 2003." Parker gave the wine a rare score in the range of 96 to 100 points out of 100. (He would give the wine an exact score after it was bottled in 2006.)

In his view, the Pavie property possesses "one of the greatest terroirs," and its limestone and clay soils "were perfect for handling the torrid heat of 2003." He was bullish on the wine's ability to age too. "The finish is tannic, but the wine's low acidity and higher-than-normal alcohol (13.5 percent) suggests it will be approachable in 4–5 years," he wrote.

Jancis Robinson was unimpressed with Château Pavie to almost the same degree: she gave the wine a score of just 12 out of 20, describing it as having "completely unappetizing, overripe aromas. Why? Porty-sweet. Port is best from the Douro, not Saint-Emilion. Ridiculous wine, more reminiscent of a late-harvest zinfandel than a red bordeaux with its un-appetizing green notes."

The Pavie debate helps to crystallize the differences between two of the most powerful figures in the world of wine. They approach their subject from almost opposite perspectives. When it comes to scoring wine, Robert Parker is acknowledged to be the world's most influential critic. Jancis Robinson is considered one of the best writers for chronicling the people and places in the wine world. Knowing about their training and experience helps to understand these differences and how they influence the wine we drink.

No one in the wine world is more followed or feared than Robert Parker. Few topics provoke more controversy than his 100-point scale. Retailers refer to the "Parker effect": a wine he scores above 90 can't be bought (because demand for it is so high), and one below 80 can't be sold (because drinkers think it's inferior).

Parker seems to attract both honors and controversy. He's been presented with two of France's highest civil awards; and he raised $24,000 at a U.S. charity auction from a bidder who just wanted to dine with him. He's also been slapped with a libel suit and has received death threats. His palate is viewed as the vinous equivalent of Michelangelo's right hand.

Parker has been described not just as the most powerful wine critic, but as the most powerful critic in any particular field.

As Adam Gopnik wrote in the *New Yorker* in 2004, "Not since Bernard Berenson made his lists of true and false Italian pictures had an American expert on the arts so fundamentally changed the economics of European culture. As with Berenson, what mattered was not so much that the list was right—who could tell for sure?—as that the list existed."

How did this happen to the man who was born a dairy farmer's son in a small Maryland town in 1947? Parker's parents didn't drink wine, or even milk—they were Coca-Cola folk. He was twenty before he discovered wine. During Christmas vacation from university in 1967, he went to France to visit his high school sweetheart, Pat Etzel, who was studying at the University of Strasbourg. Since they were eating on student budgets, Etzel encouraged him to drink the local table wines, which were cheaper than Coke. Parker was immediately smitten—both with French wines and with Etzel, whom he later married.

Parker rose to stardom on the flood tide of wine appreciation in late-1970s America, as a newly moneyed middle class developed a thirst for the finer things in life. But the country didn't have a traditional wine culture, nor the knowledgeable merchants of Britain. (Wine was, and still is, sold through a three-tier distribution system that effectively keeps most of the importers who taste the wines well away from the consumers who buy them.) Although the domestic wine industry was making strides, Americans tended to choose from a far wider range of wines than did Europeans, who mostly drank their local wines. Those fledgling U.S. consumers had few resources to guide them, so they quickly latched onto Parker's guidance—particularly since he seemed to be an ordinary person like themselves, not some bow-tie connoisseur. His newsletter, now called the *Wine Advocate*, quickly established itself as the *Consumer Reports* of wine and today has some forty-five thousand subscribers.

Parker considers himself the Ralph Nader of wine. Like Nader, this self-taught critic crusades on behalf of consumers rather than cozying up to the industry. "When I started, most wine writers existed at the largesse of the wine trade," he explained to me when we spoke by phone. "But I went to law school during Watergate, and the professors really beat into us what a conflict of interest was."

The *Advocate*'s front page announces that it "relentlessly pursues the goal of providing valuable, uncensored, totally independent and reliable information on wine and issues affecting wine quality to those consumers in search of the finest wines and best wine values." The newsletter's graphic, a corkscrew, is designed in the shape of a Crusader's cross.

"Early in my career, producers offered me Napoleonic music boxes, a Porsche, and their daughters," Parker tells me with a chuckle. One enterprising Burgundian winemaker, Dominique Lafon, once took it upon himself to include two free cases of his 1987 vintage with Parker's order—knowing that Parker's daughter was born in 1987. But Parker deflected the gesture: he sent Lafon a check for the wine he'd ordered, and a note saying that he had donated the estimated value of the 1987s to charity.

Another time, when Parker sardonically observed that one vintner's wines tasted good with microwaved food, the producer actually sent him an expensive microwave oven. Parker had the appliance delivered to a local liquor store and told the vintner to pick it up there or it would be donated to charity. By now, he says, most vintners know that such tactics are a "no-go."

Yet Parker has been criticized for co-owning with his brother-in-law an Oregon winery that produces pinot noir. He tries to head off any accusations by declaring this interest publicly in the *Wine Advocate* and by giving his colleague Pierre

Rovani responsibility for evaluating wines from the Pacific Northwest and Burgundy.

What established Parker as the world's leading critic was going head-to-head with several leading writers of the time by declaring the 1982 Bordeaux vintage to be one of the best ever. (He calls it the vintage that allowed him to leave the law.) Those who believed his assessment scrambled to buy the wines from that year; and eventually, consensus moved to his side. Subscriptions to the *Advocate* leapt from seven thousand to ten thousand. (One Chicago retailer recalls a taxi driver coming into his store brandishing the newsletter: he wanted to buy all his cases of the 1982.)

The Bordelais were delighted, of course, though they haven't always welcomed Parker's judgments. For one thing, he has the annoying habit of ignoring the 1855 classification. To their horror, he has even rated unclassified wines ahead of the established châteaux. In the good old days, their system meant that top-tier wines could command hefty prices even in poor years. (If you thought the wines tasted unripe or bitter, you were told that you just hadn't developed a palate to appreciate their elegant restraint.) Parker has turned that hierarchy upside down for the benefit of wine drinkers; and many Bordeaux vintners now wait to price their wines until he has sampled and rated their products.

Parker himself puts it this way: "I don't give a damn that your family goes back to before the Revolution, and you've got more wealth than I could imagine. If the wine's no good, I'm gonna say so."

In 1993, President François Mitterrand recognized Parker's contributions to raising public awareness of French wines and presented him with the l'Ordre National du Mérite. In 1999, President Jacques Chirac awarded Parker the Légion d'honneur (an award created by Napoléon Bonaparte in 1802) and described him as "the most respected and influential critic of French wines in the entire world." No French wine writer had ever won that coveted award. Other American recipients have included Neil Armstrong, Colin Powell, and Ronald Reagan.

Part of Parker's success is that his passion for wine leaps off the pages. When he likes a wine, he tosses around descriptors like "gobs of fruit," "prodigious," "mind-blowing," and "immortality in a glass." Unlike more traditional writers, he doesn't hedge his opinions. There are few *somewhats* or *appears to be.*

Jancis Robinson describes him as "completely untroubled by self-doubt" and says that "you don't have to have a keen grasp of the English language to understand his views, or what is a Parker pick." She also thinks he's a purely American phenomenon: Britain could never produce a Parker. "The British traits of self-deprecation and irony are at odds with the Parkeresque pitch of omniscience."

Fellow Brit Hugh Johnson has harsher words for Parker. In his 2005 autobiography, *Wine: A Life Uncorked,* Johnson writes, "Robert Parker deals in absolutes and castigates those he sees as backsliders." Parker, he says, assumes that there is "better" and "worse" when it comes to wine, whereas Johnson himself perceives differences. He even compares Parker to the George W. Bush administration, linking "imperial hegemony in Washington" with "the dictator of taste in Baltimore." In the past, Johnson writes, taste was largely a matter of harmless fashion. Today, in American hands, "it feels more like a moral crusade."

Along with its moral tone, the *Wine Advocate* has been described as a triumph of content over style, especially when compared to the glossy, full-color magazines filled with photos of celebrities holding glasses of wine. Parker's beige-colored pages, printed in basic typeface, carry no ads or pictures. If the

Wine Spectator looks like a *Town & Country*–style photo album of a society wedding, the *Advocate* resembles the prenuptial agreement. But its simplicity is part of its success: the no-frills format makes it easy for wine stores to photocopy for their shelves, and for subscribers to pass along—which is part of the reason its readership is much higher than its subscriber base.

The other reason is the scores themselves. Although Parker didn't invent the 100-point scale, he was one of the first critics to use it consistently. Consumers embraced his ratings because they were easy to understand and their mathematical judgments seemed unbiased. Think of school grades: 90 or more (points or percent) is an A, 80–89 is a B, 70–79 a C, between 50 and 69 a D or E, and anything below 50 is a failure. (Wines, it seems, are rarely rated below 70.) As a result, many North American critics now use the 100-point scale, including the *Spectator*, *Wine Enthusiast*, and *Wine & Spirits*.

In a 2005 biography of Parker entitled *The Emperor of Wine*, Elin McCoy writes that the wine scores "tapped into a deeper fascination with numbers and ratings that was peculiarly American. To outsiders, Americans were preoccupied with who or what was numero uno—whether it was a baseball team, a rock album on the top-20 chart, or the person with the highest IQ." She quotes British writer Andrew Barr, who observes that wine scores are "a victory of American pragmatism over French mysticism."

In 2001, Robinson started using a 20-point scale in response, she tells me, to her readers' request for scores. But only on her Web site: her books are "point-free zones" as is her *Financial Times* column. "The 100-point scores don't mean anything to us in Europe," she observes. "Points will never be as emotive on this side of the Atlantic. Traditionally, if scores were used here at all, it was simply to achieve consensus on a tasting panel."

She also believes that the most useful assessment of wine comes from a single palate rather than a panel, which drags distinctive wines into the "innocuous middle ground of communal assent." However, scoring wines was "so inimical to traditional British wine lovers that when in 1985 Hugh Johnson was sent proofs of Parker's first book on Bordeaux, he thought [the ratings] were printer's marks."

Johnson himself refuses to rate wines at all. "It's a very useful shortcut for people who don't want to make up their own minds or become involved, or even bother to read tasting notes," he writes. "The idea that you can score quality is fundamentally strange . . . I've never seen it tried on works of art."

Besides, he points out, great wines "never end in an exclamation mark . . . they always leave questions unanswered. They tease you. Short wines just say what they have to say and shut up, but all great wines stay with you. They keep asking you to come back, try me again, see what's happening to me."

The French find rating wines odd. As Adam Gopnik writes in the *New Yorker*, "A man who makes love to fifty-some women and then publishes a list in which each one gets a numerical grade, would not be called a lady's man. He would be called a cad. And that, more or less, is how a good many Frenchmen think of Parker: they don't doubt his credentials; they question his character. A real man likes moles and frailties; a real man marries his wine, as he marries his wife, and sees her through the thin spots."

Can critics even quantify something so elusive, ethereal, and subjective as wine? Many wine lovers believe that the numeric system lends a spurious air of scientific accuracy to what is simply someone's opinion. After all, an emotional response can't really be captured mathematically. The problem with scores, Robinson observes, is that there is no absolute objective truth when it comes to wine. The easily understood shorthand of scores is actually quite difficult to pin down. Is an 85 good, very good, or great? Is there really a difference between wines rated 91 and 92? Even good critics have their off days, blind spots, inconsistencies, prejudices, and palate differences. To compensate for this and for the fact that wine changes and evolves over time, some critics (like Parker) retaste wines every few years to see if the rating should be changed. Parker points out that his scores rarely change by more than a couple of points, if at all.

Language, a more descriptive tool than numbers, has its inadequacies too: Is brilliant better than outstanding? Is zesty better than refreshing? At her first formal tasting, Robinson recalls a gathering of writers, including Hugh Johnson. "The most extraordinary thing was that they all used contradictory expressions and yet acted as though they were in complete accord." She felt reassured that "wine appreciation is an entirely subjective process."

I didn't score wines for the first five years I wrote about them. But like Robinson and others, I eventually responded to readers who wanted them. Many people buy their wine as they do their toothpaste: they want to make a quick decision, but a good one (or at least, a safe one). A good score may give novice drinkers the confidence to make that precipitous leap from bladder-box swill to bottled poetry. So I'm conflicted: while I agree that the essence of wine can never be trapped in a number, I do want as many people as possible to experience the pleasure of wine. If that means using a tool they can relate to, so be it.

Points don't represent the essence of the wine itself, but rather your opinion of it. The debate over scores is a testament to how wine makes us feel and to our need to both quantify and qualify the feeling in a way that we don't with other food and drink. We certainly don't rate orange juice, and there are no cabbage critics talking about the leaf set each year.

In a bolded disclaimer on the cover of the *Advocate*, Parker himself acknowledges, "There can never be any substitute for your own palate." Then again, his success is built on the fact that most wine buyers don't rely on just their own palate. Those who mindlessly follow his recommendations, replacing their own judgment with his, are dubbed "Parker sheep." Winemakers who craft their wines to get high scores are said to "Parkerize" them. They make their wines denser, darker, and more alcoholic to cater to his apparent preference for "fruit bombs."

The grapes for these brawny wines (dubbed TEC for their use of technology, extraction, and concentration) are picked much later in the season than usual, so that they're riper and have more grape sugar. This converts into higher alcohol levels and rounder, fruitier flavors. The downside is that they lose their balancing acidity and the tannins that give a wine structure but need time to smooth out. These wines tend to muscle out other wines in tastings, much like steroid-fueled weight lifters strutting on a beach of ninety-pound weaklings.

Parker disagrees with the charge that he only likes big wines. He claims to be a "wine omnivore" and asserts that he especially likes French wines, which are often balanced and elegant. However, as McCoy points out in her biography, "With few exceptions, the wines that received 95+ scores and set the markets moving had certain things in common—rich texture, intensity and concentration, plush fruit, and, for reds, low acidity. In fact, they were mostly red. The 100-point wines were most often those Parker described as 'massive and powerful.'"

Some vintners feel it's not so much Parker himself they're

trying to woo, as the consumer tastes he represents. In their eyes, his reviews just reflect the ratcheting up of our entire sensory environment, from spicier sauces on our food to bigger special effects in the movies. Still, even if vintners are just responding to market tastes, the scores themselves have some redeeming qualities for the wine industry too. They can help to recognize excellence in winemaking and to weed out faulty or poorly made wines. They can help consumers in liquor stores, particularly in those without knowledgeable staff. (Even when the staff is highly trained, many customers don't know what questions to ask.) Shelf slips that offer ratings and tasting notes can guide buyers in their decisions. The downside is when some dishonest retailers misuse such information by posting the same shelf slips for wines of different vintages, or more egregiously, for entirely different wines. Parker has actually hired a law firm to send warning letters to those who misuse his scores.

Whether it's Parker or the market driving public demand for the big new style, tasting these wines is a punishing exercise. I know that no matter how dedicatedly I spit, the buildup of alcohol and tannin will eventually numb my palate. It's a marathon for the mouth. Everyone thinks how wonderful it must be to drink wine all day; but really it's quite sobering to face fifty cabernets at eight A.M. Reviewing wines also means avoiding many strong-tasting (and delicious) foods and drinks that can skew your palate: coffee, soft drinks, juices, chocolate, sweets, garlic, and spicy dishes. This is the difference between drinking wine for enjoyment and tasting it as a piece of information you need to do your job.

There's also the problem of olfactory adaptation: after a few glasses, I stop smelling certain aromas because I've got so used to them. (It's analogous to the way some women stop smelling their own perfume after a few hours of wearing it—even though others may be reeling backward in the wake of their scent.) When tasting, I perceive each wine relative to the one before; so after twenty or thirty wines, it's mostly those big, alcoholic fruit bombs that shock my palate out of its stupor. After sampling seventy-odd wines, I can barely move my lips, and my tongue feels riveted to the parched roof of my mouth. (After one parent-teacher interview that followed a tasting, I discovered that pressing my face into my glass to smell deeply had left a large purple stain across the bridge of my nose.)

Where I taste about three thousand wines a year, Parker tastes ten thousand (more than a quarter million wines over his career so far). He tastes as many as a hundred wines at one sitting, spending about a minute on each one, sniffing, swirling, and spitting. To compensate, he drinks ten glasses of water a day to keep hydrated and sprays his nose regularly with saline solution. His doctors check his mouth and liver three times a year—and, yes, a clause in his disability insurance really does insure his nose for a million dollars.

That en masse tasting is the wine critic's dilemma. If you only drink one bottle a night with dinner, you don't taste enough to find the range of good wines readers want recommended. But tasting large numbers of wines distorts your perception and takes them right out of the context in which readers will eventually consume them. I've often been surprised by how much I love a certain wine in a tasting and then later find it monstrously heavy with dinner. It's like meeting a person at a noisy bar who seems interesting; but when you bring him home, he doesn't lower his voice—or shut up.

The *New York Times* wine critic Eric Asimov once described the challenges his paper's tasting panel faces. "We do the strangest things in the name of judging wine," he wrote. "If we're visiting a winery, we stand in cold, dank cellars spitting wine into buckets, scribbling notes on smeared slips of paper. In the office, we sit around a table with dozens of glasses of wine before us, sipping and spitting, sipping and spitting, scribbling notes on smeared slips of paper. From these artificial situations, we try to extrapolate how a wine will taste when it's ready to be drunk, or we try to imagine how a wine will accompany various types of food."

It almost seems, Asimov mused, as if he and his colleagues "taste wine every way but the most natural way: slowly with friends or family at a meal, with plenty of time to savor—and swallow—a glass or two."

Still, Parker himself is confident of the wines he likes among the thousands he tastes. Anyone lucky enough to find his favor feels the effect almost immediately. Case in point: California winemaker Donald Patz. Critics had panned the entire Californian 1989 vintage, and it was tough selling for all winemakers, including Patz. Then a friend of a friend gave Parker a bottle of the 1990 to try—and he gave it a rating of 92, with an effusive note on the *Advocate*'s back cover.

"The phone lit up like a Christmas tree," Patz recalls. "Customers were begging to get on our mailing list, and distributors were calling back every fifteen minutes like stockbrokers: 'I've got five cases, I can move five more.'" In an industry increasingly dominated by megacorporations, favorable ratings are often the only way for smaller wineries such as Patz & Hall to get recognition.

The euphoria didn't last. "We've had high ratings from Parker since then, but never quite the same response," Patz noted. "We weren't the hot new label anymore, so it didn't have the same impact. But you can't ever discount his influence: when he speaks, people do crazy things."

Parker clearly has more impact with high scores than low

ones. According to a 2005 study by economists at National Institute of Agronomic Research in France, Parker's scores can affect bordeaux prices by up to 15 percent. The researchers found that his score could add up to $5 to the price of a bottle and that the "Parker effect" is strongest on Pomerol wines from the right bank, of which he's a big fan.

Despite the genuine effect of his influence, reports of it can sometimes be overstated. When Parker decided to delay tasting the 2002 Bordeaux vintage, many in the wine industry believed that the move depressed futures buying in America. But other critics had already characterized the vintage as not a great one and the wines overpriced—which would certainly have dampened enthusiasm for them. And a 2005 study by the California-based Wine Opinions found that 48 percent of respondents said that Parker's recommendations have no influence when they buy wines costing $20 or more. According to researcher John Gillespie, the backlash against Parker's ratings is evident in that the negative survey response toward his scores is twice as high as for any other media or referral source. Some 61 percent rated friends and relatives as having the greatest influence on their purchasing decisions.

Even viticultural practices such as low yields and unfiltered wines, often attributed to Parker's preferences, were already well under way when he started writing about wine. Those techniques were first advocated by the French consulting enologist Émile Peynaud in the 1950s and 1960s. His efforts to improve French wines reached fruition with the famous 1982 vintage— the one that also made Parker's career.

As might be expected, Parker's scores and comments have provoked the indignation of some winemakers. However, few expressed their ire as openly as the estate manager of the Saint-Emilion estate Château Cheval Blanc. After Parker called its wine "a disappointment," the manager invited him to visit the château and retaste the wine. But when Parker entered the front door, the manager's dog, a fox terrier, attacked the critic— biting his leg hard enough to make it bleed, while the other man stood by and watched. Parker asked for a bandage; the manager instead handed him a copy of the *Wine Advocate*.

Parker has even received death threats, most notoriously from a disgruntled American wine merchant. Parker tried to pros- ecute, but couldn't: the man hadn't said that he would person- ally kill Parker, just that Parker would be killed. "He's still selling wine in New York and using my scores, but I don't buy wine from him," Parker told me drily.

Although Jancis Robinson's style may be different from Parker's, their beginnings are similar. Like Parker, Robinson grew up in a small village: she was born in Kirkandrews-on-Eden in northern England in 1950. Her parents also were not wine drinkers; they preferred gin and tonic. She too went to univer- sity to study subjects unrelated to wine, taking her degree in math and philosophy at Oxford. (Her love of food found an early outlet in reviewing restaurants for the student magazine *Isis*).

After she graduated, she took various jobs in search of a career. One job as a tour guide took her through France, reigniting her love of food: its flavors and textures, its "mental stimulation and the physical comfort." That passion eventually led her to wine, "food's quintessential companion, liquid food." She was determined to get a job that would combine her love of both; and in 1975, she started writing for the British industry magazine *Wine & Spirit*.

Robinson attended trade tastings and developed her expertise both as a writer and critic. At that time, many British writers had come from the wine-sales business or were still in it: they wrote reviews of the wines they sold to their customers. That's the cozy relationship to the trade that Parker criticizes. In his sixth edition of *The Wine Buyer's Guide*, he wrote, "Until most of the English wine media begin to understand and adhere to the basic rules of conflict of interest . . . then and only then will the quality of wine writing and the wines we drink improve."

However, Robinson had no such ties and remains independent to this day. Like Parker, she pays for her trips to wine regions; and she's even wary of being photographed holding a bottle for fear of looking as though she's endorsing the winery. ("I'm always turning the label to the back," she says, laughing.) The most egregious assault on her professionalism, she told me, came during a trip to China, when the organizer suddenly departed from the agenda. He whisked her away to a hotel room, where she found herself seated beside a winemaker for a press conference—in front of a backdrop bearing the winery's logo and brands.

"I tried to act as independently as I could," she recalls. "But I was rather thrown by the first question, from a beautifully dressed Chinese woman journalist: "Tell me, Mrs. Robinson, what, in your opinion, is the difference between red and white wine?"

The closest Robinson gets to any commercial involvement is as a wine consultant for British Airways, helping a panel to select the airline's wines for its passengers. (The other consultants are Hugh Johnson, Michael Broadbent, and Colin Anderson.) As a result, Robinson says, "I'd never write about airline wine." As well, she's a member of the Royal Household Wine Committee, which chooses the wines for the queen to serve to her guests. Both committees taste the wines blind and have no affiliation with any producer.

One of her proudest accomplishments was becoming the first person not in the wine trade to pass the notoriously stiff Master of Wine exams in 1984—a feat she accomplished while pregnant. Even as of 2005, the pass rate for both parts of the exam (theory and tasting) was only 10 percent, and there were just 250 Masters of Wine in the world. Although there are now fifty women Masters of Wine, in 1984 there were only eight.

Musing about this, Robinson thinks it might reflect the flip side of that lingering sexism: because society expects less from women, they're free to have a more relaxed relationship with wine. "Men, to a certain extent and in certain circles, are expected to know a bit about wine. There is an obligation on them to order the 'right' wine—rather like driving the 'right' car," Robinson says. "Competitive wine tasting and wine ordering is very definitely a male sport." Women, she thinks, "are much more likely to choose not the wine they feel they ought to choose but the wine they feel like drinking."

Another career milestone was becoming editor of *The Oxford Companion to Wine*, published by the venerable Oxford University Press. The book stands as one of the best endorsements of wine as a serious subject. Until then, writing about wine (like other niche writing, such as food, sports, gardening, and home décor) had long been considered as belonging to the "how-to" service category, rather than to "real" journalism, and still less to literary or scholarly writing.

Now in its third edition, *The Oxford Companion to Wine* features the work of more than a hundred contributors. It covers over four thousand topics, with six hundred grape varieties and seventy-two countries, including newly emerging ones such as Ethiopia, Korea, Thailand, Vietnam, and even Nepal. Robinson edited nearly a million words for the tome.

In 1999, as a tribute to her work, the readers of the leading British wine magazine *Decanter* voted Robinson (Wo)Man of the Year. Members of the British Circle of Wine Writers voted her Most Influential Writer as well, with three times the votes of runner-up Robert Parker. In 2003, she was appointed to the Order of the British Empire for services to broadcasting and journalism.

In her autobiography, *Tasting Pleasure*, Robinson writes about her "old-fashioned need to see ticks and 'VG' in her exercise book," referring to the teacher's check marks and very goods on her homework when she was a student. She adds, "The more I read biographies of women writers, however, the more I am convinced that this need to achieve has nothing to do with education and probably reflects some sort of driven escapism."

Robinson believes that it's mostly been an advantage to be a woman in a traditionally male-dominated field: based on traditional etiquette, she was often seated beside the host at winemaker dinners and tastings. This allowed her to get the inside scoop or, at least, a more detailed story than the journalists sitting farther away. She also says that "medical specialists acknowledge that the tasting faculties are generally better in women" and that many male vintners have told her that their wives or girlfriends are far better tasters than they are.

In all of her career, Robinson can recall only a couple of instances of sexism. One was just after the *Sunday Times* of London had appointed her its wine correspondent in 1980. "I was at a tasting in the financial district of London, run by one of these pin-striped wine merchants," she recalls. "I wasn't taking notes, but most of the other people there weren't, and they were treating it more like a social gathering." One of the fellows peeled off from his group, came over to Robinson, and asked, "I say, do you come to these things to taste for your boss?"

"For once, I *did* think of a suitable riposte," she reports with satisfaction. "I said, 'Not unless you count Rupert Murdoch'— who had just taken over as owner of the *Times* newspapers, so was effectively my boss."

Then there was the time she had just been appointed one of British Airways' wine consultants. When Robinson told an airline manager how pleased she was to be on the panel, she was informed, "Well, we thought we needed a woman."

Reflecting on her own approach to writing about wine, Robinson says in her autobiography, "As a visitor I try to be scrupulously polite; but in print I find myself being dispassionately objective, even sometimes to the point of brutality. I try never to think of the effect of what I write on its subject until after I have written it. Perhaps this is all a reaction against the relatively indulgent school of wine writing that prevailed when I started out."

She says that most American wine writers believe that critics should remain as distant as possible from those who make and sell wine for fear of clouding their judgments with personal feelings. But how, Robinson asks, are we to learn about wine without spending time with the people who make and sell it? In her experience, "wine people are congenitally generous hosts." This, she observes, "may occasionally bring the wine writer into dangerous contact with not only the wine producer but also his family. Perhaps our critical faculties might be swayed by exposure to a pretty wife, wise parent, or particularly cute child?"

In this way, Robinson differs vastly from Parker. Although she was the first to introduce British wine lovers to Parker through her *Sunday Times* column in 1986, she observes "one has the impression that he would really much rather stay at home in Maryland and [have] anonymous glasses pushed through a hatch for evaluation." By contrast, Robinson's own views are openly subjective. Her Web site, www.jancisrobinson.com, welcomes visitors to a "very personal, obsessively updated, completely INDEPENDENT source of news, views and opinion on fine wine and food."

Robinson relishes the human context that surrounds wine. "For me, wine is so much more than a liquid in a glass; the liquid is merely our link to what is so often a fascinating story, a spot on the globe, a point in time, a fashion in winemaking, an argument between two neighboring farmers, rivalry between old schoolmates, perhaps proud new owners who want to make their mark at any cost."

Those differences in approach lie at the heart of the debate over both Château Pavie and the role of the professional wine writer. Where Parker sees himself as a crusader on behalf of beleaguered consumers, Robinson views her role more as an educator and entertainer. ("I don't aim to be laugh-out-loud funny, but I hope that when people read my work, they occasionally say, 'Huh!' because they're amused.") She recommends wines that are good buys at various price points and helps readers understand where wines come from.

More fundamentally, the Pavie debate also raises the issue of what wine is and what it should be. Must it always taste of its origins, the place where the grapes are grown? How much intervention and innovation can winemaking take before it becomes a soulless manufacturing operation? Are concentrated and fruit-forward wines necessarily less sophisticated than restrained and medium-bodied ones? Is a traditional wine more authentic, more honest, than a nontraditional one? Are new wines that try hard to please intrinsically less worthy than those that are already effortlessly established? Are New World and Old World palates different? Is Old Money better than New Money?

When Robinson praised the 2001 French "garage wines" for backing off the big, bold oaky style that had earlier brought them to the world's attention, Parker interpreted this as thinly veiled criticism of his own taste, according to McCoy. "It's her

British DNA taking control of her logic," he responded. "First of all, they couldn't make big rich wines in 2001 because Mother Nature didn't give them the raw materials. So they're spinning it like they're making more elegant wines. She's just parroting the viewpoint of some old reactionaries in Bordeaux, and it is surprising that someone of that stature and intelligence would do that. And it's a way of cleverly taking a shot at me—saying Parker just likes these grotesque, overweight, overly woody wines, which is a total bullshit story."

As other leading writers waded in with their opinions on the 2003 Pavie, the world of wine criticism—usually as sedate as an afternoon croquet game—started to look more like a private-school brawl. The Americans tended to line up with Parker. This included the *Wine Spectator*'s James Suckling, who also rated the wine highly (95–100), and Stephen Tanzer (92–95). Perhaps not surprisingly, British critics sided with Robinson. Michael Broadbent observed, "Parker is looking for concentration, opulence, impressiveness. He should be looking for a wine that is civilized, that is for drinking with food." Another Brit, Clive Coates, refused even to rate Pavie: "Anyone who thinks this is good wine needs a brain and palate transplant."

One of the most thoughtful opinions came from the Japanese writer Katsuyuki Tanaka. Although not a fan of the wine, he observed, "It is a true horror to imagine a stage on which wines line-dance lifelessly with the same smile on their faces. I appreciate 2003 Pavie because it stirred our conception of what fine wine should be."

Then the Pavie debate moved from critiquing wines to questioning wine critics. Michael Bettane and Thierry Desseauve, of the magazine *La Revue du Vin de France*, blamed some critics' lack of enthusiasm for the wine on personal animosity. "Perse has many enemies in Bordeaux and elsewhere. I think some tasters get carried along by this. He [should be] judged by who he is, not by the wines he produces."

Robinson had been vocal about Pavie's owner in the past: "Chief among the current practitioners of caricature winemaking is Gérard Perse, who has used a supermarket fortune to buy such extensive properties." Robinson went on to say that Perse had "just amazed le tout Bordeaux" by offering the wine division of the insurance company AXA-Millésimes more than 300 million francs for Château Petit Village in Pomerol. (Perse eventually withdrew his offer before the deal could be completed.)

Robinson also wrote, "The big force in all this, of course, is the extremely powerful (and admirably conscientious) American wine critic Robert Parker, whose points out of 100 dictate demand and therefore prices in the international wine market. However much he may write that he values subtlety, he has continued to reward sheer size. And whatever sort of wine individual winemakers may wish to produce, it is the château owners who call the tune. What they tend to seek above all is a high score from Parker."

Parker kicked the debate up a notch. On his Web site, he wrote that Robinson's review of the 2003 Pavie was "very much in keeping with her nasty swipes at all the Pavies made by Perse."

Robinson fired back, "What is the difference between a nasty swipe and a critical tasting note? Perhaps the former does not chime with the most powerful palate in the world while the latter does? Wine assessment is subjective. Am I really not allowed to have my own opinion? Only so long as it agrees with Monsieur Parker's, it would seem. I do wish we could simply agree to differ."

She also defended her dislike of the wine itself, irrespective of the maker, saying that she had tasted the wine blind, without seeing the label. "I should make it clear that these notes were written long before I knew what the wine was—and I have witnesses!" (Every March, Robinson attends the *en primeur* barrel tastings of the new wine at various French châteaux, along with many other writers. By contrast, Parker tastes samples delivered to him in his Bordeaux hotel room and he sees the labels.)

Parker wasn't buying her explanation. Robinson would have known what she was tasting, he wrote, because "Pavie is the only premier grand cru estate to use an antique form of bottle that, even when covered up, stands out like a black sheep."

Then Perse himself waded into the fray. "Never did I imagine that trying to make the best wines possible could elicit such virulent criticism and even vicious personal attacks," he fumed. "To portray those who enjoy my wines as 'imbeciles' is insulting and malicious and has no place in contemporary wine criticism." His suggestion was that some British wine critics "would have us go back to a time when they feel Bordeaux wines were made the way they [feel they] should be."

Whatever your view on wine and the role of wine writers, there's little doubt that both topics matter a great deal to an increasing number of people. Ratings, in particular, are becoming the main criteria wine lovers use to buy wines. As much as I dislike personal mudslinging, I actually find it reassuring that there's so much heat in this debate: it shows that many people care enough about wine to duke it out verbally. If we keep our passion for wine—whether it's expressed in numbers, words, or just sighs of pleasure—something vital still lives in the glass and on the page.

A Tale of Two Wine Stores

As I TRUDGE up the steep incline of Van Ness Avenue on a gusty September afternoon, voices, shapes, and shadows stream by. The view behind me looks like a giant fun slide: you could roll down, bump after bump, for several miles before splashing into the bay below. But my thoughts are on the top of the hill where I'll meet the wine savant of San Francisco.

At the intersection of three trendy neighborhoods—Russian Hill, Nob Hill, and Pacific Heights—is a modest store tucked between a stationery shop and a low-rise apartment building. THE JUG SHOP is scrolled across its blue awning, and in smaller letters underneath, a conflicting afterthought, PURVEYORS OF FINE WINES & SPIRITS. Faded boxes are stacked in the window: Gordon's Rum, Duckhorn Vineyards, Cointreau, Krug Champagne. Over them hang neon signs for Budweiser and Bud Light, and peeling decals and handwritten signs (SATURDAY NIGHT RED FOR $8) fill the window gaps. It doesn't look promising, but it's home to Chuck Hayward, whom many consider one of the most knowledgeable (and friendliest) wine experts in this city. Hayward was also one of the earliest advocates in North America of now wildly popular Australian wines.

As I approach the store, laughter drifts out of the open doors along with a Louis Prima 1930s swing tune. Inside, boozy curios hang from big wooden beams and perch on a high shelf around the store: giant liquor bottles, beer pennants and flags, oversize baseballs, and a large white horse, bedecked with tinsel. Covering the three-thousand-square-foot concrete floor are rows and rows of stacked cardboard boxes, their tops ripped off to reveal the bottles inside. The store looks like the basement of a hard-drinking sports freak, but it's not the décor that draws wine lovers to the Jug Shop, it's the staff.

Across the store, I spot Hayward, the store's managing wine buyer, chatting with a customer. In his early forties, with curly orange hair and a broad grin, he reminds me of a grown-up version of Danny from the 1970s show *The Partridge Family*. His carrot-colored T-shirt makes him glow like a neon sign against the dark wine bottles. He waves for me to come over and meet one of his regular customers, who's holding a bottle of sauvignon blanc for a dinner party that evening.

"You know the wine is too cold if you can see your fingerprints in the condensation on the bottle, and if it clouds up the glass when you pour it," Hayward says to her. "If it's too cold, you won't get those great herbal and citrus aromas."

She thanks him and heads for the cash register. "Customers are a lot more knowledgeable about wine these days," he says. "San Francisco, in particular, is one of the most competitive and demanding wine markets in the country because we're only an hour away from Napa Valley. It's also a West Coast thing: our customers are willing to experiment with New World wines, while the East Coast tends to be more Eurocentric."

The Jug Shop certainly has a New World focus, particularly on Australia. In 1990, Hayward fell in love with Australian wines at a tasting in a local restaurant. At that time, few other North American retailers were offering these wines: the wine boutiques tended to focus on classic wines from France, Italy, and California. Hayward had the idea that Aussie wines could help differentiate the Jug Shop from its competition since they were both delicious and much cheaper than Old World wines and even those from California.

Still a relative neophyte with these regions at the time, Hayward had to teach himself about Australia: tasting, reading books, and making annual visits down under to seek out new wines. He's now such an acknowledged expert on these wines that, as well as training his own staff, he's also in demand to train local wholesalers. His customer newsletter is called *Down Under Digest.*

The store now gets an extra sales boost whenever there's an important Aussie sporting event. When the Australian Rules Grand Final football match is played in September or the Melbourne Cup horse race takes place in November, the store holds themed tastings to build on the excitement. "We were one of the first ones in the city to bring in sparkling shiraz, and we sold seventy-five thousand dollars' worth in two months," Hayward says. "Who would have thought red bubbly could move so fast?" The media came calling as well: both *Bon Appétit* and the *Los Angeles Times* interviewed him about the product.

Hayward explains why Australian wines are so successful today. Vintners there aren't bound by tradition or numerous winemaking laws, so they're free to experiment and use whatever techniques and technology work best. As a result, the country is fast becoming one of the largest wine exporters in the world. In 2003, Australia edged out France as the top exporter to the U.K., long considered the epicenter of the world wine trade. Since then, it's performed the same feat in Canada and the United States. Australia is now the fifth-largest exporter (after France, Italy, Spain, and the United States). That's remarkable for a country that in 1990 produced just 3 percent of the world's wine. In 2004, a new winery opened in

Australia every eighty-six hours. And it's good stuff: the powerful American critic Robert Parker has rated Penfolds Grange as highly as French icons such as Château Pétrus.

Why the Aussie boom now? If it were simply a matter of climate, then California, Chile, and South Africa would be just as popular. One of Oz's secrets is blending, which enables vintners to create complex, flavorful wines from grapes grown in vastly different soils and climates. Vintners often ship tons of grapes thousands of miles around the continent—something that would be unthinkable, not to mention illegal, in much of Europe.

Another benefit of blending is that it reduces the economic risk from poor weather. If a vintage is cold or rainy in one region one year, vintners can still use grapes from another region to produce consistent wines. Most other New World countries don't mix grapes from as far afield as Australians do—it would be like a "North American" wine whose grapes came from Napa, Niagara, and Texas. Although some labels do mention the district and vineyard, the most prominent identifier (after the grapes) is usually just *Australia*.

No other wine region markets itself as a country in quite the same way. In France, for instance, labels may bear any one of 467 appellations and tens of thousands of châteaux—but grape names are rarely mentioned at all. Only in the past few years, as consumers have become big buyers of Australian wines and more familiar with them, have Oz producers started to distinguish subregions.

Unlike France, Italy, Spain, and increasingly America, Australia must export: its domestic consumption can't support its wine industry. To that end, Australian winemakers are often on the road promoting their wines. In fact, according to Hayward, the store gets more visits from down under winemakers than from those in California.

Australia, along with California, also pioneered the use of grape names as brands on the labels. Although cabernet and chardonnay can be grown anywhere, many consumers were unfamiliar with them fifteen years ago. The Australians had another trick up their sleeve: shiraz, the grape traditionally grown in the Rhône Valley of southern France as syrah. Renaming it made it easier to pronounce and effectively rebranded it for the Aussies.

Antipodean wines also benefit from their price. Australians have developed a full range of wines of "ladder brands" that allow consumers to move up (or down) a producer's offerings, much like designers who have "weekend wear" lines. Consider Penfolds: it starts with the $10 Rawson's Retreat and progresses up through the $15 Koonunga Hill, the $20 Thomas Hyland, and the various bin wines, until finally arriving at the giddy height of the $250 Penfolds Grange shiraz. The last has the remarkable ability to lend its cachet to the lower-priced labels without diluting its own premium image. This is because the winery introduced Grange and the higher-end bin brands before creating cheaper labels.

It's thanks mostly to Australians that wine is no longer viewed as the preserve of the upper classes, and more like liquid food. Their friendliness has made wine less intimidating. Which would a novice rather ask for in a wine store or a restaurant: châteauneuf-du-pape or Yellow Tail? Yellow Tail has, in fact, become the most popular imported wine in the United States. Since its launch in 2001, it's captured 35 percent of all Australian wine sales in North America, having sold more than 24 million cases worldwide and catapulting into the big leagues with Hardy Wine, Southcorp, and Beringer Blass. It's the first wine in the American market to sell more than a million cases in one month.

Yellow Tail is made by Casella Wines, located in the Murrumbidgee River region of New South Wales. In 1994, it was a small, family operation owned by Italian immigrants

Filippo and Maria Casella, who couldn't even afford to hire their own son John full-time as winemaker. Several factors contributed to its success. Irrigation is widely practiced in the warm river-lands of this region, and large harvests yield consistently ripe grapes. Casella started with a narrow focus—a chardonnay and a shiraz—that both reduced costs and simplified its offer to consumers. It also made the startling discovery that consumers don't really care about bottle shape, so it streamlined manufac-turing by putting both wines in the round-shouldered red-wine bottle rather than selling the chardonnay in the traditional slope-shouldered white-wine bottle. This enabled Casella to price its wines competitively: at $12, they fit into the "fighting varietals" category. That class of wines, priced $8 to $12, accounts for 63 percent of all sales of standard 750-milliliter bottles in the United States.

Casella didn't use any advertising to launch the brand; it depended on word of mouth from consumers and positive reviews from wine writers, although some have been highly critical of it. Critics claim that Yellow Tail appeals so widely just because it's sweet. The wine does have a soft structure, with several grams of residual sugar, although this isn't unusual for the commercial wines sold at this price point. That hasn't hurt its success: the winery is now built on the scale of an oil refinery. It has a 293-million-bottle capacity, and some sixty thousand bottles can go through the bottling line every hour.

Purists rail against branded wines such as Yellow Tail because they stand for everything wine shouldn't be about, in their opinion: predictability, homogeneity, security, profitability, and simplicity of taste. But Château Margaux and Tignanello are brands too; they just happen to be expensive ones. The dark side of wine brands is that they play to our insecurities about trying something new and therefore narrow the diversity of wine. With that consistency comes monotony. The thrill of wine is in its complex, mercurial nature. From this perspective, brands are anti-wines; confections of a chemistry set.

The strong branding of New World wines is one of the reasons France in particular is struggling, according to Kermit Lynch, whose eponymous wine shop is on the other side of the bay in Berkeley. Lynch has been introducing American drinkers to quirky, artisanal French wines for more than thirty-five years. In his devotion to a region and cultish customer following, he's more like Hayward than dissimilar. French wines are losing ground due to several factors, Lynch explains to me later by phone: increased international competition and decreased domestic consumption. Sales have been declining steadily for the past five years. In fact, the only categories still growing are the most expensive French wines, some 2 percent of high-end labels, along with champagne, always considered a luxury.

In 2001, the French Ministry of Agriculture published a scathing report written by Jacques Berthomeau, a senior civil servant and wine specialist. He denounced the selective deafness of the domestic wine industry that had for so long "sat on its little cloud, tipsy and uncaring, like the grasshopper in the fable." (He was referring to the La Fontaine story about the lazy grasshopper that didn't bother to store food for the winter, unlike the hardworking ant.)

Berthomeau also compared the industry's battle against New World producers to France's resounding defeat by the British in 1415 during the Hundred Years' War. "At Agincourt, we were defeated by our own self-certainty and complacency much more than by the English archers," he said. He spoke about the days when France was the reference point for all wines, but "today, the barbarians are at our gates. Australia, New Zealand, the United States, Chile, Argentina, South Africa—is the flood of wines from the New World going to sink the wine industry on the Old Continent? We stick to our own home regions just when we must begin to compete in a universe of consumers who dress in Nikes, eat Big Macs, and drink Coca-Cola. We're in the process of losing the battle for new consumers."

"In the past, French wines didn't have to compete with those from hot climates," Lynch observes. "Now France is up against New World producers who irrigate their grapes and let them ripen to such an extent that the wine is mostly an expression of fruit. It's a consistent recipe of big fruit, high alcohol, and a flash of oak. Plus they now have the technology to control the temperature of fermentation. What's happening to wine is similar to what's happening in Hollywood. Even if you tell a tender love story, you still need to finish the movie with a fire or an explosion. I liked the movie *Rambo*, but I don't want to see it several times to deepen my appreciation of it."

Several domestic trends are also affecting France's wine sales negatively. Since 1960, the country's wine consumption has dropped almost in half. The average French person used to knock back 133 bottles a year; now that figure has dropped to 73. One factor is the inevitable modern shift of the population away from the countryside, with its readily available cheap, everyday wines, and into the cities—where the young urban crowd prefers mixers and beer to the old-fashioned wine of their parents' generation. Another is that traditional wines were low in alcohol and parents served them watered-down to their children at dinner. But today's more powerful wines have alcohol levels of 13–14 percent, so youngsters don't grow up with wine as much as they used to and as a result drink less as adults.

Meanwhile, consumption in many New World countries is trending in the opposite direction. Wine now surpasses beer as the alcoholic beverage that American adults consume most often. A Gallup poll found that, back in 1992, 47 percent of drinkers said they usually consumed beer and only 27 percent said they drank wine most often. A similar poll in 2005 found that their positions had reversed: the numbers were 39 percent for wine and 36 percent for beer. According to a 2006 study by the research company International Wine and Spirit Record, America will become the largest wine-consuming country in the world by 2009, as France falls from first to third and Italy remains at number two.

In Hayward's view, making wine buying easy for the novice is as critical to wine sales as catering to the aficionados. You can try on a dress or read the first chapter of a book, but you usually can't sample the wine before you buy it (at least, not legally). Of course, you could read wine reviews before going to the store, but the sad fact is that most people don't bother—a shattering revelation for a wine writer.

"We aim to have a third of our wines be familiar brands; a third, labels you may have heard of but don't see often; and a third, producers you've never heard of unless you're a real wine geek," Hayward says. "We walk a thin red line because we don't want to scare people or bore them."

Hayward points to the shelf that rings his store: nestled among the memorabilia are two glass-fronted boxes containing soil and vine roots. He explains that they're the different soils in which shiraz grows. "We try to make what customers read come alive for them. We can talk about the technical aspects of wine to those who enjoy that, but we try not to geek out on people. Sometimes we set out clumps of soil in bowls in front of the wines we're tasting so that people can see and taste how different compositions of earth actually make a difference to the wine. Though one time a vintner came in and said, 'Hey, that's not my dirt, man!'

"Wine appeals to the liberal arts major in me," Hayward explains. "It's connected to so many facets of life: agriculture, science, commerce, culture, sociology, history, religion, art. I couldn't work in retail with any other product. And I meet so many different people I otherwise wouldn't: doctors, carpenters, travel agents, teachers, mechanics, judges. I'm helping them with their pursuit of pleasure—what could be more satisfying?

"It's all about matching wines to people, finding the right bottle for the right occasion," he says. "Most folks just want to be reassured that the wine is good. The question I'm asked most frequently is 'What do you like?' I'm also asked to suggest wines for weddings, divorces, baptisms, and wakes. You become part of people's lives." (For wakes, he suggests whatever the deceased liked to drink. For divorces: something strong with a bitter finish.)

"A woman once asked me which wine would be best for seduction." Hayward laughs. "She was planning a dinner at her apartment to put the moves on a man. I told her she needed a 'whammy wine' such as a full-bodied Australian shiraz." Apparently, the evening was a success: the woman and the man both came back regularly to buy more of that shiraz.

Hayward fills me in on a little of shop owner Phil Priolo's history. Surprisingly for a man who works in a business that makes passions run high, he has no particular passion for wine. His father died when he was just thirteen, and to support his mother and three sisters, young Phil took the first job that came along—working in a wine and spirits shop owned by a friend of the family's, Dave Ravetti. (Like the Priolos, Ravetti was part of the city's close-knit Italian-American community.) A few years later, in 1965, Ravetti opened the Jug Shop on Polk Street. Priolo joined him as a partner, took over when Ravetti retired, and in 1979 moved to the current location. (This shop was originally an auto repair garage, though now the only evidence of its former life are some fading paint lines on the floor and a few grease stains on the wall.)

Although Priolo may not be a wine expert, he certainly knows the retail industry. The Jug Shop quickly established itself as a reputable business, especially after Hayward joined in 1985. The store currently has a staff of fifteen people and generates $6 million in annual sales. Its success, Hayward says, isn't just due to Priolo's good management, but also the vibe of the place. "We're like a small bookstore that specializes in detective stories or children's books," he explains.

It's also just the right size. Unlike in many small wine boutiques, most of the Jug Shop's wine labels aren't pricey or obscure. And unlike large chains such as Costco and Wal-Mart, which must deal in enormous volumes, the Jug Shop is happy to offer its customers small-production wines and to change its inventory based on what they ask for. It even wants customers to know what they want before they buy it. Back in 1979, it became one of the first liquor retailers in North America to have a built-in wine-tasting bar.

Hayward has since become a recognized expert in the international wine community as well and is often called upon as a guest speaker at conferences. He recently attended one in New Zealand where he discussed the consumer reaction to the screwcap. He's a firm believer in sealing wine bottles with a metal twist-off cap instead of the traditional cork made from the bark of cork trees in Spain and Portugal.

Natural bark corks can contain a chemical compound called 2, 4, 6 trichloranisole, or TCA. Some studies have estimated that 5–10 percent of all wines are corked, a defect rate that would be unacceptable in almost any other industry. Today, methods are improving to lower the incidence of corked wine, but the problem persists.

Even a mild case of taint from natural corks strips wine of its expressive aromas, and a severe one makes it smell like moldy cardboard. Knowledgeable consumers can recognize this and return the bottle to the store or restaurant. But inexperienced drinkers just assume that they don't like the wine, not realizing it's faulty. That can damage not only the reputation of the individual winery, but also the whole industry as yet another potential drinker resigns himself to the fact that he'll never "get" wine.

In 2000, some Australian vintners decided to bottle some of that vintage with screwcaps. It worked: none of the capped wines were faulty. News of their success spread to other winemakers down under, especially to those in neighboring New Zealand. In 2006, nearly all (90 percent) New Zealand wines were bottled under a screwcap. Its adoption rate was much faster than that of most other countries, due to its small size, which required an all-or-nothing approach for the sake of cost efficiencies in making the bottles and caps.

Another problem with cork is that it makes wine more difficult to open than, say, beer, and hence less accessible. As Larry Lockshin, director of the Wine Marketing Research Group at the University of South Australia, puts it, "If you were developing a new fruit beverage today, would you put it in a glass bottle that comes in only one size and requires a special implement to open?" Hayward notes that screwcaps are especially good for senior citizens with arthritis, bartenders who can twist and pour wines quickly, and picnickers who forgot their corkscrew. (Synthetic corks haven't caught on as quickly as screwcaps: they have the aggravation of seeming to require a pneumatic drill to open them.)

Although screwcaps better protect the wine and make it easier to open, consumer acceptance has been slow. The market reveres tradition, especially one that goes back to the early 1600s. Compared to the ritual of uncorking a bottle, unscrewing a cap has all the ceremony of opening a bottle of beer with your teeth. Still, more and more upscale producers are moving away from cork and toward the metal caps.

In North America, Bonny Doon was one of the first premium wineries in the country to use screwcaps. "You won't need any specialized hardware to open a bottle of 2001 Big House Red or White. Opposable thumbs will do," read the press release. Randall Grahm first put screwcaps on his Big House wine and now uses them on most of his lineup. In 2002, to garner some publicity and encourage consumer acceptance, Grahm hosted a "Death of the Cork" dinner in New York City. Pallbearers marched a coffin full of corks through Grand Central Station to the restaurant Bacar, where Grahm presided over a mock funeral for "Thierry Bouchon"—a play on the words *tire-bouchon*, French for "corkscrew." The mortal remains (a man's suit stuffed with corks laid out in an open coffin) were eulogized by Jancis Robinson. "Oh, Corky, Corky Cork! How we shall miss thy cylindrical barky majesty!" she declaimed.

After the funeral service, a ten-course, black-themed dinner was served. It included dishes such as corkscrew pasta in a squid-ink sauce, seared black cod, black olives, and blackened almonds, all served on black-rimmed plates, with black linen. Grahm got the idea from J.-K. Huysmans's nineteenth-century novel *Against Nature*, which he characterized as "a hysterically funny fin de siècle novel about aesthetes who have such hyperrefined sensibilities that normal pleasure no longer satisfies them."

Consumer approval is growing, according to John Gillespie, of Wine Opinions: "A very small percent of U.S.-produced wine, by value, is in screwcap, but about twenty-five percent of U.S. consumers have purchased a screwcap wine in the past few months. Acceptance is growing quickly, and I expect to see an explosion of these packages in the next two to three years."

Screwcaps have a few of their own minor design problems, but the industry is working to eliminate these issues. Jamie Goode, a British scientist who has written extensively on the subject, believes that screwcaps perform well overall and are a better seal than cork. Even Robert Parker predicts that wines closed with corks will be in the minority by 2015. Personally, I agree with both of them and mention when a wine is closed with a screwcap in my tasting notes, along with the word *Yahoo!*

To help customers ease into new closures and new wines, several other Jug Shop employees are specialists in other regions: Paige Granback focuses on Spanish wines, Floribeth Schumacher on Italian. Together, they've developed an in-store library of tasting notes, books, and magazines. In fact, most of the wine recommendations come from the staff, though a few shelf slips bear the scores from Robert Parker or the *Wine Spectator*. One staff note declares, "Loooooong finish. Stunning fruit. Massive spicy shiraz." Another reads, "The best parcels of grapes for this wine are kept separate. We love it!"

While we're chatting, a woman in her thirties pushing a child in a stroller asks Hayward to recommend a California cabernet. He walks her over to the right-hand wall, which is lined with bottles from the state. "I really like this one," he says. "But it depends on your budget. If you want to go a bit higher, try this bottle.

"Selling expensive wine is easy," Hayward says, after she leaves with her bottle. "Many people think if it's pricey, it's good. But expensive brands already have a following. All you have to do is play classical music and walk around with a grim expression and your hands behind your back, like you're in a morgue." He says this with a straight face, but I laugh because I've met some of the wine boutique stiffs he's talking about.

"What's really challenging is selling a bottle that's underpriced, even cheap," he says seriously. "That's because I know that the winery produced more of its top label that year than it could bottle, so it put some great vino in its value brand."

He's proudest of promoting the 1997 Kenwood cabernet, the most basic red wine from that California winery. "We had it for $4.99 and I was raving about it because 1997 was a fantastic year. People don't think about vintage variation for lower-priced wines. But really, that's just snobbery because the weather changes the nuances of all wine, not just the expensive ones. When you track what's happening by region each year, you can help customers find gems that they'd otherwise overlook. You want to take all this passion and knowledge and do something with it. We had customers lined up out of the store for the Kenwood."

Some of the cost difference between a $200 wine and a $20 one can be attributed to lower yields, better barrels, marketing costs, and so on. It's like the difference between factory-made clothing from Taiwan and hand-stitched haute couture from Paris: if that kind of nuance and quality matters to you, then you're willing to pay the premium. However, these cost factors still don't tell us why a $200 wine doesn't always taste ten times better than a $20 one. As wines get more expensive, price depends more on intangible factors such as rarity, prestige, critics' scores, and the winemaker's ego.

In *Tasting Pleasure*, Jancis Robinson wrote, "The difference in price between the world's most expensive and cheapest wines has widened to such an extent (ironically, at a time when the gap in quality is probably narrower than it has ever been) that I shall probably never feel able to buy the seriously sought-after wines again. Farewell first growths, grand crus, Penfolds Grange, top Italians and the rest."

Hayward introduces me to Floribeth Schumacher, thirty-nine, a petite woman with dark hair and big brown eyes. She travels to Italy once or twice a year to find wines from lesser-known regions and villages. "When I help people discover a new wine, I feel I'm really doing my job. I love it when they walk in and ask me, 'What's next?'" she tells me in her melodic Mexican-Brazilian accent. She recently hosted a seminar on small-production barolos, those robust red wines from northern Italy. Forty-five customers attended and she sold seventy cases. Angelo Gaja, one of Italy's most renowned winemakers, also hosted a seminar and sold 106 cases. During the store's "Italian Month," she hosted a tasting from one region of that country every day.

"Not everyone can travel to Italy," Schumacher says, "so we try to bring Italy to them, or at least, to their palates. Most customers don't have time to become experts on any region, but tasting helps them learn what they like."

Schumacher also enjoys the challenge of matching wines with food. Often customers bring in multicourse menus to get her advice. Cooking schools sometimes fax over the dishes their students are preparing, and she chooses wines from the store and ships them to the school. The store charges for the wines, but the consulting is free. Schumacher provides her expertise because "I love doing this for customers. It's something we can do that the big chains can't."

As well, she says, "It's important to recognize that most people don't drink wine on its own, even though it's sold that way." Her point is underscored when a woman comes up to her and opens her grocery bag, to reveal four cheeses, and asks for a pairing suggestion. Schumacher smiles and says she has just the wine as she guides the woman to a case of valpolicella, a light red from Italy. She explains that the wine has the acidity to complement the saltiness of the cheese. She also shows her some dessert wines with enough sweetness to do the same thing.

Over the next hour or so, I see the drop-in democracy of

wine as a cross-section of society passes through the Jug Shop. A sous-chef in his white kitchen uniform comes in to buy wine for a reduction sauce. A man pulls a gallon jug of wine off the shelf; he's wearing coveralls with WILLY'S AUTO REPAIR stitched over the left breast. Another man chats animatedly on his cell phone, apparently with his wife, about which cabernet they drank at a friend's house. A burly motorcyclist in a black leather jacket and pants gently cradles a bottle of merlot.

Meanwhile, Hayward has asked Paige Granback, a cherub-faced blonde who is thirty-five, her opinion on a wine kit that a sales rep is trying to sell him. The kit provides buyers the materials to taste wine "blind" so that they don't know what the wines are before they make guesses. It also includes two bottles of shiraz, a notepad, a blindfold, and a CD with music from down under.

"C'mon, let's go for it—I really want that CD!" she says, smiling.

Hayward laughs. "Booze and a blindfold? I don't think people will buy it just to taste wine! It would be perfect for the Las Vegas market." But they take the sample and tell the sales rep they'll get back to her.

Since the store seems to do so well with its personal approach to wine sales, I'm curious about the Internet. With increased competition from both chains and small boutique stores, Hayward and Granback explain that the only way for midsize stores like theirs to thrive is to become known as specialists both within and outside their geographic area. That means selling via the Internet. In 2005, the U.S. Supreme Court reversed a law that had banned cross-border shipping of wine among the states, removing a major impediment to online sales. But a confusing tangle of laws still remains that varies by state, made even more complex by a three-tier distribution system that includes producers, distributors, and retailers. Each state must decide whether to allow all wineries to ship to their residents or none of them. A state cannot discriminate by allowing only those wineries within the state to ship to residents.

Hayward believes that wine is similar to products like records and books: they're all research-intensive purchases, and the Internet is good at providing in-depth information to buyers willing to do their homework. That's consistent with a purchasing theory called the Long Tail, developed by Chris Anderson, the editor of *Wired* magazine. Anderson explains that the average Barnes & Noble store carries 130,000 book titles. The size of the store and amount of shelf space limit sales. However, more than half of Amazon.com's online book sales come from outside the top 130,000 titles. A book purchase on Amazon.com fuels the suggestion for another: if you liked this book, you'll probably like this other book. "For too long we've been suffering the tyranny of lowest-common-denominator fare, subjected to brain-dead summer blockbusters and manufactured pop," Anderson writes. "Hits fill theaters, fly off shelves, and keep listeners and viewers from touching their dials and remotes. But most of us want more than just hits. Everyone's taste departs from the mainstream somewhere, and the more we explore alternatives, the more we're drawn to them."

Anderson believes that we need both ends of the curve because hits still attract consumers in the first place. Great Long Tail businesses, he says, can then guide consumers further afield by following the contours of their likes and dislikes, easing their exploration of the unknown. The parallels to the wine market, in my opinion, are uncanny. Of all alcoholic beverages, I believe that wine best fits the Long Tail concept. Even the largest wine brands own less than 5 percent market share. Compare this to spirits, for which the leading brand can easily own as much as 50 percent market share, or the ten best-selling light-beer brands, which comprise 99 percent of the market.

Even though the Web may be a larger piece of his future business, Hayward doesn't believe that it'll ever completely replace bricks-and-mortar shops. "The downside of the Web is that you can't read people," he says. "When people ask for a recommendation in the store, I suggest a style and a price range based on my impression of them. But I always look to see how they react and modify my suggestions accordingly."

It's true: I know from my own experience that wine attracts people who love to touch the labels and who don't know what they want until they see it. Such people also like to talk about their passion with other kindred spirits. Often when I'm in a wine store pondering a bottle, a stranger beside me will say something like "That's an awesome wine" or "You know Parker gave that wine a 90?" That never happens when I'm shopping for furniture, a much more expensive purchase. People just aren't as passionate about sofas as they are about shiraz.

As the afternoon slips into evening, the lineups at the two cash registers are building. There are an amorous couple in their late twenties, a businessman who seems jet-lagged, and a thin, heavily made-up woman whose affections seem to be negotiable. Despite how busy the Jug Shop is, like most small to midsize shops, it is faced with serious pressures from various sources. "Rents are going way up, margins are thinner," Hayward says. "Wineries and wine stores are consolidating, and the survivors will likely be the big guys, the chains." Indeed, according to the Wine Institute in San Francisco, warehouse retailers, such as Costco, Price Club, BJ's, Trader Joe's, Sam's Club, and Wal-Mart, now account for a third of wine sales in America. In Britain, the figure is even higher, at 75 percent. Costco and Sam's Club rang up more than $1 billion in wine sales in 2004, according to the market research company ACNielsen. In fact, Costco is now the country's largest seller of first-growth Bordeaux.

These changes in the retail and distribution channels present substantial challenges for wineries, of course, because the big, powerful players have much more bargaining power than small liquor stores. Smaller vineyards often find it difficult to secure shelf space with Costco et al., and all wineries find themselves facing pricing pressure from distribution channels.

While the wineries may not like these changes, and the small retail shops may find the competition daunting, consumers seem to benefit. They can purchase quality wines at much lower prices and appreciate the convenience of being able to buy wine alongside food and other drinks. That's certainly what happened in the U.K.: the surge in wine consumption in recent years has been led by the supermarket chains making wine widely available, easy to buy, and cheaper.

Still, Hayward is optimistic about his own business. As he sagely points out, "You can either compete on price and distribution or else on service and selection. That latter is our niche. The small specialists will survive." In fact, Hayward tells me, in a few months the shop will be moved across the street to much snazzier quarters; this store is being torn down to build condos. The new space will be more modern and sleek, with wooden cabinets and recessed lighting.

The challenge, he says, will be to preserve the store's quirky culture. "I'm going to miss this place," he adds wistfully, as he walks me to the door to say good-bye. "But then again, things have changed so much since I started here twenty years ago—and I'm still lovin' it."

Hayward's remarks about the differences between East Coast and West Coast wine buyers make me curious enough to visit several wine shops in New York City. I've also gained enough confidence to spend the day actually working in Discovery Wines, which fellow wine lovers have told me is one of the most cutting-edge retailers in the city. The notion of working in a wine store has long appealed to me: I'll gossip with fellow wine geeks as we sip on samples; take a long, boozy lunch (followed by a nap in the stockroom); and spend the rest of the day being flattered by sales agents trying to get their wines listed. So imagine my surprise when Ellisa Cooper, one of three owners of Discovery, told me, "Wear comfortable shoes—it's exhausting being on your feet for ten hours."

As I walk to the store, I can already feel my left heel chafing slightly in my weekend-wear Manolo Blahniks. No matter. It's one of those freakishly mild December mornings when you begin to think that global warming may have an upside. A lavish loneliness wraps around me as I wander through the Village in the early-morning quiet. Most of the storefront gates are still down, and the sun spills over the rooftops into the street. The awning of a Chinese restaurant flaps gently in the breeze. The newly gentrified shops nudge impatiently at the still-weathered ones beside them.

Cooper, thirty-eight, a Meryl Streep look-alike in jeans and a sweater, welcomes me in her soft Kentucky accent. Bottles line the wall, their sensuous shoulder curves glinting in the morning light. They're displayed like art in open oak cabinets with gallery spotlighting. Some half dozen bottles of each stand in single file, like soldiers waiting for orders. It's so different from the Jug Shop's homeyness, yet welcoming in its own way.

Cooper tells me that she grew up "wedged between those who still believe that you'll go to hell for taking a sip of the demon alcohol and the bourbon-swilling good ole boys." Her parents enjoyed a glass of wine, but were careful to put the wine and glasses away at the end of the evening because "you never knew who might drop by in the early morning and discover that you were sinners.

"I started throwing parties for my friends when I was just eleven, and as soon as I was old enough to drink alcohol, I remember loving wine," Cooper tells me. "With wine, the subject itself is fresh every day: new vineyards, new winemakers, new styles. Just learning enough to be conversant on the subject is a challenge. It's daunting and exciting."

As a result, she tried various jobs that involved wine, such as wholesale distribution, restaurant management, catering, and event planning. But she realized that she didn't want to work for anyone else, so she got together with two men whom she'd met through her work and shared her passion for wine and independence: Tony White and Scott Reiner.

As Cooper chats with me, White comes to say hello. Before he opened Discovery Wines with Cooper, the tall, slim African-American designed store layouts for the consumer brands company Nielsen, created an inventory-tracking system for National Wine and Spirits, produced a documentary on the Cognac region of France, and taught film studies at Columbia University.

"In both displays and videos, I learned how to make the bottle the hero," he tells me. Discovery's theatrical lighting is a big improvement over the harsh fluorescent lights of most retail outlets, which make customers look as though they're suffering from salmonella. I also like the open hardwood floors and the wide aisles, which prevent what retail psychologists call butt-brush—the sales-killing effect of customers bumping into each other. There are also no stacked cardboard boxes, no jumbles of bottles in wire bins, and no ladders leaning against the wall to reach high-up shelves. The Zen-like symmetry of this small store is soothing compared to the overcrowded shelves of others, where I feel a rising hair ball of panic. Imagine if Baskin-Robbins had thirty-one thousand flavors instead of thirty-one.

Selling wine has come a long way since Prohibition, but the hangover from that period still lingers, giving the wine business some of the tightest and most complex laws in the retail sector. "The problem is that we still see selling alcohol as a sin!" Cooper says, rolling her eyes. "We really need to separate church and state."

For merchants, achieving economies of scale is difficult (or even illegal), as is selling to customers outside your own state or province. Margins have become razor thin as retailers have proliferated, from specialists such as New York's Italian Wine Merchants and the Burgundy Wine Company, to mass-market retailers, grocery chains, and warehouses like Costco and Wal-Mart.

Then there are auctions, direct-shipping wine clubs, the wineries themselves, and the Internet. NYC retailer Sherry-Lehmann makes 20 percent of its sales from its Web site, and 80 percent of its customer purchases are delivered. Cooper isn't concerned about Internet-only wine retailers; in her view, they appeal mostly to people looking for cheap prices rather than interesting selection. "That's why we still browse in bookstores, even though there's Amazon," she points out. Much like Hayward at the Jug Shop, she hopes to leverage her expertise beyond this neighborhood through online sales. She also views her services as an important extension of her stock: in addition to personal advice and wine tastings, she offers the magic of modern technology in the store. Big video panels mounted on the wall give customers electronic advice: they double as both price-check points and electronic encyclopedias.

To illustrate, Cooper puts a bottle under one of the video screens. It scans the bar code and pops up not just the name of the wine and its price, but also its vintage and the grapes in its blend. Pressing other buttons brings up Cooper's own tasting notes (which are mercifully short and jargon-free). There's even information on how the wine was made, the history of the vineyard, a map of the region, and the mandatory picture of the smiling winemaker in muddy overalls standing by a barrel.

Intrigued, I try searching for wines based on the type, region, price range, and food matches. The kiosk is as easy to use as an ATM, and I can even print off the information I find. It's perfect for customers who are too intimidated to ask the staff questions. But isn't there a danger, I ask Cooper, of overwhelming customers with too much information?

"Wine is one of the most information-intensive purchases we make, but many people don't want to ask questions because they're afraid of looking stupid," she says. "Some people don't even know what questions to ask. This technology makes the buying process a bit easier because people aren't forced to reveal how little they know."

The kiosks appeal to both genders for different reasons, Cooper says. Men like them because they don't have to rely on another person to make a decision; women like the kiosks because they like to discover new wines. Men want to get in and out of the store as quickly as possible; whereas women like to linger and seek advice. Despite 2.5 million years of evolution, men are still hunters and women are still gatherers. Perhaps that's why women buy 77 percent of wine in America and drink 60 percent of it, according to a 2005 *New York Times* article.

The electronic information makes it unnecessary for Discovery to post those printouts of purple prose that clutter shelves in many other wine stores. This place doesn't even bother with ratings. "If we did, most people wouldn't look at a wine that scored only eighty-nine points, say, even though it might be delicious and a good value," Cooper says pragmatically.

"Parker has overpowered the market; he directs too much of the retail business like a silent hand."

I have to wonder, is this just vinous envy? Do retailers want some of that power for themselves?

"No, we want people to develop their own palates," Cooper says firmly. "Palates are like fingerprints, every one is different. We want people to explore wines from a secure base, so they'll try new ones. Part of the beauty of wine is its diversity and ever-changing nature, from vintage to vintage. But most of us cling to what we know—or what the critic knows. We're reluctant to risk wasting twenty-five dollars experimenting with something new. Many people who drink wine are dying to learn about it—the only thing standing in the way of them becoming card-carrying wine geeks is the lack of information."

You might think these kiosks would allow Discovery staffers to slack off. But the opposite is true: the store's seven employees all derive great satisfaction from fielding the questions customers ask that are too difficult for the system. (Example: Which wine pairs best with pickled boar's feet? Answer: perhaps an off-dry riesling or even an herbal sauvignon blanc.)

Several assert that theirs is the best possible retail job for wine lovers. Not only do they get to try thousands of wines a year, they also get to talk about them all day long. Jobs in wine stores tend to attract people who enjoy inventory lists as bedtime reading and who love to tell stories about the winemaker they met last summer. As one salesperson told me, "In any other job, I'd be considered weird—here, it's what I do." As he also pointed out, "Selling wine is about selling stories: your own stories about discovering the wine, the vintner's stories about making the wine, and the customer's imagined stories about enjoying it."

As I help Cooper set out glassware for the afternoon tasting, I start to worry. How can I possibly be cheerful for hours with aggressive, short-tempered shoppers? How can I solve other people's domestic problems when I'm so absorbed in my own? How will I be able to hold back comments such as "You really have no taste" or "Don't be such a friggin' tightwad"?

Finally, it's opening time. The day's first customers trickle in, most seeming to know one another. They fall into easy conversations about their kids' schools, the movies, the latest restaurant opening, where to buy good radishes. They are mostly apartment dwellers buying only what they need for tonight, or for this week, since few have a cellar or even a large kitchen.

One woman clicks her way over to the champagne section in high heels, a couple is in running outfits, and two young men are in jeans and baseball caps. The place has the feel of a small neighborhood shop. I'm an insatiable eavesdropper, so I spend the first few hours pretending to shop while listening to snippets of conversation.

"She wants Montrachet; she only drinks Montrachet."

"Do you have a great wine for artichokes?"

"All wines have sulfites; they occur naturally. Why don't you try an organic wine since they have far fewer sulfites than most other wines?"

"This wine tastes like grass."

"Is the winemaker single?"

With my ears pointed forward like antennae, I sidle up beside Cooper, who's chatting with a woman in her thirties.

"I need something for tonight."

"What are you eating?"

"Glazed ham, with snow peas and yams."

"Then you want something with just a touch of sweetness, like this German riesling."

"Is it a good wine?"

"Absolutely!"

Cooper's experience tells her that most people don't want a detailed analysis of the wine; they just want someone they trust to tell them what's good. After all, why should it take twenty minutes to make an $8 decision? Australian professor Larry Lockshin found that most buyers spend an average of thirty-eight seconds on their choice—and they base it almost entirely on the label. Few consumables are as fraught with social meaning as wine. At social gatherings, it's the only consumable we put on the dinner table in its original packaging. The label is like a billboard: it tells your hosts and guests just what you think of them and how much you're willing to spend on friendship. You want to show everyone that you have taste and sophistication. Buying wine is a search for comfort ("I hope it tastes good"), nostalgia ("It'll bring back happy memories"), approval ("I hope my friends will like it"), and even adventure ("I hope I'll find something new I like").

"Most people just want some point of reference," Cooper says. "There's so much about wine that's a mystery, and it really shouldn't be that way. Saying that a wine 'smells like lead pencils'—that makes no sense to many people. They figure, why pay two hundred dollars for a bottle of 'liquid lead pencils' when I can buy the kind that write much cheaper in a stationery store?"

She recalls one customer who had bought a pinot noir, brought back the empty bottle, and said it was bad. Cooper gave her a new bottle and asked her to bring back the unfinished wine if there was a problem so she could find out if it affected the entire case. The woman did come back later, with the bottle opened. Distraught, she blurted out, "This wine smells like, like fertilizer!"

Cooper, relieved, explained the problem: "Hon, you just don't like the style of pinot noir. They're supposed to smell like shit!" It's true: earthy, barnyard aromas can be a characteristic of that type of wine. She got the woman a cabernet sauvignon instead.

Meanwhile, Scott Reiner, a former banker and wine importer, is over in the Burgundy section talking animatedly to a man about that region's pinot noir. "When you sip it, the heavens will open, and light will shine down and you'll say, 'Oh, baby!'" He laughs. The man must be convinced: he buys three bottles.

After a few hours of watching and listening, I tentatively decide to start helping customers myself. I'm determined not to be one of those salespeople who wield "May I help you?" like a pickax. They're the ones who stalk you around the store like the Man from Glad, popping up to solve problems you didn't know you had.

So I bring out my happy-to-help smile, with a nonaggressive half-glance for anyone who looks my way, until a young woman asks me, "I'm looking for a nice dessert wine to go with a crème caramel."

"Try this Monbazillac," I say, holding up the amber bottle of French elixir with both hands, like an infomercial idiot. Fortunately, it's a dessert wine I've tried before with a rich, honeyed sweetness so I know it would be a lovely match.

"How much is it?"

"Just $9.99," I say, suppressing the impulse to add, "And if you buy three bottles, we'll throw in a free Thighmaster because this little sweetie sure packs a caloric punch."

"Fabulous! It looks a lot more expensive than that."

A short, sober lunch comes and goes. Now the store is filling up. Discovery Wines doesn't sell what its owners consider the fast foods of the wine world: E&J Gallo, Mondavi Woodbridge, Fortant de France, Mouton Cadet, Wolf Blass, Lindemans, Jacob's Creek, and Yellow Tail, among others. This isn't snobbery: most of the wines in the store are reasonably priced, with 70 percent costing less than $20. The owners buy from small artisanal producers, which is why they tasted some 5,000 wines before choosing 650.

A short, balding man, whose beady squirrel eyes glitter with greed, walks well into my personal space before asking me, "Can you give me a great wine for less than five dollars?"

I choke down the words "Sure, if all you want is a wet tongue."

"Not really," I say sweetly. "But I can suggest some real gems for under twenty dollars."

"So, you're saying you get what you pay for?" he challenges me.

"Well, yes and no," I say, with unassailable conviction.

My words pour out of me like oatmeal, runny with explanations and clumpy with *um*s and *ah*s, as I try to explain to this unpleasant little fellow how wines are priced. (It doesn't help that he keeps staring at the part of me that is eye-level for him.) As we walk through the store, I suggest that he get to know a few reputable wineries in regions known for producing reasonably priced wines.

I also advise Squirrel Man to stick with the grapes that are a region's strengths, the ones with which they're most experienced and make their best wines. In Italy, for example, go for sangiovese (which makes chianti) rather than cabernet. Cool climates such as northern France, Germany, and New Zealand are ideal for the elegant, food-friendly wines made from pinot noir, riesling, and sauvignon blanc. Hot climates such as California, Chile, and some regions of Australia focus on bigger, bolder wines, such as robust chardonnay, shiraz, and cabernet sauvignon.

Look for lesser-known regions within wine-producing countries, such as Washington State rather than Napa Valley; southern Italy (Campania, Sicily, Sardinia) rather than Piedmont and Tuscany; in Spain, Priorat or Rueda rather than Rioja; and in France, the Languedoc, southern Rhône, and Loire regions rather than Bordeaux or Burgundy. There are also Old World regions, such as Germany and Alsace, that have never gained mainstream popularity in North America and therefore offer great value. As well, certain grapes (riesling, grenache, mourvèdre) and wine styles (sherry, madeira, dessert wines) have never become as fashionable as chardonnay, merlot, cabernet sauvignon, and shiraz and are therefore often good deals.

At last, he scampers away with a Chilean cabernet, gleeful about saving $1.29. And before long, I get to consider the opposite end of the price spectrum.

"I'm spending serious money today," says Deep Pockets, a middle-aged man in a Burberry coat and hat. "I want the best."

It seemed to me that this man didn't really want the best wine; he just wanted to want the best wine. Even I often succumb to the myth that if a bottle is expensive, it must be good (and the unfair corollary that cheap wine is bog water). According to the wine accounting and research company Motto Kryla Fisher, sales in the premium category are now 3 million cases annually, with a value of $1 billion. The category is growing by 25 percent a year. When we're willing to pay $5 for a cappuccino, we're willing to stretch on wines too. However, the equation isn't linear: high prices don't guarantee great wine, and some expensive wines are better values than others.

I frisk my mind for suggestions for the man, nervously patting my pockets as if the answer might be in them. Then I remember a tip from a sales rep in my own hometown: buy the "second labels" of the great Bordeaux châteaux. These aren't second-class wines; they just don't meet the winery's exacting standards for its top labels. In fact, some châteaux declassify up to half their production every year. The grapes may come from less advantageous vineyards, or from younger vines. Established châteaux must replant some portion of their vines every year; and while the new plants will produce decent fruit after only three or four years, it takes about ten years before the vine roots have reached deep enough into the soil to absorb the range of nutrients that will give the grapes complexity.

Still, grapes in second-label wine grow in the same excellent soil, receive the same winemaking care, and are usually aged in the same first-quality oak as the great wines. As a result, they often have the same elegant style—but are ready to drink much earlier and are often only a third to a half of the price. For the stellar 2000 vintage, *the Wine Advocate* scored certain second labels an average of 90.2 points, not so far below the 99 for the first growths—and yet the grands vins sold for an average of $405 on their release and the second labels for $54.

Of course, even mediocre years can be good for buying from the great houses, as the château may decide not to make any grand vin at all that year and will use the whole production for the second label. (As my former finance professor used to exclaim, his eyes aflame with the glories of capitalism, "A magnificent opportunity for arbitrage!")

All five of the first-growth wineries make second labels. Deep Pockets finally leaves clutching a bottle of Les Pagodes de Cos, a second growth, and a steal compared to the price of its grand vin cousin Cos d'Estournel. The concept of the second label isn't exclusive to Bordeaux; vintners from around the world now produce them. Examples include Grand Archer (Arrowood Vineyards, California), Robert Mondavi Private Selection (Robert Mondavi), Y Series (Yalumba, Australia), and Preiss (Dopff & Irion, Alsace).

Just then, a customer comes in looking for a certain red blend from southern Italy. "We're getting that one next week," Reiner tells him. "Would you like me to e-mail you when it comes in?" He takes the man's business card and enters it into the store's database. This tracks all customer purchases and sends out a biweekly e-newsletter with wine tips and news of promotions and sales.

In fact, Discovery is fast becoming a full-service operation for wine lovers. The store now features a fully equipped kitchen (complete with a large-screen TV) for wine appreciation classes and corporate events. Other retailers are also embracing the one-stop shopping concept and offering cellaring services and consultation, auctions, and adjoining restaurants. That makes sense: most of us want wine to relate to our lives. How does it compare to other wines I've enjoyed? Will it work with dinner? Will our friends like it?

Four of the wine distributors who work with Discovery have set up tasting stations, which give the store a festive feel of a mini–wine show. One of them, Andrew Bell, offers a German riesling to a couple of customers sitting on barstools at the back of the store.

"Thirsty?" he quips to the eager participants, who hold out glasses to be filled. "Do you need a straw?"

To a middle-aged woman, he says playfully, "May I see some ID, please?" She laughs, flattered, and perches on a stool for a sample.

"This one will make you salivate," Bell says, getting into his spiel. "Acidity is the skeleton of a white wine—it's like Liberace playing the scales up and down the sides of your mouth." This wine must be well made because acidity is one of the hardest aspects to get just right. That's why cheap whites are more difficult to produce than cheap reds: it's easy to destroy the balance between acid and fruit, and end up with what tastes like battery acid.

It's now late in the afternoon and I've developed a code-blue blister on my left heel and my hamstrings are on fire. (Damn those beautifully fashionable shoes.) Working in a wine store, I decide, is a lot like life: you spend most of it waiting around for just one or two memorable moments (which you can easily miss because you went to the bathroom).

But the experience makes me think more about the process of buying wine. For instance, it puzzles me why so many wine stores (even this one) organize their products by country of origin or by grape rather than by taste or by which dishes they'd go best with. Surely this kind of organization must make customers feel like they're outsiders. What about an end-aisle display of zippy whites to complement Asian dishes? Or a barbecue set with spicy reds set out enticingly on the grill?

I mention this to Cooper, and her response does make sense: she says that system would require many wines to be stocked in several different sections. Not all wine merchants agree, though. Joshua Wesson, who owns the Best Cellars stores in Manhattan and several other American cities, believes in trying to put his customers in touch with their "inner wine child, their true pleasure center." He groups his wines under eight adjectival headings: fizzy, fresh, soft, luscious, juicy, smooth, big, and sweet.

The toughest challenge for most people buying wine is still mental. Buying wine is a lot like buying a computer: we assume that we're stupid because we don't understand technology. Similarly, when we buy wine and then don't like it, we chastise ourselves for knowing so little.

So what can you do if you're feeling at a loss in a store that doesn't have Discovery's handy kiosks? You don't want to look like an uncultured tightwad, but neither are you keen to empty your wallet to impress your hosts. Start by cultivating a relationship with reputable merchants—people who will get to know your tastes and suggest things you might like. When I tell my local wine-store staffer that I'm looking for a full-bodied red in the $15 range or a medium-bodied white for less than $20, he knows just what to suggest. Or I might mention a wine I've liked in the past and ask him to recommend something from the same region or grape.

My next suggestion: cut yourself some slack and pick a wine that's easy to pronounce without having to cough to disguise the attempt. Sure, Balthasar Ress Hattenheimer Schützenhaus Rheingau Riesling Kabinett is a wonderful German wine, but do you really want to attempt such a tongue twister if you're just starting out? When you want just a few good simple choices, keep it short.

German winemakers and other Old World winemakers are now clueing into that difficulty. Many now offer user-friendly names pioneered in the New World: monikers such as Bend in the River, Devil's Rock, Cuckoo Hill, Winter Hill, Deer Leap, Spice Trail, Riveroute, and Perth Pink. In fact, the new brand of wine snobbery likes to take potshots at the old wine snobbery, with names such as Meat Market Red, Fat Bastard, Space Shuttle White, Love Goat Blush, Good Ordinary Claret, and Rude Boy Chardonnay. One British supermarket has even created a line called "Great with"—Great with Chicken, Great with Pizza & Pasta . . . (There's also Great with Friends, which should really concern anyone who stops to think about it.)

If wine names can be misleading, the back label copy is often about as believable as a Harlequin romance. In this purple prose, every vintage is spectacular and every wine goes perfectly with chicken, beef, pasta, and cheese. That's why I love the sense of humor of Californian vintner Sean Thackrey. He parodied this nonsense on one of his wines with a label that reads simply, "The object of Pleiades Old Vines is to be delicious, delight the jaded, and go well with anything red wine goes well with."

I usually advise people to skip the blurb, or at least not make it an important factor in their decision. As well, avoid slick labels with lots of gold foil: I can smell the marketing plan from across the store. I'm also suspicious when the owner's signature is scrawled on the label: Massive Ego Alert!

At this point in the afternoon, a young woman with big blue eyes asks me if there's much difference between a wine labeled Napa Valley and one that just says California. I tell her that the more specific the place name, the better. When a region is narrowly defined, quality guidelines and laws are more stringent, so it's less likely that grapes from good and bad vineyards will be blended. (Though blending can also improve the wine's complexity—it just depends on the producer.) For the same reason, estate-grown grapes are usually better than those bought from growers, since the winemaker has more control over vineyard practices.

Bottles that are specific about their contents, such as the grapes, aren't necessarily better than ones that don't put this information on the label; but they're safer buys for a novice. Most regions have laws about how much of a grape, by percentage, must be in a wine for it to be labeled with that grape. But the laws vary vastly. In California, a merlot must in fact contain at least 75 percent merlot. In Bordeaux, though, merlot, cabernet sauvignon, and cabernet franc are usually blended to produce the final wine, with nothing mentioned on the label. And some branded New World wines skip the grape information entirely, carrying only a proprietary name such as Opus One, Dominus, or Pinnacle.

A novice buyer might also be seduced by fancy label terms such as *reserve, proprietor's reserve, vintner's blend,* and *cellar selection.* While these may sound good, they don't necessarily mean anything at all in most New World regions. They're not regulated, or even defined, so they can mean whatever the winemaker wants them to. Some low-end wineries put *reserve* on every bottle they make. In fact, that word appears on some 10 percent of U.S. wines, making it as meaningless as blurbs about "wines handcrafted from the finest grapes." Conversely, in Old World wine regions, *reserve* often does indicate a higher quality level (though still no guarantee of good wine), but the laws and definitions of what constitutes a reserve wine are labyrinthine.

Most European countries have quality designations for wines that meet certain standards, much like France's *appellation d'origine controlée* (AOC). These are based on industry controls for aspects of grape-growing such as irrigation of the vines, yield per acre, etc. You don't really have to know the minutiae of such regulations though—just think of it as the difference between a genuine Prada handbag and a knockoff. These quality designations won't guarantee you delicious wines, but they do tell you exactly where they come from—and often identity is equated with quality.

What about vintages? Unless you have the palate of a pachyderm, avoid labels that claim, "February was a good month to box this wine." The year the wine was made certainly makes a big difference in cool climates because a harvest can be glorious one year and a bitter disappointment the next. The Bordeaux 2000 vintage was spectacular, whereas 1991 and 1992 were disappointing. In Tuscany, 1997 was declared the vintage of the century and the wines made that year will age for decades, whereas in Bordeaux, the 1997s were recommended for short-term drinking. Hotter climates are easier: weather doesn't vary as much and most years produce decent wines. For example, nine out of ten years in Chile are similar to a top year for the Médoc, according to Jean-Guillaume Prats, the general director of Château Cos d'Estournel in Bordeaux, whose father owns vineyards in Chile, Portugal, and South Africa. Still, knowing the vintage will tell you how old the wine is and how long a life it has left. Most value-priced wines today are meant to be consumed as soon as they're released, within a year or two at most. They're not made for aging.

Another factor to consider is the alcohol content. For a dinner party, you may be tempted to choose a high-alcohol wine that'll anesthetize you for that tortuous first thirty minutes of small talk. But consider how alcohol affects wine and in turn, the dinner. A full-bodied wine generally has 13 percent alcohol by volume or more and goes best with hearty dishes such as rich stews and steaks. More medium to light-bodied wines (8 to 12 percent) are better matched to lighter dishes, such as seafood and pastas.

Back at the store, I'm ready to say good-bye to Cooper, White, and Reiner. I feel so advice-weary that I need someone to dictate the rest of my day. Evening light now streams into the store, burnishing the gold labels and making the white spaces glow like little tombstones. The few remaining customers stand in small, chatty groups like characters released from an F. Scott Fitzgerald novel.

Something unfastens in my head and a gale-force migraine blooms against my brain, and I realize that I'm not destined for the world of wine retail. Released from my sales duties, I reclaim the privileges of a customer. I limp over to one of the distributors like a wounded animal and ask him to pour me a sample—or six. For once, I don't even look at the label.

SIX

A Glass Act

HE'S HANDSOME, TANNED, and trim, with courtly manners and a soft Austrian accent. His eyes, the azure of Alpine skies, gaze into mine over the restaurant table and several glasses of wine. I know that he will change my life forever, bring me years of domestic bliss. We barely touch our food since we're both quivering with anticipation. But, alas, he's no Captain von Trapp, I'm not Maria, and this isn't really a romantic dinner. It's a gathering of wine enthusiasts in Ottawa to meet Georg Riedel, who represents the tenth generation of his family to make crystal stemware.

The Tyrolean mountains of Austria may be alive with the sound of music, but the Riedel Glass factory in Kufstein is abuzz with the noise of production. The company now makes some 5 million lead-crystal wineglasses every year. Riedel is in town to convince any skeptics that the shape and size of a glass profoundly affect the smell and taste of the wine it holds.

"Now this," Riedel says, picking up a puny glass, "is the enemy of wine." His disdain is so palpable that we all glare at the vessel like a village outcast. It looks like something from the sorry little collection of chipped and unmatched specimens I had as a student years ago. Riedel calls such an object a "joker": it's here tonight for contrast.

In front of us are four gleaming Riedel glasses, all containing a little of their namesake wines: sauvignon blanc, chardonnay, pinot noir, and cabernet sauvignon. Both the chardonnay and pinot noir glasses have more rounded bowls than the sauvignon blanc and bordeaux glasses, which are more tulip shaped. These tall glasses, with their elegant lines, look like lithe supermodels beside the joker glass, which sits empty like a parched troll.

I'm dreading a stemware slipup such as confusing the chardonnay and cabernet glasses, then being branded a Dixie Cup Chick. Perhaps my feelings come partly from Herr Riedel himself: one senses he has patrician sensibilities that it would be easy to offend. He's famously fastidious; he has even planned the wines to be served at his own funeral. At fifty-four, he looks just like the debonair actor you'd imagine in an ad for Riedel stemware. He wears a crisp navy suit (made from Italian fabric by a Viennese tailor) and has the svelte figure of a marathon runner.

He asks us to first taste some chardonnay from the joker glass and then again from the proper wineglass—which he calls his "precision tool." He talks animatedly about the "velocity of wine entering the mouth," and how it makes love to the palate, caressing it. He gazes shyly at his own precision tool as we taste. I want to throw the glass over my shoulder and declare, "Let's just get away from here!" But I'm distracted by the genuine difference in the smell and taste. The wine we drink from the small glass is as predictably bad as the "other brand" in a Tide commercial: it tastes sharp and alcoholic.

"Now we will go to the repair shop, to heal the palate of the bad experience," Riedel says, as we pour the wine back into his glass.

And it's true: the difference is immediate. As I bring the glass up to my nose (my "smelling instrument"), I'm enveloped in an aroma cloud of ripe pear, peaches, nutmeg, and a kiss of oak. Damn. I had wanted to hate this glass, if only to preserve my preconceived notion that fancy glassware is more about marketing than about true function. But I just can't; the wine really does smell and taste remarkably better. I'm reluctantly coming around to the view many enophiles share: a good glass makes good wine taste even better, accentuating its character. But it can't actually make bad wine taste good. "I can't work miracles," Riedel says humbly.

Expanding on this theory, Riedel explains that the air just above the glass not only contains suspended molecules, but that they're layered like a cake. At the top are the lightest floral aromas, then the fruity ones, then the mineral and earthy notes; and finally, at the bottom the heaviest aroma elements, wood and alcohol. Good stemware, he says, minimizes the congestion of these elements by eddying the aromas. Okay, if you say so. I'm ambivalent about swallowing Georg's gospel of glassware. Granted, bad glasses are a delusional form of wine democracy. But doesn't marketing 103 different glasses make wine more complicated and pretentious? Have we traded wine snobbery for glass snobbery?

Riedel has a specific design for almost every major grape, including different ones for recent and mature vintages of bordeaux. For the highly aromatic pinot noir, there's the Grand Cru Burgundy Sommelier glass. It's almost a foot tall and holds thirty-seven ounces—leaving room to spare even after pouring in an entire bottle. Wine lovers do actually imbibe from this glass, but with a rim circumference of twelve inches, it's also suitable for steam facials after you finish drinking.

In fact, Riedel is always coming up with new designs. As new styles of wine emerge, he creates a glass for them. He generally tries at least twenty different shapes, enlisting the help of a panel of experts to taste wine from them all before settling on one. He used that process to develop a new style of tasting glass. It has a hollow stem to hold exactly five eighths of an ounce, so that a bottle can be precisely divided into thirty-five tasting samples. By contrast, the sauvignon blanc glass holds $12^{3}/_{8}$ ounces. The design allows it to be rolled onto its side (without spilling the wine) to coat the glass with wine and maximize the aromas. The latest model is opaque black to use at blind tastings where participants don't know the identity of the wine.

The Sommelier Series is Riedel's top line: handblown, made with 24 percent lead crystal, and selling for as much as $95 apiece. The Ouverture line is cheaper and made from glass rather than crystal. Three of its glasses have shorter stems and so fit into the dishwasher.

Riedel now has glasses for other kinds of liquor: tequila, cognac, single-malt scotch, and even water. (However, he doesn't yet differentiate between sparkling and still waters, or mineral and spring: evidently there's a vast untapped business.) The Sommelier water glass sells for $60, proving that even glass makers have a sense of humor. But such is Riedel's cachet that he could design a glass for Kool-Aid and charge big bucks for it.

"My father was interested in glasses, but I am interested in the wine," Riedel says. In 1973, Georg's father, Josef, designed "history's first wine-specific glassware," according to the company's Web site. Georg says that his father was a genius, a "glass professor" who spent sixteen years studying the physics of delivering wine to the mouth. Riedel senior believed in the Bauhaus aesthetic that form follows function, which led him to deduce that content commands shape. (But anyone who has ever bought a bra already knows that.)

Glass itself has an interesting history. Although some form of it has been made for four thousand years, the lead crystal for which Riedel is famous dates back only a few centuries. It was invented in the late seventeenth century in England, then quickly spread to other glass-making regions, such as northern Italy and the Bohemian region of what's now the Czech Republic. Both glass and crystal contain sand or silica; but true crystal also has a small quantity of lead in the mix, which gives it clarity, strength, brilliance, and weight. The brilliance not only adds sparkle to the tablescape, it also allows drinkers to see the color of wine without distortion, as there is in cut or colored glass. The weight of these glasses gives them a luxurious feeling while holding and swirling them. Crystal has a slightly rougher surface, which supposedly allows the swirled wine to release more aromas.

Lead-crystal manufacturing is much more demanding and expensive than for glass. The furnaces have to reach temperatures of up to 1,500° Celsius, compared to 1,260° Celsius for glass. The product is fragile: for every hundred glasses made, thirty are rejected for imperfections and ten are broken. It used to be a manual process, but few glasses are handblown today—most are made by machine. The entire industry turns out more than 50 million glasses a year, but Riedel's products are still acknowledged as the best—the Pradas of stemware. They're the only glasses on display in the permanent collection of New York City's Museum of Modern Art.

Riedel believes that the best way to convince drinkers to buy good stemware is to show them what a difference it can make. Hence his series of taste-offs for those in the wine trade as well as for consumers. His strategy seems to be working. Several years ago, Riedel pitched his wares to some top winemakers who were also consumate marketers. Robert Mondavi, after tasting his product from a Riedel glass, said, "I never dreamed that my wines were this good." Riedel got a similar reaction from Angelo Gaja of Italy. Now Riedel has been on tour longer than the Rolling Stones.

Riedel's main message is one echoed by wine lovers every-where: the glasses in most common use, in restaurants and at home, are terrible for tasting wine. Those golf-ball-size cups are just too small to concentrate the wine's aromas, let alone to allow you to swirl the liquid without sloshing it on your shirt. You'd be better off drinking from a jam jar. Such glasses are like seats too close to the orchestra: all you hear are isolated sounds from the instruments, rather than the harmony that comes together farther back.

"Good stemware changes our perception of wine due to physics, not chemistry," Riedel explains. I dropped both subjects in high school, so I'm easily impressed. What he means is simple enough though: the glass doesn't change the wine itself, but rather the way we smell and taste it. Riedel glasses are like loudspeakers: their shape, volume, and rim diameter amplify a wine's inherent qualities. Pinot noir benefits from a large bowl to capture its aromas, for example, whereas champagne flutes are long and narrow to preserve the bubbles. The shape of the rim is important too. Thick ones act like speed bumps in front of the mouth and don't deliver the wine to the tongue evenly. Thin ones spread the liquid evenly across a broad section of the palate, like a smooth highway on-ramp.

Riedel's stemware science is his tongue map, which he brings out to show us the five basic tastes: sweet, salty, sour, bitter, and umami, a Japanese word for the savory character in food and drink. Until the 1990s, it was believed that the tip of our tongue detects sweetness, the sides of our mouth sense acidity, the inside of the mouth and gums pick up the dryness of tannin, the back of the mouth gets any bitterness there may be on the finish, and umami was detected all over as a total sensation. So Riedel designed his glasses to deliver the wine to the area of the mouth that would best appreciate it. For instance, the glass for the acidic sauvignon blanc directed the wine toward the middle of the tongue, away from the acid-sensitive sides of the mouth. However, several studies have since proved the "geography of the palate" a myth, as all of our taste buds can detect all five tastes to varying degrees. But no one here seems to be debating the scientific theories—we just want to drink. Maybe there's something wrong with my technique, though: within three nanoseconds of "initiating flow," the wine covers all of my mouth.

On the pretense of scientific thoroughness, I ask for more wine in all of my glasses. I'm convinced that a $95 stem can beat a tin mug when it comes to nuances, but how about his competitors' top stemware? I ask Riedel about this since all he's brought for comparison is the joker glass.

"They walk behind our tractor as we plow the field," he says cryptically. "But there's still a lot of unplowed field out there."

In fact, the competition in the upscale stemware market is stiff and includes companies such as Baccarat, Schott Zwiesel, and Waterford. One of my favorites is the German manufacturer Spiegelau. The brand is a great value for those who still want to send their kids to college after buying stemware: its Vino Grande series is a lower-priced knockoff of Riedel's Vinum line. (Riedel bought the company in 2004.)

Riedel's advice on choosing stemware reminds me of those diamond commercials that advise you to spend two months' pay on the engagement ring, if you really love her. He says that drinkers should spend as much money on one glass as they would on an average bottle of wine—the more expensive the wine, the more important the glass. He also recommends choosing the glass style for the wines you like best.

My problem with that: if I owned a different glass for every type of wine I like, I'd have to build an extra room onto my house and then hire staff just to clean them all. And really, some of the larger glasses are not just impractical to store and wash, but cumbersome to hold as well. By all means, move beyond a golf ball on a stick, but not to a fishbowl on a mast.

"Aesthetics and excellence are my criteria, not mere convenience," Josef Riedel said when he created his stemware back in 1973. For purists who also say convenience be damned, washing glasses requires as much attention as buying them. We know that the dishwasher, the housekeeper's best friend, is the worst enemy of good stemware: its soap will etch a fragile surface after repeated washings, so crystal glasses should always be washed by hand. Allow cold glasses to come to room temperature before washing them, as extreme changes in temperature can weaken crystal. Most wine lovers prefer not to use any soap at all, because even the slightest residue can affect the wine. Rinse glasses thoroughly under warm water. The most finicky people use distilled water, as the chlorine in some city water can also leave a taste on the glass.

Hold the bowl rather than the delicate stem or the base, which can make them snap. For an extraclean gleam, do what Riedel himself does: hold the glass over a kettle of just-boiled distilled water, so that the steam from the spout cleans the bowl. Then wipe it dry with a lint-free cloth (though not one that's been washed with fabric conditioner since that too can leave a film on the glass).

As my evening with Georg Riedel winds down, the gentle clinking of the glasses reminds me of children's voices and the soft strains of "so long, farewell, auf Wiedersehen, good night." He may not have sold me on the virtues of his brand above all others, but he has convinced me that the glass makes a difference. As he puts it, "Life is too short to drink good wine out of bad glasses."

*

Although glasses do influence our experience of wine, what matters more to me are people and places. Some of my most memorable wines were sipped from plain tumblers, sitting on a sun-drenched terrace overlooking the sparkling Mediterranean. Wine may lend itself to technical analysis, but tastings aren't just for serious connoisseurs. So I'm going to host my own wine tasting with friends, and instead of comparing stemware, we'll compare our favorite wines. I also think it's more fun to get together to drink than to buy Tupperware—unless, of course, you're drinking from the Tupperware. An in-home tasting is also a lot less intimidating than a formal event. You don't have to dress up, look serious (always difficult after several glasses), or listen to someone droning on about how the 1956 September rains ruined the riesling crop in the Rheingau. Most people just want to socialize over a good glass or two (or three); and it's just a bonus if they can also learn something.

An informal wine tasting can be a creative twist on cocktail or dinner parties; it's a lot less work than cooking a full meal or even setting up all the ingredients for a cocktail bar. It's also a great way to get to know your neighbors better, perhaps by inviting them over for a barbecue and matching big red wines. (Perhaps I should do this soon to clear up the misconception that I'm a lush based on my recycling bins overflowing with empty bottles.)

I decide to invite over seven of my girlfriends. Between six and twelve people is a good number for a tasting, both to encourage lively conversation and to make it easy to divide each bottle into moderate tasting samples. You don't want everyone inebriated by the end of the evening, unless you have a guesthouse that sleeps twelve. Over two or three hours, people may consume the equivalent of two or three five-ounce glasses— about half a standard 750-milliliter (26-ounce) bottle. The best sample size is two to three ounces, which is just enough to get a good sense of the wine. This increases the number of wines you can try because you're not knocking back a full glass of each.

For my choice of wines, I have to decide whether I want a "vertical" or "horizontal" tasting. This doesn't actually refer to which position you assume as the night wears on, but rather to comparing wines by certain variables, such as grape, region, or years. For example, if you compare a selection of Australian shirazes from different wineries, that's a horizontal tasting. Similarly, trying various kinds of shiraz from Chile, California, and Australia, all from the same year, is a horizontal tasting. But comparing the shirazes of one Australian winery for each year from 1998 to 2004 is a vertical tasting.

I've got all kinds of ideas for the event based on themes I've heard about over the years. These include asking everyone to bring a memorable bottle and share its story—perhaps they drank it to christen a new apartment or at their first dinner in Venice. Another is to choose stereotype-smashing wines, such as dry German wines or Canadian pinot noir. Book clubs can choose the wines featured in their novel, such as a sherry tasting while reading "The Cask of Amontillado"; or ones that are made where the story is based, such as Italian chianti for *Under the Tuscan Sun.*

Another option is a blind tasting, in which you brown-bag all the wines and taste them without knowing their identities. At the end, everyone votes on a favorite and then all is revealed. Guests can rank them in order of preference, with a score of one to ten—or even play the Roman emperor, giving the vinous "combatants" a thumbs-up or thumbs-down. (In the end, they'll all go down without a struggle anyway.) I've always thought it would be fun for the host to slip in a Chilean cabernet among the California cabs, or an expensive wine among cheaper ones, for example, just to see if anyone can spot the ringer.

Food matching is also a great way to theme a tasting: deciding which wines go best with seafood, cheese, desserts, hors d'oeuvres, artichokes, vinegar, and so on. The only flavors to avoid are volcanically hot and spicy dishes since these can numb the palate. The food doesn't have to be elaborate; nibbles are fine. We're doing potluck, with each woman bringing an appetizer. The idea is just to give us something to absorb the booze, since alcohol hits the bloodstream harder on an empty stomach than a full one.

For our event, I decide to go with a modified horizontal tasting: a mix of wines in the $10 to $20 range, four whites and four reds. Several wines grouped together for comparative tasting is called a "flight" of wine. I'm hoping that everyone will find at least one wine she likes for her shopping list. There'll be time enough to get more specific if we all agree to hold another event.

The big day arrives and I feel surprisingly nervous. My friends all know I write about wine, so they probably have high expectations for this tasting. I open all the wines and try them so I can find out if any of them are corked, otherwise spoiled, or just plain awful. I also put a glass of water at each place. Not only is alcohol dehydrating, but guests won't drink as much wine if they have water to slake their thirst.

Fortunately, I have enough stemware for the evening. For those who don't, options include asking guests to bring their own glasses from home; renting glasses for the occasion; or (for longer-running groups) pooling funds to buy dedicated glassware for the gatherings. Apart from wine tastings, though, how many glasses do you need for weekday dining or even entertaining? You could buy the full Sommelier line, but even if your cellar has complete verticals of Margaux and Cheval Blanc, a full set isn't really necessary. Instead, just buy two all-purpose styles: the bordeaux glass is the most versatile for reds, and the sauvignon blanc glass works for most whites.

About twenty minutes before my guests are due to arrive, I pour the first flight of white wines. I want them to be at the right temperature by the time we taste. Wine is often served at the wrong temperature: too cold and its complexity and aromas are numbed; too warm and it tastes alcoholic and flabby. To get the most from white wine, serve it chilled to about thirteen degrees Celsius; and when you pour, your glass should feel cool but not ice-cold—it shouldn't mist over. The quickest way to chill whites is to submerge them in ice water for about thirty minutes—chilling them in the fridge can take two to three hours. Don't even think of putting them in the freezer unless exploding bottles are to be part of the evening's entertainment.

Red wine is much easier: store it away from heat and serve it just below room temperature, about eighteen degrees Celsius. Reds are often served too warm. This faux pas probably comes from the long-established advice to serve them at "room temperature," which actually refers to the temperature of a chilly eighteenth-century castle rather than to today's centrally heated homes. However, some light reds, such as beaujolais, are better served at cooler temperatures, between red and white wine, to capture their freshness.

Some wine lovers like to "condition" their wineglass before drinking from it. They pour an ounce or two of wine into the glass, swirl it around so that it coats the sides, then dump it, supposedly along with any residual odors, but my hands are too shaky to do that.

The women arrive, one by one and a few together. (Carpooling is a good idea for tasting parties, and so are taxis.) We chat and nibble for a while before sitting down at my glassware-laden dining room table. I explain that we'll taste from left to right at first, but later we can go back and compare. Taking notes is optional, but might be helpful if they like the wine and want to remember its name so they can buy it. So I've provided sheets of white paper and pencils too.

I tell them that the only way not to get tanked when tasting so many wines is to spit out some of their samples after they swirl them around their mouth. If you swallow all the wine you taste, not only will you get drunk, but you will be unable to smell or taste the later samples: alcohol numbs the palate after a while.

Lisa looks disappointed, presumably about not getting sloshed; Natasha seems disgusted. Many people consider spitting or "expectorating" as crude as spitting out gobs of food or wet tobacco. And in a social setting, a force stronger than gravity impels most of us to swallow whatever's in our glass. Europeans, however, are much less inhibited—just as they are about so many other things, from nude bathing to May–December sexual liaisons. The French consider it no sin to *recracher* onto the vineyard earth, down winery drains, or even on the barrel-room floor.

I'm not aiming to take us that far, though: even I don't think it's a mark of European sophistication to spit on a floor that's finished in bird's-eye maple or covered with Persian carpets. That's why, for this charming tradition, I've set out mugs at each place as ersatz spittoons. (They're opaque rather than clear to preserve the much needed illusion of delicacy.) The bottom line: nobody should have to swallow wine they don't like or be forced to drink too much, which is another reason that you should provide some sort of spittoon.

"Do you mean like a big, horking spit?" Shelley asks me mischievously. "Let's see you do it first."

It's not a common request from one girlfriend to another, but I'm happy to oblige since I'm now a practiced spitter. Alas, it wasn't always so. This odd little demo makes me recall one of my first unfortunate attempts in a winery tasting room. It happened just as I was about to release a mouthful of robust cabernet into the spit bucket: a large man suddenly leaned on the tasting counter in front of me, blocking the spit bucket. He had his back to me and was chatting merrily with his group, oblivious to my presence, as the tannins started to erode my tooth enamel.

I should just have given up and swallowed, but I had ten more wineries to visit that day and was stubbornly determined to follow standard procedure. In my panic, I made a foolish mistake: I tried to say "Excuse me, please" out of the corner of my mouth.

As I opened my lips, wine dribbled down my chin; I tried to gulp after it and managed to inhale a good ounce of wine. I choked, lungs burning and tears streaming down my face. I scaled to the summit of my humiliation as I sprayed out the remaining wine all across the counter, the tasting sheets, and the brochures; though I narrowly missed the large man's white shirt.

All the other visitors went quiet for a moment. Then the young girl behind the counter, with the compassion of a nurse to some poor soul who has just lost bladder control, offered me a paper towel and asked, "Would you like this one to wipe yourself?"

I shake this sad little incident out of my mind now as I take Shelley up on her challenge. I show my friends the technique: after you have tasted some wine, you just suck in your cheeks, purse your lips into a slightly open O-shape, lean close to the bucket (or mug), and expel in a steady stream. It's considered bad form to dribble, spray, or have your wine ricochet back at you.

It sounds simple, but it takes some perfecting. Some people prefer to start in the shower, then move on to the bathroom sink—and only when they're finally ready to work without a net will they graduate to the dining room table. In our case, there were many slurping laughs as my friends tried to master the art of expectoration. I told them not to sweat it as tonight was about enjoying ourselves rather than sticking to procedure.

Now we get to the fun part: actually tasting the wine. I fill the glasses with a towel wrapped around each bottle, to keep its identity a secret until later. I explain about the five basic aspects to examine: look, smell, taste, texture, and finish. The first means we need good light—though as always that means striking a balance between creating a cozy social setting and being able to see what we're doing. Candlelight isn't ideal for judging the color of wine, but we also don't want a harshly lit lablike environment. So we compromise with the lights on a medium setting.

When I say we'll look at color, several of the women immediately hold their glasses up to the chandelier. Although this is a standard approach in movies (poorly made ones without a wine adviser on the set), it's useless: all it tells you is what the wine can reflect from your wallpaper. Instead, tilt the wineglass on its side a little against a light background, such as a white tablecloth—if you're willing to risk getting wine stains on it. I'm not, so we use our pieces of white paper.

The color tells us how old the wine is. Young whites are usually green at the edges and become a deeper yellow or gold with time; reds are usually purple or ruby in youth and turn to garnet or brick in age. We can also tell how clear the wine is and whether there's anything floating in it (usually not a good thing).

If white wine is dark gold or brown, it may be oxidized. Too much oxygen is an enemy of wine, as it is of so many other substances. Overexposure to air makes nails rust, fruit turn brown, and wine taste unpleasant. Even mild exposure while the wine is being made, aged, bottled, or stored makes low-acidity wine smell cooked and high-acidity wine smell burnt. Prolonged exposure causes wines to smell and taste of vinegar, which eventually evolves into an aggressive smell of glue or nail polish remover.

For reds, young wines should ideally be a vibrant red or purple; while lighter reds, such as gamay and pinot noir, are on the brighter-red end of the spectrum. Robust reds, such as cabernet, zinfandel, and shiraz, are darker purple. Only mature reds, such as aged bordeaux and barolo, will have hues of mahogany, brick, or even faded brown because of their long, slow exposure to the air in the bottle. This is accompanied by smooth, integrated flavors, which are nothing like the stale taste of oxidized wine due to a dried-out cork that has allowed too much air into the bottle. This usually happens when a bottle is stored upright, rather than laid on its side so the wine inside keeps the cork moist.

Fortunately, none of our wines is oxidized. We give our glasses a good swirl to aerate the wine and release its aromas. If you're nervous about doing it with your glass actually in the air, try the training-wheels version with the glass on the table. Then lift the glass to your face and inhale deeply. I tell the women not to be shy about this inelegant move and to get their noses well inside the glass.

Although we can detect only five tastes with our mouths, we can smell more than two thousand aromas with our noses. Try sipping wine with your nose plugged and you'll taste the difference. Wine's aromas are considered the determining factor of its character. This scent factor is also why I've asked the women not to wear perfume, as it interferes with the wine's aromas.

The other thing about smell is that it's so evocative. I ask the women what the wine reminds them of: wood chips, cherries, apples, their aunt Mildred's spice cake? This is a subjective judgment, but it becomes sharper with time and experience.

"This one smells like putty," Robyn says, looking puzzled.

"I get cinnamon," says Debbie.

"It just smells like wine to me," Shirley says. She isn't alone: beyond a few basic adjectives, such as *fruity* or *smooth*, most people find it difficult to analyze how a wine smells and tastes. Indeed, the first time I listened to two wine-loving friends discuss a merlot, I thought they were speaking some ancient tribal language. It reminded me of British illustrator and satirist Ralph Steadman's description of an Algerian wine: "Very soft and very round, like sheep's eyes with square pupils. The hint of promise got steeper and sparser yet, and it began to taste like dull pewter covered in dust and cobwebs stuck to the roof of my mouth."

Some wine descriptions seem to be far removed from the actual experience of smelling and tasting wine. What's prompting this proliferation of purple prose? Perhaps it's the thousands of new wines coming onto the market, all of which need to be described? Then again, perhaps wine critics are looking to secure their niches through comparisons so obscure that nobody can question them. Perhaps wine retailers also see full-bodied writing as a good way to get more cash for *vin ordinaire*. But on the bright side, it could represent a renaissance of wine appreciation, this demand for new ways to talk about one of civilization's oldest drinks.

Dr. Adrienne Lehrer, professor emerita of linguistics at the University of Arizona, has been studying this topic for twenty years. According to her book *Wine and Conversation*, wine description is using new words and metaphors. A wine today isn't simply balanced, it's *integrated* or *focused*. In contrast, an unbalanced wine is *muddled* or *diffuse*. A full-bodied wine is now *chunky* and *big-boned*; a light-bodied wine is *svelte* and *sleek*.

"I'm interested in this from a linguistic point of view, because wine writers are enriching the language and making up metaphors," Lehrer says. "When critics try to describe thirty California chardonnays, they often find that the wines are similar—but it would be boring to read the same thing all the time. So they jazz up the descriptions to keep readers engaged."

When compiling her glossary of frequently used wine adjectives, Lehrer discovered that the tasting terms included *barnyard funk, intellectual*, and *diplomatic*. "*Funky* was used a lot," she says. "I don't know whether it has any specific meaning that's different from the way that it's used elsewhere."

Then there is the new generation of wine writers trying to make wine talk less intimidating and more relevant by including pop culture references. *Wine X* magazine claims to "provide a new voice for a new generation of wine consumers." Describing one California cabernet, it asks us to "imagine Naomi Campbell in latex." An Australian shiraz is a "Chippendales dancer in leather chaps—tight, full-bodied and ready for action." A New Zealand cabernet merlot is like "a Victoria's Secret fire sale: smoky charred wood, leather, spicy and very seductive."

Is *Wine X* simply the same old juice in a newly accessorized bottle? Some critics think that trashing grammar and mixing metaphors makes wine writing irrelevant, not irreverent. Walter Sendzik, publisher of the Canadian wine magazine *Vines*, which also reaches out to young drinkers, admits that traditional wine description can sometimes be too esoteric. But you can also go too far in the other direction, he says wryly: "I've never smelled or tasted Naomi Campbell in latex."

Serious attempts have been made to standardize wine-tasting vocabulary. The accepted template is now the Aroma Wheel, developed in the early 1980s by Ann Noble, professor of enology and viticulture at the UC Davis. The inner circle of its concentric rings notes the most basic wine adjectives, such as *fruity* and *floral*, while the subdivided middle and outer rings provide more descriptive terms such as *grapefruit, strawberry jam*, and *asparagus*.

But wait: Isn't wine made from grapes rather than asparagus or grapefruit? Well, there is some sense behind this descriptive noble rot. The molecular structures of wine are in fact similar to those found in fruit, flowers, vegetables—and can even smell like "wet dog" and "cardboard box," indicating spoilage. For example, scientists have identified the chemical compound isobutyl methoxy pyrazine, which has the aroma of bell peppers, in sauvignon blanc. That same compound is also found in high concentration in—you guessed it—bell peppers.

Our culture is visually oriented, and so much of our language refers to sight cues. Of all our senses, smell is the most under-developed—perhaps because we no longer have to hunt for our meals and worry about poisonous plants. Even taste fares better: most waiters can come up with mouthwatering descriptions of a restaurant's dishes. But unless they've taken a wine appreci-ation course, many are hard-pressed to offer equally rich descriptions of the wines on the list.

Yet for all that, we have only four genes for vision, but one thousand for smell. Input from the other senses must first go to the hypothalamus and then on to the cortex for further analysis; but smells are routed directly to the areas of the brain responsible for emotions and memories.

The renowned French gastronome Jean Anthelme Brillat-Savarin recognized the importance of smell in his book *The Physiology of Taste*, published in 1825. "I am not only convinced that without the cooperation of smell there can be no complete degustation," he wrote. "But I am also tempted to believe that smell and taste are in fact but a single sense, whose laboratory is in the mouth and whose chimney is the nose; or to be more precise, in which the mouth performs the degustation of the tactile bodies, and the nose the degustation of the gases."

The good news is that most of us can recognize a far wider range of aromas and flavors than we think ourselves capable of. It just takes a little discipline, some concentration, and lots of practice. It also means paying attention to everyday smells—literally, taking time to smell the flowers and even the grass in your garden. Sniff the bread before you put it in the grocery cart, smell the cinnamon on your toast and fruit and vegetables just after you cut them open to eat or cook.

The goal of democratic wine description is to develop a common vocabulary that's widely understood and can be used over and over. It shouldn't create a caste system that sets those in the know apart from those who confine themselves to margaritas for fear of looking foolish.

Now at our tasting, we finally get to taste the wine. I tell the women to swirl it around their mouths, to coat all the taste buds, and to aerate it by sucking a little air into their mouths. This further enhances the taste, though it may be another technique best tried first in the shower. We talk about what flavors we're picking up, concentrating on the most common ones such as fruit and oak. We also discuss how the wine feels in our mouths, whether it's heavy as cream, light as skim milk, or somewhere in between, like whole milk.

We take another sip and swallow a little of the wines that we like best. That tells us how long the wine's flavor impression lasts—its finish. As with so many other pleasures in life, the longer the better. A long finish means you can still sense the wine in your mouth for eight seconds or more after swallowing. A medium finish is four to seven seconds, and fewer than four seconds is short.

We taste both flights, chatting about them and turning our thumbs up or down for our favorites. By this time we're all feeling quite festive, and any initial shyness about commenting on the wines has dissipated completely. In fact, multiple conversations are going on, and at times I enjoy listening to the musical quality of their voices, without trying to figure out what they're saying. There are high notes of excitement, soft notes of understanding, and tinkling punctuation notes of laughter.

Finally, as the evening draws to a close, I amuse and shock my friends by pouring the leftover wine into the sink.

"Is this what you do every night, Natalie?" Debi asks me with mock horror. "Dump all kinds of good wine down the drain?"

"Well, yes and no," I tell her. "I don't do this for the really good ones. But I do pour away a lot of the free stuff wineries send me to try because much of it isn't that great."

Debi says half-jokingly and half-longingly, "I still wouldn't mind taking home your rejects."

As we say good-bye and the women head out into the dark blue night, warm and light-limbed, I contemplate the practical side of wine tastings. With tens of thousands of wines on liquor store shelves, the choice can be overwhelming. You have to kiss a lot of frogs to find a prince, that delicious and reasonably priced bottle. Group tastings stretch your wine budget since you can sample several bottles for the cost of the one you bring. That's especially useful to choose wines for dinner parties when there are multiple courses that require different styles.

Looking back on the evening, I realize that wine is as much about camaraderie as taste. When we share good wine with good friends, we also share what makes us human: sensual pleasure, conversation, and connection. That's the magic hospitality of wine: you can give it all away and yet feel filled to the brim yourself.

SEVEN

Partners at the Table

EVERYONE WILL BE here in three hours. A thread of sweat stitches my blouse to my back. Whose idea was this anyway? Surely, not mine. As a party animal, I fit somewhere between a desert lizard and a night worm. But now I recall that febrile moment a month ago when I thought a dinner party would be a wonderful way to celebrate Thanksgiving with friends.

Every month, though, I read some grim article about the Death of the Dinner Party. The writer calls them démodé, ousted by the more democratic potluck gathering. But if the recent surge in sales of fine china, table linen, and fancy candlesticks is any indication, reports of the dinner party's death are premature. Surely all of this finery isn't stored in cupboards, awaiting a fiftieth wedding anniversary? Even increased house sales augur well for such events: the third *C* of home ownership, after comfort and convenience, is conspicuous consumption—which requires inviting people over. As well, food is the new entertainment. You can watch Emeril, then be Emeril, with your own handpicked audience.

However, after a full day's work, taking my son to after-school soccer, working out, picking up the dry cleaning, putting plant food in the dead fern's pot, shopping for a new air filter, and defrosting dinner, I wonder, why even host a dinner party? Well, offering hospitality is one of life's greatest pleasures. It gets us out of our separate solitudes and gathers us together to celebrate special occasions, to enjoy good food and wine, and to brighten otherwise ordinary evenings. The risk, though, is that dinner parties put your personal life on display. Opening your home allows your guests to see if you have taste (home décor), culture (art, books), hygiene (housekeeping), connections (family photos), and personality defects (PEZ stick collection). Even parenting skills are up for review: our six-year-old has now mastered slipping in for a quick hors d'oeuvre and then dashing out again, skipping the tiresome introductions. This is why evil guests can trash your reputation: they have so much material to work with. Maybe that's why I'm down on my knees, feverishly combing the rug fringes with my fingernails, just after tossing *People* magazine into the cupboard and leaving *Anna Karenina* bookmarked on the side table. ("Oh, so that's where I left my book!")

The flip side of such personal revelation and vulnerability is the chance for hosts and guests to develop a deeper friendship. While restaurant tables can usually accommodate a large group, only a few people can sit down together in most home dining rooms. This gives the guests an exclusive feeling and makes hosts feel more responsible for their happiness. That's especially important to us tonight because this is the first Thanksgiving meal we'll make ourselves: in all our years together, we (like our friends) have always traveled home for the holidays. But this year we're on our own in the kitchen.

Or rather, Andrew's on his own—he's the cook in the family. He actually enjoys cooking, whereas my forte is pulling corks. To be blunt: I don't cook, I don't know how to cook, and I'm not interested in learning how to cook. I come by this aversion honestly: my mother disliked kitchen work too and we ate many frozen dinners when I was a child. What she did do, as a single parent and full-time teacher, was foster in me a life-long love of reading, writing, and financial independence. And once I started dining in good restaurants as an adult, there was no turning back: I was like a devotee of classical music who can't bear to take piano lessons because her appreciation is so far ahead of her ability.

However, Andrew is adventurous and likes to experiment with food. Living with me, he's come to enjoy cooking with wine—though one of his first attempts involved unwittingly pouring Dominus into the osso buco. This prestigious California cabernet, which sells for about $150 a bottle, is usually best savored from the glass.

Still, this *vincident* started me thinking about wine the way cooks do: as a seasoning, like herbs or garlic. Wine is one of the quickest and simplest ways to add flavor to food, giving some softer grace notes to a hearty dish or richness to a light one. Tonight, Andrew adds a splash of red wine to the gravy, substitutes a cup of white wine for water in the rice, and drizzles champagne over the panna cotta for dessert. (It helps that our cellar is well stocked in these basic ingredients.) The bonus is not only that wine is fat-free, but also that its natural glycerin helps to bind sauces, which minimizes the need for oils or other fats. And because it adds so much flavor, many cooks find that they don't need as much salt, or even any at all—a plus for those on low-sodium diets.

The reverse is also true: food can elevate the flavors of a wine. An austere and tannic young cabernet may taste too harsh on its own, but soften to voluptuousness in your mouth alongside a juicy steak. However, the wines we like to drink on their own aren't necessarily the best companions to a meal. If they're assertively flavored, with lots of ripe-fruit aromas or buttery oak, they can overwhelm food.

Of course, in Europe, wine has long been considered a natural part of a healthy Mediterranean diet. In France today, wine-makers are lobbying the government to get it officially desig-nated as food. (Though that has more to do with propping up flagging wine sales than fueling a passion for reduction sauces.)

In North America, the wine industry has also tried to posi-tion the product as more healthful than other alcohol. In the book *Spinning the Bottle*, Harvey Posert describes the public relations efforts of Robert Mondavi and other California vint-ners in the early 1990s to counteract the messages of alcohol opponents. The winemakers hosted conferences featuring health researchers, social scientists, and other experts; funded medical research on the health benefits of wine and issued their findings to the mass media and to health journals; and hosted wine tastings for doctors and medical students.

In 1991, two scientists, Dr. Serge Renaud, of Lyon University, and Dr. Curtis Ellison, of Boston University, were interviewed on the investigative television show *60 Minutes*. They described the French paradox: even though the French eat more red meat and fatty foods than North Americans, smoke more frequently, and exercise less often, they still suffer far fewer heart attacks. They concluded that it was because of the effect of moderate drinking of red wine, which reduces the risk of heart disease. After the show aired, sales of red wine soared in America.

Still, most of us aren't thinking of our blood platelet activity when we smell slow-braising meat in a rich wine sauce. In fact, classic French cooking has long depended on wine for such techniques as glazing, deglazing, macerating, marinating, and poaching. Many dishes can't be made without it: think of boeuf bourguignon, coq au vin, and coquilles St. Jacques. Those clas-sics depend on wine to impart its rich and textured flavors— variations on the ones we enjoy in the glass.

At one point, I imagined all the shabby-chic dishes that Andrew could concoct to gussy up our weeknight dinners with the finest wines: macaroni and cheese made with French champagne (Kraft Dinner avec Krug), and for dessert a dash of Penfolds Grange with gelatin powder mix ("Hoe-di-doe, now that's Jell-O!"). But this would just be a waste of money: the complex nuances of an expensive wine don't survive cooking. If you pour champagne over the roast, all those lacy liquid pearls simply bubble off. That's like lighting a campfire with a hundred-dollar bill.

Beware, though, of the pernicious substances sold as "cooking wines" in some grocery stores. They're often thin, sour wines that have been denatured with food coloring, salt, soy, sugar, garlic, and preservatives. Unfortunately, cooking wines have generally become a dumping ground for what we consider undrinkable. A bottle of this grape juice–turpentine will not make your pasta sauce a work of art. Flavor in, flavor out: it's a myth that the bad taste of poorly made wine will be cooked off. For better or worse, heat accentuates a wine's character as it reduces it to the essential flavors.

Fortunately, as more cooks today use wine in their dishes, "cooking wine" has earned new respect. Now it's usually a bottle that Andrew is happy to sip from as he cooks—though I always decant the Dominus safely into a carafe and put it on the dining room table first.

Decanting is a simple enough practice, but few topics are more controversial among wine geeks. Surprisingly, there's a philosophical chasm between "decantists," who insist that most (if not all) wines benefit from being exposed to oxygen when they're poured from the bottle into some other vessel before drinking; and "bottlists," who think that the practice is unnecessary, even harmful. The latter believe that decanting is simply another way for wine snobs to show off and for sommeliers to earn a bigger tip (or even take a free swig of your wine).

Like most areas unsupported by science, the topic of decanting generates a lot of heat but not much light: it's one of the least-understood aspects of serving wine. But there are several good reasons why people do it. The least contentious is to get rid of sediment. The grape juice from which wine is made contains organic matter, and as wine matures, these particles fall out of the wine as sediment. The wines that throw the most sediment tend to be mature, full-bodied red wines and vintage port. Tawny and late-bottled vintage ports don't need decanting: their sediment is removed earlier, before they're bottled. White wines tend not to have sediment because their skins are separated from the juice during fermentation.

As bottles are usually stored on their sides (to keep the cork wet and the wine from oxidizing), the nasty-tasting sludge settles along the bottom side. That's why the bottle should be stood upright for several hours before decanting: to settle the sediment at the very bottom. These days, many wines are clarified and filtered before bottling to suit the taste of consumers who like their wine clear, even though this can strip the wine of its character. For these wines, decanting is often unnecessary.

The second reason to decant is to let the wine breathe. This is controversial because oxygen is both friend and foe to wine. As anyone who's left a glass of wine out overnight knows, too much air can turn wine into vinegar. But oxygen is necessary for wine to mature and to release its aromas. One reason why many wines are aged in oak barrels (apart from imparting an oak flavor) is that tiny pores in the wood allow just the right amount of air in. The same was believed of corks: their pores, along with the air space below the cork, allow the wine to develop further in the bottle. (Researchers are still trying to determine how plastic corks and screwcaps affect wine's ability to age in the long term.)

Many people believe that aerating wine helps to warm up a wine that's too cold, soften any harsh tannins, and open up its aromatics. This is especially true of young, full-bodied ones such as cabernet sauvignon, zinfandel, brunello, barolo, bordeaux, rioja, shiraz, syrah, and northern Rhône reds. These wines can be rough around the edges, with some tannin that needs to be smoothed out. Airing such wines not only softens their tannins, but some drinkers believe it also diminishes out-of-balance elements such as too much oak. Even excess odors of sulfur can dissipate with a little air time.

While there's no scientific evidence to support decanting in general, it has been proven that simply uncorking the bottle is useless. A professor at the University of Milan, Dr. Pier Giuseppe Agostoni, once measured the oxygen levels in five bottles of uncorked wine at different intervals. He concluded that there was no positive benefit. Wine can no more breathe through the bottle neck than we could breathe through a pin-sized straw. To get the full benefit, you have to aerate the liquid by pouring it out of the bottle and into another container, be it a carafe, decanter, or a water jug.

Even decanting hard-liners admit that some wines aren't really made for airing out. Delicate red wines such as pinot noir aren't usually decanted because their subtle aromas can quickly dissipate. The same goes for zesty whites, such as ries-lings and sauvignon blancs, since they can quickly lose their crisp, refreshing edge. Others are more borderline: full-bodied whites, such as oaky chardonnays and some sweet wines, may benefit from decanting.

Many wines I've tried improved after being decanted for half an hour—they taste smoother and more integrated. Young reds benefit most from a two-to-three-hour air time. Older wines don't really open up any further after an hour, but neither do they fall apart like some geriatric scuba diver coming up too quickly and getting the bends.

Tonight I'm decanting two red wines, which means two decanters. I've developed my own slightly obsessive ritual for doing this: First, I wash the decanter with warm water but not soap, using a long brush to reach into the narrow necks. I shake out the excess water. I'm equally obsessive with the bottle. Once I've removed the foil and pulled the cork, I use a lint-free cloth to clean the mouth. Finally, I sniff the bottle to make sure that the wine isn't corked or otherwise faulty. If it is, decanting won't do a darned thing to help—I'd take it back to the store for a refund.

Luckily, none of tonight's wines is faulty. The first wine is a Rosenblum zinfandel from California that doesn't have much sediment, but needs to breathe: when I take a sip, it makes my mouth pucker. I use a duck-shaped decanter because it's large enough to hold a full bottle and still allow lots of air space over the wine. Before I bought it, I'd use a water jug or a carafe. And sometimes, I'd just pour the wine into the glasses to about one-third full, which also helps it to breathe.

I've selected a different decanter with a narrow neck for my second wine, a 1966 Château Palmer, because it just needs its sediment removed. When I was choosing this bordeaux from my cellar yesterday, I noticed that it had sediment, so I left it standing upright for a day to settle the gunk at the bottom. (Sometimes, I forget to do this—well, okay, often I forget to do this or I just don't notice. When that happens, I don't stand the bottle upright before I decant it since that just mixes the sediment back into the wine. Instead, I leave it reclining at about forty-five degrees as I uncork and pour. Granted, this is awkward; but at least most of the sediment stays in one place in the bottle.)

Either way, to pour the wine, I stand a flashlight on the table so that it shines upward with a stronger light than a lit candle, which is more about pageantry than practicality when you're at home. Then I place the decanter beside it and pour the wine so that the light shines through the neck of the bottle. This lets me see when the sediment is approaching the neck so I can stop pouring.

Done properly, there's clear wine in the decanter and an inch or two of dregs left in the bottle. I throw these out, but one friend pours them on her fern—she has a very large fern. I lose half an inch or so of wine, but that's a small sacrifice for not having bitter wine.

I leave younger wines in the decanter for an hour or two, and older wines from fifteen minutes to half an hour. I taste them periodically to see how they're opening up (and more often when I'm nervous about the dinner, so that I open up). If I decide that the wine has peaked before it's time to drink it, I drape a cloth over the decanter to slow aeration. (In summer, this also helps deter the pesky fruit flies that like to high-dive into my wine. I seem to breed a connoisseur class of pests that enjoy a good vintage as much as I do.) Conversely, if the wine is still tight when the guests arrive, I try to speed up the aeration by double-decanting: pouring the wine back and forth slowly several times between two containers.

Of course, like any ritual, decanting can be taken too far: some enthusiasts treat their wine more like a sacrament than a drink. Tonight, I've waved off the hot air on this debate and focused on the beauty of the cut-crystal decanter filled with dancing rubies in the candlelight.

I like to greet our guests with a wine that doesn't need

decanting: champagne. In France, the traditional aperitif was once the highly alcoholic vermouth. But in my opinion, sparkling wine is much better. It stimulates the appetite, its lower alcohol content reduces the risk of guests breaking out into spontaneous karaoke before dinner is finished, and it adds a celebratory note to any evening.

Champagne is also part of several classic cocktails that whet the appetite before dinner, such as Kir Royale. Modern politicians who want to stay in office could learn a thing or two from Félix Kir, who became mayor of Dijon, France, in 1945 and held the post until 1968.

His secret? A little cassis cordial made from two local products: four parts aligoté, the region's basic white wine, and one part crème de cassis, the black-currant-flavored liqueur. The same soil and climate conditions that nurture grapes are also good for black currants—a fact not lost on the sixteenth-century monks who first created the bloodred cordial as a cure for jaundice and "wretchedness" (an antidote that might also benefit a political career).

Kir, who loved to entertain, always served his aperitif at official receptions. As time passed, the drink became known simply as Kir. For the sparkling version, Kir Royale, he used champagne instead of white wine, but any young, dry sparkling wine will round off the sweet flavor of cassis.

Another classic champagne cocktail was invented when Prince Albert, Queen Victoria's husband, died in 1861. The bartender at Brooks's Club in London felt that champagne alone was too festive to drink at a time of national mourning, so he "veiled" the bubbly with equal portions of the dark Irish stout Guiness, and named it Black Velvet.

One of the few downsides to champagne is that many of us (especially women) are scared to open a bottle of it. When the

British retailer Marks & Spencer surveyed five hundred women on their wine habits, 75 percent said they always ask a man to uncork the champagne. They were afraid that the cork would fly out and hit them in the face or break something. It's not an unfounded fear: the American Academy of Ophthalmology warns that many people injure their eyes every year that way. Corks flying out of champagne bottles have been clocked at fifty miles per hour.

Since I write about wine, friends and family usually hand me the champagne bottle to open. The conventional method is simple. First, ensure that the wine is properly chilled, since warm wine doesn't taste refreshing and foams out of the bottle faster. The ideal temperature is about seven degrees Celsius for nonvintage bruts and ten degrees for the vintage wines. Chilling it too much numbs the aromas, especially the finer ones of a prestige cuvée. (Twenty minutes in iced water works best, but an hour in the fridge will do too.)

Now ignore those Formula One winners who shake the bottle before opening it. If you actually want the wine in your glass, as opposed to showering your guests, handle it gently. Remove the foil and wire cage. (Some say that the cage should stay on as a safety measure, but you'll need to untwist the bottom anyway to allow the cork to move. I find keeping it over the cork makes removing both more awkward.) Angle the bottle away from you, pointed at the ceiling rather than at a guest or that vase on the mantel, just in case the cork flies out prematurely. Keep one hand firmly over the cork while using the other to slowly turn the bottle. The pressure inside the bottle will start to push the cork out by itself, with no corkscrew required. I usually drape a small towel over the cork, just in case it comes out a little too fast and foamy. Ideally, this happens with a postcoital sigh rather than a slam-pop and it's over too soon.

Over the holidays last year, I got a bit daring and decided to try the saber method. Legend has it that after winning a battle, one of Napoléon's soldiers had used his sword to shear off the top of a champagne bottle. I felt that if I could manage this stunt, I'd strike a blow for women cowering from champagne bottles everywhere. Stylish though the technique may be, it has almost died out in France: most diners today would find an armed host (or sommelier) disconcerting.

Fortunately, I had the hardware. I was a Scottish Highland dancer as a child and still have my trusty sword. I also had a basic grasp of the physics involved. When molten glass solidifies quickly into a bottle, the crystalline structure incorporates many tiny imperfections or microfractures, especially around the mold seams. The place where the side seam meets the head of the bottle has the most imperfections and is therefore the weakest point. The idea is that a clean slice at this spot, together with the champagne's internal pressure, will easily shear off the top. The only problem is that if you don't do it correctly, the bottle, with its ninety pounds of pressure per square inch, can explode in your hands.

Fearless as I may have felt, I wasn't going to try this out on Krug or Grande Dame, nor in front of guests. Instead, I bought some budget bubbly and went out to the backyard to practice. I pointed the bottle away from me at a forty-five-degree angle and used my fingernail to find the bottle's side seam. Then, holding the bottom of the bottle in my left hand, I placed the sword blade flat against the bottle, over the seam, about six inches below the cork. Pressing firmly (and taking a deep breath), I slid the blade quickly up to the neck and the top joint. A sharp, but surprisingly small tap was all it took to break the neck cleanly off and send top and cork flying together into my neighbor's yard. The champagne didn't even foam out: it seemed as stunned as I was that I'd actually managed the feat. To calm down, I poured the wine into a flute and knocked it back.

This is an entertaining party trick but I wouldn't recommend it for anyone who doesn't want to risk spending dinner with one eye swollen shut or a cork burn on your cheek. I'm definitely not trying it tonight for our Thanksgiving soirée.

The doorbell chimes and I assume the posture of Casual Elegance; then decide that Confident Simplicity is a better bet. Dashing for the door, I mentally flip through the "The Good Host" chapter: How many times should I let the doorbell ring before answering so I don't appear more eager than a cocker spaniel?

Couple by couple, the guests arrive. Our Scottish, Latin American, and French backgrounds collide awkwardly as we greet each other with the pigeon-pecking air-kiss dance, unsure whether to shake hands, kiss one cheek or both. We all have children with whom we'll have a family dinner tomorrow; but tonight we're giving thanks for the pleasures of adult conversation.

"Here you go," Sharon says, thrusting a potted geranium into Andrew's arms and then bear-hugging him—nearly flattening the plant into a corsage against his jacket. Jeff tentatively hands me an Australian shiraz, sheepishly acknowledging that it's the equivalent of bringing tea to China.

"You have nothing to worry about as long as you bought an expensive label," I reassure him, winking. He lunges forward a bit, as though to retrieve the bottle, then smiles.

Sheila and John bring truffles. Nancy and David arrive last, with homemade preserves. In other cultures, follow-up gifts the day after are more the norm so that the host doesn't have to abandon guests to put a bouquet in water. Flowers, chocolates, cheese, potted plants, coffee-table books, household gifts, and bath products are all good ideas. (How do you think Crabtree & Evelyn stays in business?)

A bottle of wine can be a good gift, but don't expect the host to open it right away: she's probably already planned the wines to suit what's she's serving. If you have a bottle that you really want to drink, call ahead to ask your host if it'll complement the meal. Short of decanting the wine in the car, this should adequately make the point that you want to drink it that evening. Of course, if the host consistently opens her own stock, don't bother bringing one you want to drink.

When I'm the host and someone is brave enough to bring a bottle, I ask, "Do you think it's ready to drink? Should we try it this evening or save it for another special occasion?" This may be a distinctive bottle that the guest has schlepped all the way back from Napa and is dying to share with me. What matters most with any gift is the symbolic recognition of the time, effort, and expense your hosts have already invested in the evening. Relax, you couldn't possibly do worse than the grandfather of Kingsley Amis, who, the late novelist recalled, once gave his host a bottle of HP sauce.

Traditionally, the up-front token was part homage, part payment; but the debt wasn't fully repaid until the guest reciprocated with an invitation. Hosts throughout history have tried to outdo each other with lavish parties in order to make their guests indebted to them. (What's the good of money if you can't wave it under people's noses?) In ancient Rome, hosts often invited some people not wealthy enough to reciprocate: they called them parasites. They were seated in the least desirable places, ate the most meager food, took the butt of jokes, and were expected to flatter the host. Of course, today we wouldn't dream of designating parasites—they tend to designate themselves.

Even today, being lavish can become a form of social isolation.

Guests may be so intimidated that they feel they can't possibly invite you over to their own homes. This is a sad loss for hospitality, which is embodied more in the gesture than in the execution. The problem is worse when people think of you as an expert on wine or food. In *An Alphabet for Gourmets*, M. F. K. Fisher writes of her loneliness among friends who thought her palate too sophisticated for their own humble fare:

"Behind the far door to the kitchen I have sensed, with the mystic materialism of a hungry woman, the presence of honest-to-God fried chops, peas and carrots, a jello salad and a lemon meringue pie—none of which I like and all of which I admire in theory and would give my eyeteeth to be offered. But the kind people always murmur, 'We'd love to have you stay to supper sometime. We wouldn't dare, of course, the simple way we eat.'"

On the way home to the "spinsterish emptiness of my one room," she'd stop at the local Thriftymart to pick up a box of Ry-Krisp, a can of tomato soup, and California sherry to eat while surrounded by "a circle of proofs and pocket detective stories."

I felt a keen pang for Fisher after reading that, since many of my own friends have often expressed their performance anxiety about bringing wine to my home or, less frequently, serving me wine at their place. No matter how often I protest that I'm happy to drink cheap Chilean cabernet, they never seem to understand that I come to spend time with them, not to evaluate their wine cellar.

Tonight, there's no loss of camaraderie: Nancy and Sheila are talking about the schools their kids attend, while the other five are discussing the hit movie *Sideways*, which takes place in California wine country. As they chat, I retreat to the kitchen to get the drinks. Much as I enjoy being with my guests, there's also something magical about being at the outside edge of a gathering. Perhaps this comes from my childhood, when my relatives had boisterous *ceilidhs* (Celtic for "parties") in the summer evenings. I'd sit out on the veranda in an oversize rocking chair, warmed by the laughter and light spilling from the windows.

I return to our group with a tray of champagne flutes frothing at the brim. As we all raise our glasses, I say, "May our friendship, like wine, improve with time. And may we always have old wine, old friends, and young cares." We clink glasses. Though secretly, I'd rather repeat the naughty verse of Dorothy Parker, one of the wits of the Algonquin Round Table in New York City in the 1930s: "I wish I could drink like a lady, I'll have one or two at the most. Three and I'm under the table, four and I'm under the host."

I may not be bold enough to say that tonight, but at least I've made a toast—another social grace in decline today. If proposed at all, they usually involve no more forethought than "Down the hatch!" or "Here's to Jack and Jill!" But it wasn't always that way: the custom used to be a good deal more formal. Back in ancient Greece, for instance, toasts usually involved kissing up to the gods first. You looked up to the sky, then spilled some wine on the ground as an offering.

The word *toast* originated in ancient Rome, when the Senate was ordered to honor the emperor Augustus with a salutation at every meal. Faced with quaffing acidic *vin ordinaire*, the senators started dropping a piece of burnt bread into their goblets. The charcoal smoothed the wine and masked its nasty flavors (making this the Roman equivalent of overoaking flawed wines). This piece of bread was called *tostus*, Latin for "roasted" or "parched"; and the ritual eventually took on the name.

Present-day toasts are tame affairs compared to those proposed in less civilized times, when camaraderie and treachery were often dinner guests at the same table. When ancient Greek hosts toasted their guests, they drank first from a common bowl to show that the wine wasn't poisoned. If the host showed no signs of oxygen deprivation, the guests drank too. This was also the point of intertwining hands, so that guests drank from each other's glasses, and of clinking glasses, so that a little of your wine spilled into the other person's glass. Even though poisoning is no longer fashionable, touching glasses still reminds us that the wine originally came from one source and so is a symbol of unity. Some toasters still like to smash their glasses after the toast—the old fireplace toss, perceived as a way of binding the toast. (Think twice before doing this with your Riedel stemware.)

As we drink our toast, I look around at our friends, whom Andrew and I know well, but who don't know each other. In high school, I went to chemistry class mostly to see what I could "accidentally" blow up. Now, being older and no wiser, I'm doing the same thing socially, trying to detonate conversations with explosive personality combinations. As the playwright Alan Bennett commented, "People on their best behavior are rarely at their best." Of course there are limits; even I wouldn't invite a Greenpeace activist and the captain of the *Exxon Valdez* to the same dinner, any more than I'd drink Château Pétrus with a chocolate bar. Nor do I invite people from the same industry, for fear they'd talk shop all evening.

With no script, dinner party conversation can be more unpredictably entertaining than theater. The plot thickens tonight when David goes on about sports being a waste of time to Jeff, who's coach of his son's Little League Baseball team. At another dinner party, my husband, a high-tech investor, used the acronym VC while discussing the economy. Another guest, who was working for a social services agency, asked, "Vietcong?" "No," my husband replied, "venture capital."

As we chat and nibble on hors d'oeuvres, I serve a crisp and refreshing Kim Crawford New Zealand sauvignon blanc. I consider it our house wine—why should such a useful concept be confined to restaurants? It's a wine to call our own, one I always have on hand for weekday meals or to offer friends who drop by unexpectedly. It's also a consolation if a new wine I try turns out to be a disappointment. The ideal house wine is reasonably priced, readily available, appeals to many palates, and is reliable. It shouldn't fall apart after being open for a day or two and should define your taste. The downside is that it can make you fall into a rut. Every now and again, I feel I need a wine makeover. In a few months, I think I'll choose a new *vin de maison*.

Twenty-four canapés later, it's time to move to the table. The guests find their places. I've deliberately separated spouses so everyone talks to someone new. (Besides, they can analyze the evening on the way home.) Andrew brings his first course to the table, and murmurs of appreciation escape from the guests like wisps of steam curling off the food. To give a twist to the traditional Thanksgiving dinner, Andrew starts with pan-seared foie gras with port-marinated figs and apricots, drizzled with port. To drink with it, I open an Inniskillin riesling icewine from Niagara. Usually, I serve the driest wines first and the sweeter ones later, so that no wine tastes bitter compared to the previous one. But dessert wines have the necessary richness to match the luscious texture of the foie gras and the perceived sweet taste of the fat.

Generals may lead with the sword and philosophers with the pen, but dinner party hosts lead with their forks. Our guests are too well-bred to dig in before Andrew and I do, so we do it immediately and with relish. For the second course—roasted loin of lamb with a crust of black trumpet mushrooms—I'm pouring the Château Palmer. The wine releases the earthy essence of its vineyards in 1966, as well as deep aromas of blackberries and cigar box. Cabernet sauvignon is the classic match for lamb. It's also better to drink before the zinfandel, since I want to start with more subtle (or lighter) wines and progress to more full-bodied ones.

Sharon is a foodie and asks me if I match the wine to the meat in the dish. I tell her that it's one of the secrets of pairing wine with food: even though the meat or fish is supposedly the star, it's often not the dominant flavor to guide wine matching. Chicken, for example, is the chameleon of food; its taste depends on how it's prepared. It may be spicy, barbecued, roasted, buttery, fried, or grilled. In fact, many meats are often just a vehicle for the sauce. So barbecued chicken would work best with a spicy shiraz or zinfandel, whereas chicken supreme would call for a round, buttery chardonnay or even a riesling to cut through the cream. Roast lamb with rosemary is classically matched with red bordeaux, but when lamb is cooked with garlic, a spicy zinfandel is more suitable.

In Andrew's dish, the mushrooms are the main attraction: they have particularly assertive flavors. The same is true of black or white truffles, which are usually the central theme of the dish they garnish. They go beautifully with the Palmer but also with earthy, gamy wines such as pinot noir, a red blend from the Rhône Valley, or a barolo or barbaresco from Piedmont.

Andrew has kept all the portions small, so we're not feeling as stuffed as the bird that now enters ceremoniously for the main course. The heady aroma of turkey and trimmings wafts through the house as he bears in the platter. He stuffed it with oranges for a lovely, nontraditional citrus flavor.

"Red wine with white meat?" Sharon asks me with mock horror, as I pour the zinfandel.

"We just follow the rules when they suit us," I tell her, winking.

Like other wine lovers, I find old rules of pairing white wine with white meat and red wine with red meat can be restrictive, boring, and often unreliable. They may once have been a good place to start, but they were formulated decades ago when both wine and food were more homogenous. Back then, things were simpler: white wines were light and fruity and red wines were heavy and tannic. Continental wines went with continental food. Men drank port and discussed politics. Women sipped tea and knitted doilies. But new cool-climate red wines, such as New Zealand and Canadian pinot noir, can be light and fruity; and white wines, such as California chardonnay and Rhône Valley blends, can be robust and full-bodied. Weight counts for more than color now. As well, fusion cuisine means that flavors on the plate are also crossing traditional boundaries. (And the only doilies I use are paper and come in packs of twenty-four.)

The idea behind matching food and wine is to find affinities that give you a richer dining experience, with more tastes, textures, resonances, and sensations. When the marriage of food and wine works, each enhances the other, making the meal greater than the sum of its parts. The wine and food rise up to meet each other and bear you aloft on a new cloud of sensual pleasure. In fact, sometimes I think of wine matching like a personals ad: "Vivacious young redhead seeks rich, beefy companion." That's why certain classic matches have survived changes in food fashion: Stilton cheese with port, foie gras with sauternes, boeuf bourguignon with Burgundian pinot noir, mussels with muscadet, goat cheese with sauvignon blanc.

For turkey, I encourage my guests to experiment: I always set out glasses for both red and white wine on the table. I've chosen both a German riesling and the zinfandel for their fruitiness.

Although I'm an iconoclast, I'm not a masochist: I wouldn't match any red wine with turkey. Young red wines, such as cabernet sauvignons, barolos, and syrahs, aren't usually a good match because of their tannin, which gives a puckery dry-mouth feeling that accentuates the dryness of the turkey. Instead, I'll save young reds for a juicy steak, since tannin and rare meat are excellent companions. The meat proteins and the tannins bind together so that the meat is tenderized by the wine's tannins. (That's why the chemical process of softening a hide into leather by adding tannin-rich bark is called tanning.) In turn, the wine's tannins are made less harsh by binding to the meat's proteins.

Of course, Thanksgiving dinner is about more than just turkey. Andrew has outdone himself: he's made spicy sage and thyme stuffing, giblet gravy, chestnuts, rice, buttery mashed potatoes, creamed onions, candied sweet potatoes, squash, brussels sprouts, cranberry sauce, and succotash. Finding one wine to accompany all these hearty flavors is enough to make even die-hard enophiles throw up their hands in despair.

So let's do away with the myth of the One Perfect Wine—that unless you find the ideal wine for your meal, you're missing out on some ultimate experience. This approach is not only frustrating and expensive, it's also dishonest. Not even wine writers can always say with certainty exactly which wines go with which dishes; the most we can do is offer general guidelines based on our experience. (Claiming to have all the answers is how some charlatans succeed in this business.) After all, there are hundreds of thousands of wines on this planet, millions of food combinations, and billions of palates.

That range of flavors in a traditional Thanksgiving dinner actually works to your advantage, because there are many complementary wines. The combination of flavors can help determine what wines will work particularly well—a task that's

made easier because most of the trimmings are served independently of the meat. Since the meal is usually banquet-style,
where people choose the side dishes they like best, why not do
the same with the wines? Offer both a red and a white wine,
with a couple of each open on the table. As British food writer
Elizabeth David observed, "One of the main points about the
enjoyment of food and wine lies in having what you want when
you want it and in the particular combination you fancy."

Some advice on wine and food pairing, such as the preciously
detailed kind, is a form of snobbery. It's part of wine's intimi-
dation, like guessing the name and year without seeing a label.
It's easy to just accept the weight of wine's tradition, but for the
sake of your own pleasure, it's imperative to question it. So go
ahead and experiment with different combinations of food and
wine to discover what pairings you like best and to broaden your
range of possibilities. But don't sweat it: if you spend too long
analyzing all the flavors and textures in the food, your dinner
will go cold. Forty years ago, Dr. Spock told anxious parents,
"You know more than you think you do." Today, I'm telling you
the same thing about wine: "Trust your sense of taste."

First and foremost, drink what you like. Think of wine like
clothing: most of us choose it based on comfort, not fashion. So
pick wines you like to drink, not because they get high scores.
I'm also a fan of starting with the wine choice and then making
up a meal to suit it, just as I buy the earrings first and then look
for a complementary outfit. Why should wine always be cast in
the role of best supporting actor in the meal? This is especially
true if you have a bottle you're longing to open: it's already made,
whereas you can still adapt your dinner to suit it.

For all the new freedom from rules, there are still a few simple
guidelines. Most of us don't put ketchup on our ice cream; and
for the same reason, we don't drink a delicate white wine with

a hearty meat dish or a powerful red with a fillet of sole—they're mismatched flavors and textures. It's true, for instance, that a little tartness in a dish makes wine seem less acidic; sweetness in food makes wine taste less fruity. Red wines tend to be carriers of flavor, whereas whites cleanse and refresh the palate. Complex food and varied flavors, such as fusion cuisine and Thanksgiving dinner, are best accompanied by simple wines, such as New World pinot noir or off-dry riesling. Conversely, complex wines, such as mature bordeaux and burgundy, are best paired with simple food, such as roasted meat.

Here's another approach: you can choose a wine that's made in the same area as the type of food it accompanies. Regional wine and cuisine tend to share the same soil and climate conditions, which makes this a safe bet. For example, you could pair pasta in a tomato sauce with a Tuscan chianti, a red wine with mouthwatering acidity and bright fruit flavors.

In fact, some of the best wines for food, such as riesling, sauvignon blanc, pinot noir, and sangiovese, have a zippy acidity that cuts through the cream and fat in certain dishes. Acidity and salt also balance each other in food and wine, just as they do when you cook. Acidity is the salt of wine: it brings forward the flavors of both the wine and the food.

The most versatile wines are like "mixer couples"—people you can invite to almost any party, because they're well-read, intelligent, and have wide interests. Similarly, the most food-friendly wines are balanced. They don't have too much alcohol, tannin, or oak; and yet, they have an interesting flavor of their own that complements a wide range of dishes. That's why two of the most difficult wines to pair with food are also two of the most popular: New World chardonnay and cabernet sauvignon. Oaky chardonnays may be great for sipping on the patio, but they're among the least food-friendly wines—they're like drinking buttered popcorn. In fact, oaky wines in general are less versatile with food. Those sweet flavors of butterscotch and vanilla don't marry with many other flavors, except those you'd also put butter on, such as corn and lobster. The same applies to wines that get awarded high scores: they can be the worst food partners. They stand out in a tasting of many wines because they're so heavy in alcohol or fruit. That's quite different from evaluating them on their own in the context of a meal.

This brings me back to bubbly, my fallback option for difficult matches. Yes, I served it as an aperitif, but that doesn't mean it can't also be drunk throughout the meal. It's low in alcohol, refreshing, has great acidity, and its effervescence elevates even the most ordinary foods—although Andrew's feast certainly doesn't require it.

Classic champagne matches include oysters, caviar, sushi, and sashimi—dishes that defeat other wines with their briny, fishy tastes. Champagne, with its incredible combination of acidity and imperceptible sweetness, glides along with them. The lighter *blanc de blancs* and blends with more chardonnay in them are ideal for poached or roasted fish. In the James Bond movie *From Russia with Love* (1963), an assassin posing as a fellow agent joins 007 for dinner in the luxury dining car of the Orient Express. With their grilled sole, Bond orders the Taittinger *blanc de blancs*—but the impostor asks for a chianti, "the red kind." Later, when our hero realizes who the bad guy is, he observes bitterly, "Red wine with fish. Well, that should have told me something."

Of course, Bond would have a much tougher time ferreting out uncultured bad guys today, since the old rules about matching wine and food are now much more flexible. But some classic matches still hold, including champagne's complement of acidity to the fat of creamy cheeses, fried foods, butter, and cream. It's also robust enough to match the vinegar and vegetable character in salads and vegetarian dishes, as well as the salt in soups, hams, and cured meats. For hot and spicy foods, a glass of champagne is as refreshing as diving into the ocean after getting a sunburn. The *blanc de noirs* and rosés, with their higher percentages of pinot noir, pair well with more flavorful dishes, such as veal, game, turkey, and rare roast beef.

Don't let champagne's luxe image stop you from enjoying it with ordinary food, the kind you might drink beer with. Champagne may be more refined, but the two share the effervescence, yeastiness, and fullness of flavor. So think shabby-chic combos like champers with fish and chips or shrimp. Marilyn Monroe's combo of champagne and potato chips in *The Seven Year Itch* is brilliant: champagne's acidity cuts through the grease and matches the saltiness of the chips. Bubbly with a touch of sweetness is perfect for Thai, Indian, Chinese, and Asian fare, spicy dishes and curry. Demi-sec and sec champagne marry well with pastries, creams, fruit custards, and pudding.

When we're all convinced that another mouthful is impossible, Andrew brings out the pumpkin pie and panna cotta.

"Andrew, you're a regular Davy Crocker," Jeff jokes.

I'm so proud of Andrew. As he slices up the dessert, I pour the tawny port. Sweetness is one of the most challenging elements: dessert wines should always be slightly sweeter than the food itself, otherwise they'll taste thin and bitter. Desserts with just a touch of sweetness, including fruit-based ones such as apple tart, often pair well with wines that are off-dry as well. But rich desserts, especially chocolate, demand wines that aren't just sweet, but also have a thick, unctuous texture. Good choices are cream sherry, banyuls, tokaji, late bottled vintage or tawny port.

After dessert, we retire to the living room as the late-evening smells of coffee, port, and brandy blanket us. Even the round-bellied snifter glasses seem full and content as they tilt lazily in our hands.

Finally, each couple shakes themselves out of their own post-prandial reveries and expresses warm thanks before leaving. Andrew and I tumble into bed, radiant with food, wine, and generosity. I'm reminded that dinner is the only entertainment we truly consume. Unlike enjoying the theater, ballet, or opera, eating and drinking are basic animal needs. But when we infuse them with creativity, we move from sustenance to culture and camaraderie. To paraphrase the poet Rilke, we turn the meal into blood, bone, and gesture. It reminds us of how fleeting life is—no record of the food, wine, or conversation is left, only memory.

EIGHT

Undercover Sommelier

UNLESS YOU COUNT the time I handed out plates at a church supper, I've never worked as a waiter. But of course, that hasn't stopped me from commenting on the service in restaurants—particularly the wine service—as if I knew exactly what I was talking about. Now, to stopper my leaking credibility, I've decided to work in a restaurant for a night.

Only the best would do, so I selected Le Baccara, an award-winning restaurant in Québec that offers haute French cuisine, with classic service. That would be just perfect for me, I thought—until I realized that as a server, I would have to deliver the classic service rather than receive it. After some pleading (and plumping of my wine credentials), I got the approval of the manager for this experiment. I'd be working with the restaurant's sommelier, Danielle Dupont. Her job is a wine lover's dream: she spends barrels of someone else's money to buy and taste the best wines in the world. Dupont suggests that I shadow her as a trainee for the first part of the evening, then work on my own.

"This is going to be so cool!" I say with an eagerness unsuitable to a sommelier, who ought to be poise personified. Dupont chuckles and before we hang up, advises me in her soft French accent to wear a jacket.

Even on the phone, Dupont embodies that mystique of a

sommelier: the equanimity of an English butler, the warmth of a pediatric nurse, and the knowledge of a winemaker. The word *sommelier* dates back to the Middle Ages in France, when it referred to the principal wine taster of a religious order or a royal household. Since making, serving, and drinking wine was serious business for both institutions, the position of sommelier was coveted.

Over the years royalty and religion became declining job markets. Sommeliers eventually became wine stewards of the people (well, the rich people) and worked mostly in fine restaurants. An 1889 issue of *Harper's* magazine described the sommelier as one "who runs from table to table, laden with bottles, and distributes here and there strange liquids."

Today, restaurant patrons are much more knowledgeable about wine; and so the role of the sommelier is changing accordingly. Instead of being aloof, sommeliers must quench wine lovers' thirst for knowledge. Ideally, they're fonts of information about wines from around the world—able to discuss grape-growing areas, châteaux, producers, and vintages. Of course, they also know which wines go best with the dishes on the menu. Sommeliers increasingly work alongside the chefs to create a complete experience for diners.

So why don't more fine restaurants employ them? One reason is that only a few carry wine inventories large enough to need professional attention. Another is that restaurant owners aren't aware of the bottom-line benefits of having sommeliers. Mostly, I think, it's just a lack of knowledge about the position. In North America, being a sommelier still isn't widely viewed as a genuine profession, as it is in Europe.

Yet such is Dupont's professionalism, you'd think she comes from generations of sommeliers. But her parents didn't drink much wine, nor did many of the other people she knew in Kingsey Falls, the small village in Québec where she grew up. Still, as a teenager, she was drawn to the dazzling world of restaurants—a world that promised mini-dramas at every table, a chance to try on different personalities every night, days without a set routine, and skills that would allow her to travel. At first she focused on the food, as a server, and got a job at Le Baccara after successful stints at several other places. Then a few years ago, wine expert Jacques Orhon came to the restaurant to teach wine appreciation to its staff. Her passion for wine awakened, Dupont decided to take his in-depth course and become a sommelier.

One of the many skills she learned was opening wine bottles with flare, which reminds me that I'll be uncorking bottles in midair as patrons pause in their conversations to watch. So for two weeks before my big night arrives, I feverishly practice using a handheld corkscrew. In my own kitchen, I always use a large lever model bolted to the counter—it makes opening bottles so easy that my manual skills have atrophied. I'm like a calligrapher who's got used to writing on a laptop.

Real sommeliers must rely on the most basic manual screw model, called the Waiter's Friend. It takes effort to learn to use it without resorting to squeezing the bottle between your knees and yanking. The first hurdle is cutting the foil cap off the top of the bottle, so you can get a clear shot at the cork. Most corkscrews come equipped with a knife that folds out, Swiss Army–style. I discover, though, that just pulling out the knife requires breaking a fingernail. I consider just leaving it sticking out, ready for action. But if I approach tables with my knife drawn, will diners interpret this as a sign of aggression? My first attempts make the foil cap flake off in silvery slivers, which I envision floating into the diners' vichyssoise.

After some practice, I hold the bottle with my left hand and, with my right hand, draw the knife around the seam just below the top of the bottle to cut off the foil cap. (If you're a leftie, you may want to reverse your grip.) For corkscrews with center wormscrews such as the Waiter's Friend, the trick is to position the point in the center of the cork and then pull it out straight. An antifriction coating such as Teflon on the screw can make this easier and smoother. Fortunately, well-made corkscrews with sharply pointed wormscrews and a leverage device decrease the amount of effort required to just a couple of pounds of pull. Just before the corkscrew goes through the other end inside the bottle, I stop so that I don't push little pieces of cork into the wine. Then I fit the notch of the corkscrew lever on the lip of the bottle and slowly wiggle the corkscrew up and extract the cork (trying not to grunt). Before pouring, I wipe off the top of the open bottle in case there's any dust or small bits of foil.

Reassured, I decide to practice my delivery. I put on a jacket and stand in front of the bathroom mirror saying, "Good evening, I'll be your sommelier tonight," with varying modulations and accents. Trouble is, I can't convince myself to order anything more than a beer. I can feel an old, familiar ball of panic rising from my stomach.

Before I started writing about wine, my anxiety dreams weren't about falling off a cliff or being chased down an alley, they were about restaurant wine lists. In my nightmare, I'd be at some stuffy restaurant where I was handed a large leatherbound book that looked like a prop from *The Lord of the Rings*. Somewhere within it was the Secret of the Ideal Wine, the one perfect bottle. It was my task to extract this vinous Excalibur from the sacred tome, as a hundred pale eyes stared unblinking at me from the surrounding darkness.

I flipped helplessly through the pages, scouring the list for an answer. Then a grim man in black approached, wheeling a trolley table. It wasn't stocked with cheese and port, as I had hoped, but with *The Oxford Companion to Wine*, back issues of the *Wine Advocate*, a vintage guide, a dictionary, a world atlas, and a magnifying glass.

"Would madam like a little pedantry with her wine?" the fellow asked with cheerful malice.

I pointed in blind confusion at the list. "I'll take that," I blurted.

"Oh, very good, ma'am: a box of the Sunset Red," he snorted in triumph. "March was an excellent month for bagging it." All those eyes silently watching me narrowed in accusation: I was exposed as a cheap, uncultured, algae-eating bottom-feeder.

I know now that I wasn't alone in that secret fear: most people would rather memorize the periodic table while getting a root canal than choose wine from a restaurant list. Even with years of experience behind me, I still dread it when my friends hand me the list. I'm worried that I'll pick a wine they won't like, or worse, one that actually tastes awful. There's so much riding on the choice that I think restaurants should tuck in a no-fault insurance policy. As I agonize over the list, my friends look like wilted dandelions. Frankly, I wish someone else would take on this task. I'd rather drink another person's choice— even one I'd never make—than watch others sip mine trying to mask their distaste.

The fact is, so many wines are on restaurant lists that nobody has the time to taste them all. The diner's dilemma isn't helped by the fact that the traditional list is organized with all the creativity of a telephone directory: most just go by color, country, and region. This gives you no sense of how the wines actually taste. That squirming, overwhelmed feeling comes from what I call the Vinous Flytraps—aspects of ordering restaurant wine that make you feel like a bug drowning in icewine.

Fortunately, some restaurants are adopting "progressive" lists: within the categories of sparkling, white, red, and dessert, wines are listed either by style or by weight, from light-bodied to full-bodied. Baccara's list has the traditional grouping of wines by regions, but Dupont helps diners find what they like. I'm looking forward to meeting her now that my big day has arrived. I walk into the restaurant as the sun streams through the thirty-foot windows. Gold and burgundy hues give the long room the feel of a royal dining hall. Dupont meets me, carrying five bottles in her graceful, piano player's hands. She's a trim five-foot-four, but her energy adds six inches to her height. Her big brown eyes glitter with playful anticipation.

"Ah, my trainee has arrived," she says. "Please carry this bottle, and follow me."

We take the bottles to the counter at the other end of the dining room. Then she balances a large silver tray on her fingertips, places twelve long-stemmed glasses on it, and moves off—quickly and silently, like a panther. I barely keep up with her, and I'm carrying nothing but my desire to make a good impression.

Dupont leads me through the kitchen, which is buzzing with evening preparations like the backstage of a theater. Someone whisks by with a large bowl of ice, and we almost run into a cart of fresh fish being wheeled in. Glasses clink out of the dishwasher, and the kitchen is filled with quick exchanges of *"Bonjour!"* and *"Salut!"* trailing in the air like friendly sky-writing.

Of the seven waiters, Dupont is the only woman. Her role of sommelier was traditionally held by sneering men who used to terrorize the beaujolais crowd, though both gender and attitude have changed in many restaurants. In this traditional restaurant, however, Dupont is the New World. Just twenty-nine, she's knowledgeable but not arrogant—guiding the helpless rich who haven't had time to learn about wine, but certainly have the money to spend on it.

Dupont also manages an inventory of some seventeen thousand bottles. These are stored in three cellars, one upstairs and two downstairs. We descend to the largest, a cavernous room containing row after row of bottles, a liquid library of grand old names. The second is smaller and temperature-controlled— it holds some of the oldest bottles, including an 1823 Château d'Yquem now worth more than $9,000. Dupont offers to let me hold the bottle, which is as brown as maple syrup with age, but I decline. I recall the bartender at another restaurant who accidentally dropped a bottle of Château Pétrus worth $10,000.

We go back upstairs to the third cellar, part of the dining room: a glassed-in, temperature-controlled room with dark oak shelves to display the bottles, candy-store style. On an oak turntable is an extraordinary vertical collection of Château Mouton-Rothschild from 1945 to 1997. It's a visual treat since the label for each year was painted by a well-known artist: Jean Cocteau, Salvador Dalí, Henry Moore, Joan Miró, Marc Chagall, and Andy Warhol. In 1978, Montreal artist Jean-Paul Riopelle created two designs for the label, both based on the circular stains left by the bottoms of wine bottles. Rothschild couldn't decide between them, so he used both, making bottles from that vintage even more valuable to collectors. In 1982, to commemorate what Robert Parker dubbed "the vintage of the century," John Huston painted a watercolor image of a ram dancing joyfully next to a bunch of grapes, under a blue sky and orange sun. For the 1999 vintage, artist Raymond Savignac again used *le gag visuel*: a frisky ram in a woolly orange sweater kicking up its hind legs (the ram is a play on the château's name—*mouton* is French for sheep). None of the artists has ever been paid in cash; instead, all were reimbursed with five cases of the wine. That's not a bad deal when you consider that the latest vintage retails for about $600 a bottle and appreciates with maturity.

There were only two years when no original artwork was commissioned. In 1953, the label bore a portrait of the family patriarch, Baron Nathaniel Rothschild, to mark the centenary of the family's purchase of the estate. And in 1977, a label with words and no art honored the queen mother, who had stayed at the château that year.

While I'm admiring the Mouton-Rothschild display, Dupont takes four bottles over to the part of the kitchen that's open to the dining room. She and the chefs are creating the fall tasting menu. I salivate as I look at the plates with morsels of duck terrine, fig confit, and warm spice cake; lobster à la nage in an emulsion of pepper squash and pistachio oil; crispy fillets of pan-fried Mediterranean sea bream, with a cèpe mushroom and artichoke tian; venison with truffle crust in a sweet-and-sour jus; and warm apple puff-pastries with an iced cinnamon parfait, topped with roasted pine nuts.

To match these dishes, Dupont has picked wines from France, Italy, and California. She pours and we all try them along with nibbles of the food. She delights in diners who choose this tasting menu, trying a different wine with every course. These by-the-glass selections help to solve the classic restaurant dilemma of how to match wines to many different dishes. Another option, if diners are having only two or three courses, is a couple of half bottles rather than one full bottle. This helps in those situations where you're having steak and your dining companion has ordered fish.

Some wines, such as riesling and pinot noir, can pair with a wide range of dishes because they are neither too full-bodied nor too light. I call these switch-hitter wines because they can swing both ways to match all but the very heartiest and lightest dishes. European wines generally tend to be more balanced and food-friendly than New World ones, which can be fruit-heavy and oaky. Of course, there are many exceptions to these generalizations, but these help to narrow the choices.

Afterward, we head back to Dupont's office, a crowded space that she shares with the maître d', the banquet manager, and several others. She sits at her computer to delete the out-of-stock wines and add the new ones.

"You're familiar with these wines and can tell the guests about them?" she asks, pointing to the list.

I swallow. The notion that I can talk intelligently about some 450 wines is absurd.

"No problem," I say.

At least I understand how she prices the wines on her list. The markup here is about twice the retail cost, though less at the high end. In the industry, that's considered fair—especially in a fine establishment such as this. Aging wine, as Baccara does, also costs money: it ties up cash in bottles, inventory carrying costs, taxes and rent on storage, electricity to keep the stock at the right temperature, and Dupont's time to manage it. That's why most restaurants don't bother and why it's generally best to choose wines from the list that are good when they're young.

The high price of some restaurant wines is also due to other overhead costs: staff wages, wastage, glass breakage, and replacement costs (because the same wine can often be more expensive when it's time to replace the stock that's been sold). In better restaurants, costs also include training their staff and buying good stemware. But high markups can also dampen wine sales, causing diners to choose beer or nonalcoholic drinks. Some diners now have drinks at home before going to the restaurant or simply don't consider going out midweek as restaurant dining is a save-up-for-the-weekend event only.

Most of us know roughly what the grocery store price is of chicken, fish, or beef, so we can tell how much an establishment has marked up its food. But with wine, especially from small producers, the wholesale cost often isn't known. That's why some restaurants keep their selections obscure, offering wines you won't find in the liquor store, so they can hide their markups—as much as three to four times the price. Robert Parker has described such prices as "legalized mugging." Of course, many restaurants offer lesser-known wines simply to give diners a unique taste experience that they can't have at home—and many others are indeed fair about their pricing.

In the hospitality industry, the adage is that customers will eat you poor and drink you rich. We now judge restaurants on the price of their entrées, but often the food isn't priced fairly relative to its cost. Restaurants have long used spirits, liquors, coffee, tea, and water as profit centers to cover the cost of food and overhead. Increasingly, they're doing the same with wine. However, it's one thing to pay $3 for a dollar's worth of coffee, but quite another to pay $30 for a $10 wine. Wine drinkers end up the persecuted majority paying for those freeloading iced-tea types.

One problem of high wine prices in a restaurant is that they're not evident in advance. Restaurants often post their menus in the front window, so we can check the prices and selection of the food, but they rarely post the wine list. That's sprung on us once we're inside and already a captive audience (like that overpriced popcorn at movie theaters).

Nor do restaurant reviewers help much. Most pay little attention to the wine, even though it's half the enjoyment of a meal for many of us—and often more than half the bill. (In fact, it's not unusual nowadays for the drinks to top the food, as a popular British restaurant guide found in a recent survey.) Many critics just throw in a line at the end of their review: "We had a nice bottle of cabernet for $50." Most likely, this is because critics are foodies first, and wine lovers second (if at all). Still, such offhandedness is a disservice to both restaurants and diners.

A good idea is to do advance research on the Internet, since an increasing number of restaurants now post their wine lists on their Web sites. Before leaving for the restaurant, take a few minutes to scan the list, maybe even look up reviews or scores online as well. Or if the wine list isn't on the Web site, call the restaurant to ask them to fax or e-mail it to you, or at least to discuss it over the phone. This is especially helpful if you'll be choosing the wine for a large dinner group and makes you look like a real hero when the sommelier arrives. Not only do you make a quick choice, but you can even toss out a few comments about the region or vintage.

I use what I call the Wolf Blass Yellow Label Index: knowing the retail price of this Australian cabernet sauvignon, I can usually figure out the markups on the other wines. Higher up the scale, I use my Veuve Clicquot Non-Vintage Champagne Barometer. One of the reasons wine price is such a sticky issue is that no one wants to talk about it. At a business event or a special celebration, who wants to look cheap? And at a romantic dinner, few of us are willing to declare out loud just how much we're willing to pay for love. So we thoughtfully peruse the whole list as if we could afford it all—we're just not quite in the mood for the $2,200 Domaine de la Romanée-Conti tonight, thank you. Many people first eye the cheapest bottle on the list, but hate to look like penny-pinchers, so instead they order the second-cheapest bottle (which was probably the cheapest bottle until last week, when the restaurant jacked up the price).

Knowing this is a delicate situation, I ask Dupont how to handle it just in case it comes up tonight. After all, the wines on her list run from $40 up to $10,000-plus. How do I guess how much a diner might be willing to spend? Do I look at the man's cuff links, the woman's ring?

No, she says. When diners don't give her hints about price by mentioning wines they've enjoyed in the past, she points to three choices at different prices—but so discreetly that only the person holding the list can see what she's doing. This allows guests to save face by pretending it's only the style of wine they're interested in, rather than the cost. Savvy diners, she says, point to the prices themselves and ask something like "Do you have anything like this that's full-bodied and well-aged?"

Good sommeliers are passionate about wines—all wines, from the moderately priced to the insanely expensive. So if you haven't already decided on the wine you want when you're dining out, ask your sommelier which wines she's most excited about on the list. Is she fond of wine from a particular region, perhaps where she grew up? If so, she may have in-depth knowledge of these wines and a superior selection. Or just ask, "What can you tell me about this wine? Does it pair well with some of the dishes on the menu?"

Of course, sometimes you may find yourself in a restaurant where your instincts tell you that the server doesn't deserve your confidence—when the sommelier has the night off, and you're left with the guy who drinks flavored vodka. There are still ways to improve your odds of choosing a better bottle. Focus on the section of the list that seems best stocked, which is usually wine that complements the restaurant's cuisine. An Italian trattoria generally offers lots of chiantis, great with pasta; a red-velour-draped steak house will likely be strong on full-bodied cabernets that pair well with meat. If you're dining in a winemaking region, such as Napa Valley or Niagara, local wines are often a good bet. They're usually cheaper; they'll complement the local cuisine; and the owner may know the producers and the wines.

Some of the best values come from lesser-known regions and grapes. Look for South African sauvignon blanc and German and Alsatian riesling. For reds, try South African and Australian shiraz; Oregonian, Canadian, and New Zealand pinot noir; Chilean cabernet; Argentine malbec; Rhône red blends; Loire

Valley cabernet franc; and Portuguese, Rhône, and southern Italian and French red blends. Conversely, some of the worst values are often the big-name grapes from big-name regions, such as California chardonnay and cabernet, or red blends from Bordeaux. That doesn't mean you can't drink wines from those regions, though; it just means you have to look for lesser-known areas and producers. In California, for example, try Paso Robles syrah or Sonoma zinfandel instead of Napa Valley cabernet.

By the time Dupont has given me these few guidelines, my feet are already tingling—it's only five P.M. (I'm hungry too—my nervous energy has long since metabolized those tasting menu samples.) We head downstairs to the staff cafeteria, where my hopes of nibbling on more foie gras are dashed: when you dine at Le Baccara, you can rest assured that your considerable check doesn't subsidize luxurious employee meals. After fortifying ourselves with something remarkably chickenlike, we go upstairs to freshen up before showtime. I repair my lipstick and Dupont straightens the bow tie of her tuxedo. (I'm wearing a starched white shirt and a black suit, an ensemble that looks as though it came from the 1988 Fall Undertaker Collection.)

We all meet in the kitchen—chef, maître d', sommelier, servers—to review tonight's specials. Sommeliers have to know the menu at least as well as the waiters do, since they must decide which wines best match the food. Dupont reviews the wines by the glass, and some of the servers ask questions. It's going to be a busy night; the maître d' tells us that the restaurant is fully booked. Then it's over. Thankfully, there's no group hug, but we all do wish each other "Good service!" I'm reminded of the ancient Roman soldiers with their chant "Strength and honor!" before battle.

For the first hour or so, I'm just trailing Dupont. This is like being a passenger in a Mercedes on a country drive: the ride is so smooth and you're so caught up with admiring the scenery, you don't really pay attention to how the driver nego-tiates curves in the road. To watch Dupont in action is to believe that some people are just born with effortless grace. She deftly handles tired tourists, flirting businessmen, chichi gold-draped women, and nervous dating couples.

I follow her to a party of four who've been studying the menus for about ten minutes. "Good evening," Dupont says warmly. "Have you had a chance to look at the wine list?"

Their glances ricochet nervously from one to another and then back up to her, seeking help. Soothingly, she asks them if they've chosen their meals yet—it seems they're all having different game dishes. Leaning slightly toward the man with the list, Dupont indicates a few wines on it and briefly describes how they would complement their meals. Although Dupont's knowledge runs deep, she doesn't get too esoteric with her descriptions: she knows that most customers aren't trying to earn a sommelier certificate over dinner. Still, if she senses that the diner is interested, she likes to tell a story about the wine—the sun-drenched hillside where the vines grow, the family that runs the winery.

After the quartet's spokesman makes his choice, she tells them that the wine has an earthy character that will dance a duet with their game. They seem pleased. Then without missing a beat, Dupont asks if they'd like to start with a glass of cham-pagne. Sold.

While they're enjoying the bubbly, Dupont presents their bottle. Like all good sommeliers, when she presents it to the host, she confirms the grape, vintage, winery, and region. This isn't as standard a practice as it ought to be; some waiters do the Vintage Shuffle, either intentionally or not. You order a wine from a certain year and you're brought a different one. The year may not sound like a big deal, but it can make a real difference for wines from cool-climate regions, where the weather can vary drastically from year to year. For example, French wines taste mostly of acid, tannin, or oak in bad years: there's not enough fruit to balance the wine because the grapes didn't ripen fully. Even New World regions sometimes have years that are better than others. California cabernets, for example, were much better in 1997 than 1998. Older wines, as well, may taste faded if they're well past their prime.

If you do get a wine from a different year than the one you ordered, your server should point out the fact to you. That way, you can decide whether you want the alternative bottle or if you'd rather a different wine. If it's a worse year, the restaurant should discount the bottle. But if they only have a better vintage, rather than the one advertised on the list, they should charge you the same price as for the one you ordered.

Some restaurants also capitalize on the fact that diners may recognize the names of the big châteaux but haven't memorized a fifty-year vintage chart. So you may think the Château Latour will be spectacular, since it's certainly priced that way; but it actually comes from a mediocre year. Lists that don't even mention the vintage are highly suspect. Either the owner doesn't know or care, or he's trying to pass off inferior goods at high prices.

Beware too of a so-so producer from a prestigious region, such as Tuscany, Bordeaux, or Châteauneuf-du-Pape. No region's wines are 100 percent fantastic, nor are one producer's wines. You may recognize and respect the Mondavi name from California; but that winery, like many others, makes wines that range from the high-end Robert Mondavi Reserve to the lower-end Mondavi Woodbridge. Remember too that new management or a new winemaker can make a big difference at a winery, pro or con—but the product's price on restaurant lists may take a while to register such a change.

Other people are lured not so much by prestigious names as by awards, taking the *Wine Spectator* honors as gospel. The magazine's restaurant-list awards have three levels, beginning with the Award of Excellence for offering at least a hundred well-chosen labels. Next is the Best of Award of Excellence for places that have four hundred or more labels; these should include selections from several vintages of top producers and strengths in specific regions. Wines that harmonize well with the menu are also considered. But the Grand Award is given only to establishments with a hefty inventory, and at least 1,250 different labels, including older vintages, rare wines, and large-format bottles. Only those considered for this last award are actually visited by *Spectator* staff; the rest are chosen based on the restaurant's own description of its menu, wine list, and wine program.

For restaurants, waiting for these awards to be announced is like waiting for Moses to come down from the mountain: first there's a lot of speculation and then everyone scrambles frantically to see what's on the tablets. The tough criteria discourage those without good lists from even applying, but some thirty-five hundred around the world do every year, and 80 percent of them get one of the awards. Le Baccara has won the *Spectator*'s Best of Award of Excellence for several years.

Now it's time to actually open the wine for the diners. To my relief, Dupont rests the bottle on an elegant wooden pedestal near the table. Evidently, the midair corkscrew act won't be required of me tonight. Still, I wish it were customary to open the bottle out of sight behind the bar or in the kitchen, rather than near the patron's table. But that custom has its roots in the bad old days, when unscrupulous restaurateurs might try to pass off Mateus as Margaux.

Traditionally, sommeliers used to taste wine themselves before pouring it for the customers, to ensure that it wasn't corked, faulted, or even poisoned. Hence the sommelier's little silver cup, called a tastevin, was traditionally worn on a chain around their necks for a practical purpose, not because of an odd passion for ashtray accessories. However, this practice has all but disappeared. Patrons are more informed, and some get nettled at the sight of the sommelier nipping into their expensive bottle. Dupont still does taste, from a small glass, old or rare wines that need decanting, but not the ones that customers drink right away.

Dupont pours an ounce or so for the host to try. This tasting ritual isn't to embarrass anyone or for showmanship, but to check the wine's quality. The man nods his acceptance and Dupont pours for everyone.

As we move away to the side of the room, I notice that Dupont constantly monitors all twenty-five tables without being obvious about it. (I'm trying to learn the art of invisible service, but have so far only mastered arranging myself like a tall ornamental shrub.) "A good sommelier knows when to approach a table," she says. "You don't want to interrupt a conversation, and yet the service must flow at the right pace. And you must also know how to break off gently with customers who want to chat, because if you spend too much time with one table, others suffer."

It's eight P.M. now, the time appointed for me to flap my tiny wings. Dupont gives me a firm, motherly nudge. "Be confident, you are the sommelier," she whispers.

Wishing I had drunk some liquid courage, I approach my diners. The foursome, two big burly fellows and their equally stout female companions, are sitting at a table beside the window. One of the men has the wine list, but his back is to me. I'd have to be Spider-Woman, crawling down the wall beside him, to get to his right, the traditional side for serving customers. What to do? Then I recall Dupont's advice: try not to frighten customers by suddenly looming up over their shoulders. I know

I don't like it when sommeliers hover over me as I decide on the wine. I can't imagine a scowling chef standing beside me as I hesitate between the scallops and the steak. I approach him from the left. Fortunately, this man knows what he wants—a big bordeaux, a 1961 Château Talbot, at $500. Ka-ching.

Nodding respectfully and withdrawing, I mentally scold myself for not asking to be in on the tips. In fact, Dupont doesn't share in the tips either—she's on salary, as are many sommeliers in fine restaurants. This reduces their incentive to sell every diner the liquid equivalent of a Porsche.

As I bring out larger stemware on the silver tray, I wonder when that tremor developed. The *liteau*, a white linen napkin, is draped over my right forearm for classic French service. I'm afraid it's going to drag all the cutlery and dishware on the table with it as I swoop in to set the glasses in front of the diners. But somehow I place them, even though they wobble like tops before stabilizing.

Next, I present the bottle to Mr. Big Bordeaux, and he nods curtly. I take it to one of those handy pedestals to open it, but realize I've got a toughie after all: red wines here are brought from the cellar lying down in wire baskets so that the bitter sediment at the bottom doesn't mix in with the wine. It's tricky getting the bottle out of the basket to pour it without tilting it upright or dribbling the wine. (Red wine seems to have a magnetic attraction to white linen tablecloths and shirts.) I almost pour the man's sample into his water glass, but just in time manage to inch it over into his wineglass.

He nods, so I make my way around the table, serving first the women, then the men. Finally, I return to the host and fill his glass to the one-third level that's considered ideal: the empty space allows drinkers to swirl the wine around and appreciate its aromas. I discover that pouring wine while standing three feet above the glasses is vastly different from doing it sitting down: it's difficult to tell how much you've filled them. I have an urge to check the levels by squatting down to table height, like a golfer on the putting green.

I've nailed every pour and feel like a gymnast who dismounts from the parallel bars with a backward flip and a perfect landing. I stand over the table like a beaming penguin, expecting the man to look up at me approvingly with a raised eyebrow and say, "Nice pour." But somehow my virtuosity is lost on him.

Not on Dupont, though, who was watching carefully. Back at the bar, she has an appreciative smile and a warm word of praise for me. Also a tip: "You're tall, so you tend to bend over. If you put your left hand behind your back, you'll maintain a straight, clean line." Uh-oh, I think—first, the aerial basket extraction, now I need one hand tied behind my back. What'll be next: a blindfold? But I try it with the next pour and realize that she's right.

Next, I serve a friendly couple who order an Alsatian riesling. While I open the bottle, they're debating whether Alsace is in France or Germany. I bite my lip trying not to jump in uninvited, until the woman turns to me with the question.

"France!" I blurt out, like a kid who's able to clinch the spelling bee. But I'm learning from Dupont's diplomacy: since the man chose Germany, I add that the region has been part of both countries over the years, and its wines share similarities of style with each.

I've never felt so omniscient, even though I've answered much tougher questions in my writing. I realize that it's easy to appear an expert with a wine library and the Internet at hand, but it calls for an entirely different kind of intelligence to draw upon that knowledge on the spot.

I long to play this game again, but my next couple isn't interested: they just ask for the house white. Of course, at Baccara these are not the cheap and nasty house wines found in lesser establishments. The notion of the house wine has sadly declined from its honorable beginnings in Europe, when wines were often locally made. They were emblematic of the restaurant's cuisine, giving a sense of the local culture on the table.

Today in North America, house wines are often the leftovers from the list: cheap and nasty stuff that you can use in a pinch instead of Liquid Drāno. They are the vinous cousins to Anthony Bourdain's Sunday buffets in *Kitchen Confidential*. Drinking them is like accidentally walking into a bad neighborhood: you'll get roughed up and robbed and will learn never to take that wrong turn again. Not only are they bad to drink, they're also usually a bad buy—one of the biggest rip-offs on the list. Many restaurants price a glass at the full wholesale price of the entire bottle. With five glasses per bottle, that can be a 300 to 400 percent markup. The first bottle can pay the restaurant for the whole case.

Yet some industry experts estimate that as much as half the wine sold in restaurants is house wine. How do they get away with rapacious margins on such vile stuff? Well, for one thing, most of us don't expect anything better. House wine is mostly about mindless convenience. We don't have to analyze the wine list or pronounce *trockenbeerenauslese*. It's much easier just to tell the waiter, "I'll have a glass of your house white please."

Yet it needn't—and shouldn't—be that way. With so many new regions making affordable wines, there's no reason not to have good house wines. House wine, like bread, is one of the first ways we judge a restaurant. You can tell that the place cares about quality when its list gives not just the wine's name ("Imported French" doesn't count), but also its region and vintage. A good house wine should marry well with a wide range of dishes and have lively, balanced fruit flavors, without too much oak, acidity, tannin, or even fruit—since all those can tire the palate and overwhelm the food. Le Baccara, for example, offers a crisp white wine from the Loire Valley and a charming red from southern France that are both reasonably priced.

After the house wine couple approves their wine, I continue working the floor. By now I'm feeling cocky. I bring a California cult cabernet to a blond woman and her girlfriend. I pour a sample, then pour for her friend, then top up Blondie's glass. But as I pull back, my wrist twitches and I leave a telltale trail of crimson drips on the tablecloth.

"Oh, I'm terribly sorry," I gasp.

Blondie blinks slowly without looking at me and purses her lips. "Sorry," I mouth again silently, as though I'm in an under-water nightmare. The woman resumes talking to her friend, but in a hardened tone. I want to take her made-up little face in my hands, turn it toward mine, and say, "Look, I'm really sorry, please forgive me!" For the first time I realize what it's like to feel servile, dismissed.

At least she doesn't call the maître d'. My wound heals gradu-ally as I serve other tables without incident, but I am still absorbed in my own tragedy. I find this reversal of the tradi-tional balance of power unfair, because as a diner, I'm used to deferring to the sommelier. It reminds me of another traumatic experience when I was traveling abroad by myself and dined in the four-star restaurant of my hotel. (I'd tell you where this happened, but I don't want to blacken the reputation of an entire nation.) I was celebrating my birthday on the road and decided to treat myself to a special wine. I had first tasted it just three weeks earlier, and the memory of its smoky cassis aromas still lingered. So what if it cost $150 for a half bottle?

So I summoned the sommelier. Unlike his confrères—the maître d', the head waiter, and a junior waiter who had brought me bread and water with civility—this functionary was a dour gentleman. He took my order with no pleasure and, looking slightly miffed, brought me the bottle. (Had I ordered the last bottle, which he was planning to serve to a favorite patron?) As he waited for me to try the wine, he tapped his index finger on the bottle—waiter code for "Hurry the hell up, I've got larger groups to serve, for better tips."

Intimidated, I quickly swirled and sniffed—and realized that the wine was corked. Those aromas I remembered with such pleasure had been pulverized by the telltale smell of moldy, damp cardboard. My stomach dropped to my feet and I wanted to crawl under the table. To buy time, I swirled and sniffed some more, as the sommelier looked ready to throttle me. The simple words "I'm sorry, but this wine is corked" formed on my lips, then died there. This may seem odd for someone who writes about wine and has consumed something equal to the annual production of several former Eastern Bloc countries, but I just couldn't do it. I grimaced and said the wine was fine; and with a parting glare, the sommelier trotted off.

As I sat choking down sips of my $150 liquid cardboard, I started to get angry with myself, the sommelier, the restaurant management, and the cork industry. In the sommelier's mind, I was probably already a loser for dining on my own, as well as a complainer for having asked to switch tables when the group beside me started smoking. Now I was about to reveal myself as a freeloader too, for drinking a whole glass of wine before sending the bottle back.

By the time he returned to refill my glass, I was trembling with rage and nerves. I couldn't face issuing a direct order. Instead, I suggested quietly that the wine might be off and asked that he try it. His narrowed eyes squished me from six inches to three as he whisked away my bottle to his tasting table with a flourish that a parade grand marshal would have admired. By that time, other diners were watching with interest. He poured a small amount, sniffed at it briefly, then returned to my table with it.

"It's fine," he said curtly, and strode off.

I stared at his departing back with my mouth open. The message was clear: shut up and drink it. The confidence I'd built up over five years of writing about wine and tasting thousands of samples vanished. I knew I was right, but I felt shattered. I couldn't even imagine what such a situation must be like for someone who isn't knowledgeable about wine. That's why so few restaurant patrons dare to assert themselves. According to the sommeliers I asked, less than 1 percent of all bottles are ever sent back. But industry statistics estimate that 5 to 10 percent of bottles are corked or otherwise flawed. Clearly, something is wrong here. The problem, of course, is that most people feel too uncertain about their wine judgment to insist and don't want to ruin what should be a pleasant evening out with a confrontation with the sommelier.

But I was certain that I had a bad bottle. And after staring at my corky wine for a while, I asked the maître d' to bring the manager—a pleasant woman in her forties. Walking out with her into the quiet lobby, I explained the situation. Fortunately, instead of dismissing my complaint, she was mortified. In fact, she was so empathetic that I burst into tears. The more she tried to calm me, the harder I cried. My crust of fear and anger had been gently peeled away to expose my shame. Who knew that rejecting a bottle of wine involved the same arc of emotions as Greek tragedy?

The manager was as efficient as she was understanding. Within a few minutes I was back in my room, tears dried and dinner served to me privately, with a full bottle of the great wine—as pleasurable as I remembered it, but now with an added layer of comfort.

So that was a happy ending, but it did get me thinking about how the situation should have played out. In fact, the correct procedure for a diner is what I did—except that it only works with staff who don't derive sadistic satisfaction from humiliating guests. If you smell and sip the wine and believe it may be off, tell the sommelier and ask him to try it. Whether he agrees or not, a well-trained server or sommelier will take the bottle back anyway, with no arguing or huffing. (And if the sommelier thinks the wine is just fine, he should never share his opinion and turn the diner into a puddle of neuroses.)

Sometimes servers are less malicious than ignorant. I once told such an eager fellow that my wine was corked. He held my bottle up to the light, said he couldn't see any floaty bits in it, but he'd be happy to run it through a sieve for me. I told him kindly but firmly that the wine had gone bad and he should bring me another bottle free of charge.

Many scrupulous people feel guilty about sending back a bottle because they believe the restaurant (or server) will suffer for it financially. But an establishment can usually return rejects to the wine merchant for full credit. Remember, too, that restaurants take the cost of returned bottles into account when they price their wines, which means that anytime you buy a bottle, you're already paying for the privilege of being able to send it back.

You might think that a restaurant's no-questions-asked return policy would leave it vulnerable to exploitation by either calculating cheapskates or by wine bores who reject perfectly good wines merely to show off. Fortunately, such incidents are rare. In fact, those sommeliers I asked said the opposite is far more often the case: the wine is actually bad but the customer (who really knows little about wine) rhapsodizes about it.

What happens, though, if a wine isn't technically faulty, it's just poorly made or lacking in character? No one should have

to drink wine he or she doesn't like, but the situation is delicate. If the sommelier or waiter recommended the wine, there
should be no problem sending it back. But if the diner chose
it himself, it could be argued that he's responsible for his choice
and should pay for that bottle even if he orders a replacement.
Others, including me, believe that if a wine is on the list, then
the restaurant implicity endorses it and should replace your
bottle free of charge if you're not satisfied.

An even more complicated scenario: what if the wine is actually good, of its kind, but the customer just doesn't like the
style? Again, if staff suggested it, they should take responsibility. If servers are going to recommend wines at all, they
should ask enough questions to determine the diner's preferences in terms of body, sweetness, and flavor; and they should
describe the wine fully so the diner has some idea what he's
getting, including whether the wine will complement his meal.

A good sommelier should also be aware that many people are
wine novices and adjust her recommendations accordingly. This
is especially important with expensive wines: some neophytes
believe that if a wine costs a lot, they're guaranteed to love it—
which isn't necessarily the case. If a novice rejects a pricey wine
because it smells of sweaty saddles and cigar boxes, all the sommelier can do is gently explain that this is the nature of that wine.

Should she, however, exchange it free of charge for another
more suited to the diner's taste? Isn't that leaving the restaurant
on the hook for customers' poor decisions? Some restaurants
have a policy of refusing to take back certain wines if they're not
faulty: bottles over twenty-five years old, for example, or ones
that cost more than $300. If such a policy is in place, it should
always be noted on the wine list. The sommelier should always
mention it to customers contemplating ordering such a bottle.

A restaurant doesn't necessarily lose money on returned

wines. Ones that are in fact good can be sold by the glass or offered to staff for tastings and education. (Those party noises coming from the kitchen? The rich twit at the next table just sent back the Latour.) Savvy restaurateurs often offer a complimentary glass of wine to regular customers as a perk.

Fortunately, no bottles were returned during my long evening at Baccara. As more and more happy diners finish their meals, pay their bills, and leave, I start to think about that other minefield of embarrassment: leaving a tip. In North America and some parts of Europe, tips comprise a significant percentage of a waiter's income. At Maxim's in Paris, the tips were so good that until the 1980s, the maître d' was required to purchase his job rather than expect a salary from it.

At most restaurants these days, the team approach is more common: hostess, maître d', coat-check attendant, bartender, bread and water back waiter, busboy, kitchen staff, and sommelier all serve the diners. Although less visible than the main servers, these folks are still important to the diner's overall experience; so most waiters "tip out" at the end of the evening, sharing their wealth. In effect, the waiter is a subcontractor: the diner tips the waiter and the waiter then tips the rest of the staff.

Tipping goes back to medieval times, when feudal lords would toss largesse to the peasants. That ancient class structure of masters and servants is now defunct, but traces of it still linger in the tradition. That said, few servers would think you're making a stand for social justice by stiffing the staff. In fact, tipping says more about what we think of ourselves than what we think of class conflict. Are we generous or gullible, kindly or demanding? Tip too little and you look like a cheapskate; tip too much and you feel like a doormat.

Most regular diners are comfortable with the basic calculations: for good service, 15 to 20 percent of the pretax cost of the meal. That means that, yes, you should include the cost of your wine when figuring out the tip. If you can afford an expensive wine that increases your meal cost and the service is impeccable, then budget for the tip. Waiters shouldn't be penalized either for your desire to splurge. Otherwise it's like buying a car without leaving any money for gas. The only exception is for truly pricey wines over $100. For those, some diners cap the tip at either 10 percent or a flat $20. They argue that presenting, decanting, and pouring the wine involves the same effort whether the bottle costs $20 or $200.

As I collect the bills from some of the remaining diners, my feet feel as though they've been on a concrete treadmill for thirty-four hours. The connecting tendons in my hips are tightening with exhaustion. Mercifully, it's eleven P.M., and the kitchen is about to close (though the restaurant remains open until the last diner leaves).

It strikes me that sommeliers are the gentle persuaders of the wine world, not so much selling wine to the customer but rather the customer to the customer. Their art is in convincing the customer she is worth treating herself to that special bottle. While this helps the bottom line, it's more about sharing a passion for wine.

I may be spent, but Dupont looks as though she's just woken up refreshed from an afternoon nap. She's coming up from the cellar with some bottles to replace what was sold tonight. I wonder how she manages to keep close tabs on an inventory of seventeen thousand bottles when I can barely keep track of my own stash at home of some eight hundred bottles. I ask her to fire me, as a favor, and she laughs.

"You've given a good service tonight," she says kindly. "Go home, sleep well, and come back soon—as a customer."

Big City Bacchus

THE RICH BROWN tones and soft lighting in the Greenwich Village restaurant Cru have a soothing effect, but not as much as I need right now. My stomach is flip-flopping nervously at the prospect of meeting celebrated New York novelist Jay McInerney. Dubbed the F. Scott Fitzgerald of his generation, McInerney captured the zeitgeist of the 1980s, with all its excesses. His first novel, *Bright Lights, Big City*, was a runaway success: it sold more than a million copies and was made into a movie.

Since then, McInerney has written seven more novels. Much as I admire his fiction, I want to chat with him tonight about his nonfiction foray into wine writing. In 1996, his friend Dominique Browning, editor of *House & Garden* magazine, asked him to write a wine column. She wanted an enthusiast rather than an expert, for a fresh take on the topic. Until then, wine had been McInerney's passion but he'd never written about it. He took to the task like chianti to pasta. Then in 2000, a friend from a small publisher approached him about collecting his columns into a book called *Bacchus & Me*. McInerney didn't expect much from it; but the book went on to sell an impressive forty thousand copies. His second collection of wine columns will be published in 2006.

I'm curious about how he—as a drinker, a writer, and a

collector—got bitten by the wine bug. While I wait at the table for him to arrive, the Cru server brings two leatherbound wine lists: one for white wines, the other for reds. Listed in these two tomes, the size of phone directories, are more than four thousand wines, ranging in price from $30 to $18,000. The list is based on the owner's collection of some eighty thousand bottles. (Opening a restaurant is one way to deal with a cellar that's grown too large.) I can see why this is one of McInerney's favorite places.

I've only got to page thirty-six by the time McInerney arrives. He looks just like his book-jacket photo, except for the ruddy face from a brisk November wind outside. He wears a blue blazer and a striped shirt open at the neck. At fifty, he still looks boyish—and mischievous.

"Good evening," he says, bending his six-foot frame into a small bow, his sapphire-blue eyes twinkling. He slides into the corner banquette beside me. All the waiters here know him and he chats with everyone who stops by the table. Wine director Robert Bohr arrives with a bottle of DeMeric Sous Bois NV Cuvée and two flutes. The champagne's silky bubbles froth up, tremble at the top, then subside with a sigh.

"Here's to our evening!" McInerney says, and we sip the bubbly. It has an almost instant effect: by now my stomach is only flopping. On the table, our flute glasses glow against the candlelight like flaming tulips.

As we peruse the wine list (before the menu, of course), McInerney tells me about his background. He was born in Hartford, Connecticut, the son of a homemaker and a corporate vice president. He spent half his childhood in Europe, but didn't discover wine until later since his parents weren't wine drinkers; they preferred cocktails. Even as a teenager, he knew he wanted to write. In 1976, after graduating from Williams

College, a prestigious liberal-arts school in Massachusetts, he landed a brief stint at the *New Yorker* magazine as a fact checker. (His protagonist in *Bright Lights, Big City* follows a similar career path.) However, he wasn't progressing on his book so he moved from New York to Syracuse to study writing at the university there with novelist Raymond Carver.

To finance his studies, he worked as a clerk in a wine shop. "As part of the regular staff larceny program, we'd take home a bottle to try each night," he says, laughing. These were cheap wines, only $2 or $3 apiece, but they gave McInerney his first taste of wine. He also recalls ordering wine on his first real date: a bottle of Mateus rosé, that popular, cheap Portuguese blush from the 1970s, which he says was also "an ideal accompaniment to the Mexican pot we were smoking at the time."

As his passion grew, he also dipped into the owner's extensive library of wine books. As he observes in *Bacchus & Me*, "The poor man, the budget drinker, is forced to make choices and sacrifices that can only sharpen his discrimination and his appreciation of competing pleasures. Starting at the top, one will miss the climb."

After his manuscript *Bright Lights, Big City* had been accepted by his publisher, he drank his first memorable wine: a 1979 Pichon-Lalande, a second-growth red from Bordeaux. "It smelled like my uncle smoking in the library," he recalls fondly.

In 1985, at his book launch party in London, he met the British novelist Julian Barnes. The two hit it off immediately and Barnes invited him to dinner in his home. With the meal, Barnes opened two legendary châteauneuf-du-papes: the 1962 and 1967 Jaboulet Les Cèdres, both robust and complex reds from the Rhône Valley. At first McInerney was doubtful, since his previous experience of châteauneuf-du-pape had been of the cheap and nasty kind. After tasting these, he realized he had a lot to learn.

"Drinking with Julian was like playing tennis with a slightly superior player—the best possible way to learn and to sharpen your game," he tells me. "Julian is a reserved classicist by nature but he loves big, flamboyant wines. Whereas I'm the opposite: a romanticist who likes elegant, classical wines." He and Barnes kept in touch about their favorite wines from opposite sides of the Atlantic. That correspondence was the forerunner of his *House & Garden* wine columns.

When McInerney realized that his first book was selling well enough to make him some money, he splurged and bought several cases of the 1982 bordeaux: Château Gruaud Larose, Lynch-Bages, and Cos d'Estournel. "If you've got the cash, the patience, and the life expectancy, track down the great vintages of these wines and then forget about them," McInerney advises. "Once you've experienced the nirvana of a great, well-aged wine, you want to repeat that experience. To do that, you need to control your access to more of those wines, which means building a cellar. This is also true if you like certain limited-production wines or those that aren't widely available in stores."

Bordeaux was his first passion because of its ability to age for decades, developing a wide range of nuances. As fine red wines age, their fresh grapy aromas are replaced by nuances of leather, smoke, and mocha. Meanwhile, the tannins soften, making the wine smoother. White wines also mellow, sometimes taking on richer, nuttier aromas, depending on the wine.

The wines that age best have the natural preservatives of tannin, acid, or sugar that enable them to mature without falling apart. Although there are variations between vintages and wineries, some of the most cellar-worthy are cabernet blends from Bordeaux and California; riesling from Germany, Alsace,

New York, and Canada; barolo, brunello, and amarone from Italy; pinot noir from Burgundy, New Zealand, and Oregon; shiraz from Australia; vintage champagne, port, and dessert wines from several regions, such as Sauternes, Canada, and Germany.

For me, starting a cellar was triggered by the craving for one particular bottle. My husband and I were admiring a gorgeous bordeaux, Château La Lagune, but realized that it should be aged for at least five years before it would be ready to drink. At that point in our drinking lives, all we had were some Styrofoam cartons (from mail-order frozen steaks): we put them in the bedroom closet and laid our bottles in their slots. Like Amelia Earhart without a plane or Miles Davis without a trumpet, we were wine fans without a cellar.

So we decided to make a few improvements. First, we bought some wooden racks and installed them in a cool, dark area of the basement. As we learned later, few environments are as potentially destructive to wine as the average home basement. Most aren't temperature-controlled, so they can swing between hot and cold, neither of which is good for aging wine. Excess heat cooks off its finer characteristics, while too much chill retards its maturation.

However, by sheer luck, our basement was close enough to the ideal temperature of fifty-five degrees Fahrenheit that wine needs to age slowly and to develop those complex aromas. We were fortunate with the humidity too, since our basement was relatively stable at about 70 percent. Too much moisture in the air causes mold and damages the labels, while too little can mean that the wine slowly evaporates from the bottle. The increased airspace inside the bottle can start to oxidize the wine, turning it brown and causing it to lose its fresh fruit aromas. That's also why wine is always stored on its side, to keep the cork wet and the oxygen out. Darkness is preferable too, even though most wine is bottled in colored glass to protect it against the damage light can cause.

To buy wine for our small cache, we visited our best local retailers. Had I been living in San Francisco, I would have shopped at both the Jug Shop and Kermit Lynch Wine Merchant, for Australian and French wines, respectively. As specialists in these areas, they're tasting these wines constantly, reading about them, visiting the regions, and arranging exclusive buying relationships with small producers. They've tracked many of the wines over time and know how well they age according to the vintage. They also know when there's been a change that might affect the quality or style of the wine, such as a new owner or winemaker. Most important, they find the obscure and up-and-coming wineries before they hit the mainstream and get more expensive. Having wines in your cellar that have doubled or tripled in price since you bought them is like being able to brag that you paid a $5 cover charge at the local bar to listen to Céline Dion before she became famous.

Another strategy is to collect wines when you travel on business or pleasure. Some wine lovers seek out well-known shops in various cities the way antique collectors do. I'll sometimes write on the back label where I bought the wine and when, like a minitravelogue, so we can reminisce about the trip when we finally drink the wine. For example, last week we drank a lovely Oregon pinot noir. It brought back memories of the wineries scattered along the Willamette Valley, which winds along the foothills of the Coast Range, cradled in the quilted silence of vineyards and farmers' fields.

Restaurants with good wine lists are another great source of ideas for cellar stock. The bonus is that you get to try the wine with a meal first before buying a whole case. To differentiate

their lists, sommeliers often offer small-production wines that
aren't available in the liquor stores. Most of them will gladly
share the name of the wine's importer so that you can order a
case yourself, if it's still available.

The Internet is also a useful resource. Two particularly good
Web sites for finding retail prices of wines around the world
are wine-searcher.com and winealert.com. Both collect data
from hundreds of retailers around the world for their search-
able databases. Most local retailers now have their own Web
sites too. *Wine Spectator* and *Decanter* track auction prices and
offer online indexes that show the trends at auctions around
the world.

Like us, McInerney stored those first cases of bordeaux in
his basement. With success came more and more wine; and
today he owns more than a hundred cases. Still, he recognizes
the dangers of that instinct to hoard: "You have to be careful
how much you accumulate. It can become a sickness."

One of the best pieces of advice I got when starting my
cellar was to go slow. The temptation is to fill your cellar quickly
once you have a space: just looking at empty racks can be as
irritating as having bare walls that cry out for art. However, it
pays to take the time to understand your own taste, to buy
bottles at reasonable prices, and to wait for the right vintages
to come on the market. Buying a mixed case, one of each of
twelve wines, is a great way to find those you love—and then
order a case of it. My cellar space is relatively small so I tend
not to buy full cases of one wine, but rather three-bottle lots.
I get to sample more broadly and yet still save a bottle or two
for more aging if I've opened the first one too early.

Even a slowly acquired cellar can create some logistical and
emotional issues. When McInerney and his third wife divorced,
he decided that moving his entire cellar from Tennessee back

to New York was too difficult, so he sold fifteen cases. "I lost sleep for nights after that," he says wistfully. Today, his collection is split between a special wine fridge in his current New York apartment; the facilities of a professional wine storage company in the city; and the cellar of the house of his ex-wife, who now lives in Southampton.

With the possible exception of an ex-spouse's place, all those are safe options for wine lovers who don't have cellars of their own. But they have their downsides. A storage facility gives you the space and conditions to store wine properly; but it means you don't have immediate access to your wines (no matter what extended hours the company offers). A fridge allows you to store your wines at home, but it doesn't usually store nearly the number of bottles of a rental space. However, models range from a fifty-bottle capacity that fits nicely under a kitchen counter, to walk-in Brink's-style vaults that can house thousands of bottles. (Don't even think about keeping wine in a kitchen fridge for the long term; it's both too cold and too dry.)

If you've got the space and the money, a high-end fantasy cellar is almost as intoxicating as the wine in it. The options make the creative juices flow faster than anything Bacchus could pour: mood lighting to evoke a Tuscan sunset, a sink for rinsing glasses, antique furniture, limestone floors, carved doors, map drawers to show where the wines originated, and even imported Bordeaux dust to sprinkle on the bottles for that instant aged look. For these projects, it's best to hire a cellar consultant or home builder who has experience with cellars to assess your current space and the possibilities of expanding it.

Andrew and I didn't have the budget to build such a den of Dionysus. Besides, we wanted a piece of furniture—low-tech, handmade, and traditional—that would be an anchor point in our home. It would be something to celebrate the romance of wine, a Château d'Yquem for the eyes. Whom to call, though, to realize this vision? Then a friend mentioned Phil Entwhistle, who's a cabinetmaker the way Joe DiMaggio was a baseball player. We explained what we were looking for; and he created for us an eighteenth-century-style hand-carved design, with curling vines, leaves, and grapes.

The internal lattice to hold the bottles was made from California redwood, widely acknowledged to be the best wood for racking wine. It's naturally odor-free, doesn't require staining, resists rot and mildew, and is strong relative to its weight. However, it's illegal to cut these trees, many of which can grow to be two thousand years old and thirty feet across. So buyers must wait until they fall on their own. The temperature and humidity are controlled inside the cabinet, which holds three hundred bottles. Bottles from Burgundy and Champagne are slightly larger than others and didn't fit in the cabinet (or standard-sized racks), so we put them in our cold storage room, originally intended for root vegetables and preserves. (Other wine lovers have told me that they've even converted old bomb shelters for this purpose.) The conditions in the cold storage room were close enough to the ideal for aging.

Large-format bottles present the same challenge for standard racks and range in size from the magnum, which equals two standard bottles (1.5 liters), to the Nebuchadnezzar, the equivalent of twenty standard bottles and which holds a table-warping fifteen liters. You'll need either larger racks or the space to store them in their cases. Some collectors are keen on these large bottles because they believe that the wine ages more slowly, and therefore, more gracefully. The theory is that the small surface-to-volume ratio reduces oxidation. There's little documented evidence for this. The oxygen at the head of bottled wine gets absorbed into the wine during the first week after bottling. After that, only an insignificant one tenth of a cubic centimeter gets past the cork each year. Other collectors think that since big bottles heat up and cool down more slowly than standard bottles, they're less susceptible to damaging temperature fluctuations. There's no doubt, though, that large bottles make for a wonderful cellar showpiece and a visual splash on the table at large gatherings.

When our cabinet was finally installed in our living room, Andrew and I could only think about stocking it. We went a little wild at the liquor store, releasing years of repressed cravings to collect. As we added to our cache, we came to realize the truth about a universal phenomenon among wine lovers: your purchases will always expand to exceed your cellar capacity. The point of a good cellar is that it creates a flow of wine over a lifetime. (Like the turn-of-the-century industrialists who believed you should give your fortune to charity and die penniless, our aim is to leave this world just after finishing the last great bottle in the cellar—maybe a magnificent 1947 Château Cheval Blanc. It's all in the timing of course.) We had already decided that our cellar would be for drinking, not for collecting dust on trophy bottles.

It's an approach that would earn McInerney's approval. "There are those who collect wine to impress their friends, others collect to make money," McInerney tells me as we polish off our second glass of bubbly. He's full of kinetic energy, shifting from one position to another, his hands gesturing like two live wires touched together. "I collect for the pleasure of my own palate. There's no Platonic notion of perfection when it comes to wine. I think most people can intuitively sense what quality is, what they like to drink, if they just trust themselves."

By this time, we've both decided to order the four-course tasting menu. However, McInerney asks for cheese to follow, quoting Ernest Hemingway: "Anyone who eats dessert isn't drinking enough." He also orders a bottle of 2001 Condrieu from Andre Perret. The white wines from this tiny region in the northern Rhône are made exclusively from the viognier grape and are McInerney's favorites.

I try some along with my first course: a gentle purée of cooked hamachi pears, with cauliflower and yogurt dressing. McInerney has warm lettuce hearts, with marinated testina (sausage), a grapefruit confit, and a red-onion vinaigrette. The Condrieu pairs beautifully with both. The wine has rich layers of apricot and rose petals over a feral muskiness. It's full-bodied and unctuous as it rolls around my mouth.

"It's haunting, isn't it?" McInerney says, as we sip. "Like Kubla Khan's pleasure dome in Xanadu."

He tells me a little more about his wine-writing history. Even though he's been writing about bottled poetry since 1996, he still claims amateur status. "I'll always be an enthusiast," he says. "I don't have the discipline to be methodical. That's the problem with wine today: many people think you have to be an expert to enjoy it."

He mentions another of America's great wine enthusiasts: Thomas Jefferson. "He was one of the great amateurs—a dilettante in the best sense of the word," McInerney enthuses. "He was a politician, philosopher, musician, scientist, and amateur winemaker. He took back vine cuttings from Bordeaux to grow them at his home in Virginia." (Jefferson astutely observed the benefits of moderate wine drinking: "No nation is drunken where wine is cheap; and none sober, where the dearness of wine substitutes ardent spirits as the common beverage.")

From the outset, McInerney's goal was to write about wine from the point of view somewhere in between the experts and "the average person looking at a wine list and saying, 'Oh, shit,

what do I do now?'" He prefers to use allusions to art, literature, and music as descriptors, rather than relying on herbs,
flowers, and fruit. "I'm suspicious of the cornucopia of flavor
analogies that some wine critics come up with," he says. "I'm
often baffled when I read notes full of huckleberries and
hawthorn blossoms."

Instead, he likes to compare an Italian wine to a dark beauty
in a homemade dress, the smoldering Sicilian bride of Michael
Corleone, the son in *The Godfather*. The same metaphor allows
him to dismiss some California wines as more like the curva-
ceous lifeguards from the 1990s television show *Baywatch*: "one-
dimensional; their homogenous voluptuosity often has more to
do with technology than with nature."

He's also not much interested in the technical minutiae of
winemaking: "My eyes glaze over when the talk turns to vini-
fication specs." Rather, he's a romantic who likes to envision
grapes being picked by virgins in gossamer dresses. (He'd rather
not call the importer and dispel the illusion with the facts.)
He's very much interested in the place where the wine is made.
Sometimes, that puts him in Santenay, Burgundy, "looking out
at the valley beyond the Romanesque church, basking in the
May sunshine and listening to the bees." And other times, his
travels have taken him to Bordeaux, where he's "standing on
the terrace of [Bruno] Borie's eighteenth-century château in
Saint-Julien, looking out over the vineyards at the end of a hot
October day, contemplating the meal and the wines to come."

"Writing this column allowed me to justify my obsession,"
he says. "I was reading wine catalogs for fun. I forget where I
put my car keys, but I can remember where and when I drank
most of the wines I've had in my life."

What animates McInerney's writing about wine, as it does
his fiction, is his sharp eye for society. In the 1980s, one book

ullitle described him as one of the "cocaine novelists." In his novels, McInerney chronicles the manic nightclubbing world of that decade, with numerous references to "Bolivian Marching Powder."

However, he considers wine the best of the recreational vices. "Snorting cocaine, then drinking half a bottle of vodka, doesn't lead you anywhere; you don't even know you're drunk," he explains. "But wine can alter your mood in a different way: a more nuanced high. I'm channeling richer paths of hedonism. Wine makes me more thoughtful. I always want to taste the next thing, so it slows me down; I pace myself. Wine saved me from rehab."

As we finish our appetizers, he observes, "Wine has also led me to food. I can't imagine dinner without it, but I also can't imagine many wines without food. That's why I don't drink during the day, I save it for the evening." When he hosts dinner parties, they're of two kinds: for "wine wonks" and for "civilians." The former, he says, appreciate the staggering diversity of wine, and particularly rare bottles. The latter are happy with a good glass of vino, but don't think much about it—and certainly don't spend a good part of the dinner discussing it.

For me, it's also this social aspect of wine that gives it an edge over other types of collecting. "Come see my coin collection" just doesn't have the same warmth as "Come share some wine with me." Collecting wine also differs from almost any other type of collecting in that you destroy your collection even as you amass it (unless you never drink from your cellar). Collecting wine is as much about letting go as it is about gathering in. Maybe that's what makes wine lovers such feverish buyers: the drive to stay ahead of your consumption and the knowledge your collection will never be finished in the sense of owning all the works of a certain artist since there's always a new vintage.

There's also the aspect of collecting for your children. The traditional notion, especially in Britain, was that you drank the wines your father laid down for you, and you collected the wines your children would drink. It's a lovely idea, especially when you can buy wines from your children's birth years. A cellar may not make you immortal, but you will be remembered as they sip a great wine you bought for them twenty or thirty years ago.

McInerney celebrated the millennium with several great wines from his own birth year: the 1955 Château Mouton-Rothschild, Château Lafite-Rothschild, and Château Latour. He drank these wines at several memorable dinner parties in London with writers Julian Barnes, Auberon Waugh, Stephen Fry, Jancis Robinson, and her husband, Nick Lander. To celebrate the new year, they also drank the 1961 Cristal and 1976 Krug; California cult cabernets from Harlan, Pahlmeyer, and Bryant Family; and a 1928 Château d'Yquem.

At another such dinner, he encountered the 1955 Château La Mission Haut Brion. "I couldn't believe a wine could be that complete," he recalls. "It was like walking through a library and smelling the leather of the old books and then standing in the Colosseum and picking up the ancient rocks."

Of all the drinkers, writers, and collectors, Jancis Robinson and Robert Parker have had the strongest influence on McInerney. In *Bacchus & Me*, he writes, "Although Jancis tries her best to pretend that she's just another girl who likes to throw back a few glasses of vino, her presence at a dinner table definitely raises the level of discourse about wine. Even if you have a crush on her you can't help but learn a little in her company. And reading her book will make you feel like you're an expert."

He's equally enthusiastic about Parker, who, he says, "created an entire generation of enthusiasts in North America; he demystified French wines for us." McInerney talks about the second great American revolution—the one for wine in which Parker played the part of George Washington. "I trust Parker because he's crazy about drinking."

Unlike Parker, McInerney isn't keen on scoring wines and doesn't do so in his own columns. "Scores are a convenient fiction that we invent to get a grip on the subject," he declares. "How a wine tastes is different every time you try it. It can depend on how the wine has evolved, the barometric pressure, the mood you're in, the people you're with, the food you're eating. As Heraclitus said, you never step in the same river twice."

With an increasing feeling of kinship, we polish off the Condrieu with our second course: he has ruby shrimp with arrowhead cabbage, banana peppers, parsnip and pumpernickel consommé. I have scallops in a bisque of sweet onions and ale, alongside hon-shimeji mushroom and tatsoi with scallions.

As McInerney reads down through Cru's massive list in search of what we'll drink next, he offers his thoughts about the various vintages of Burgundy, Bordeaux, and other regions, with their historical weather conditions.

"Did you memorize the vintage charts?" I have to ask.

"No" he says, laughing. "But the more I drink, the more that information gets internalized."

McInerney advises keeping it simple: just remember the great worldwide vintages, such as 1985, 1990, and 1995. These are when most regions had a great year, with enough sun (and not too much rain) to ripen the grapes and develop their complexities. He warns against youthful vintages from France and Italy because part of their criteria for greatness is the ability to age. Knowing that, you can find some bargains on a restaurant list or for a short-term cellar. Such wines will fade fast, but they taste wonderful in their youth. (Vintage guidebooks, such as those by Hugh Johnson and Oz Clarke, can advise when to drink various wines.)

"Big vintages cost a lot more in restaurants, mostly because some drinkers fetishize them," McInerney says. "Look for the wines that give pleasure not just in big years. Find producers you love and stick with them, even through unfashionable vintages." In fact, some expensive wines are meant to be consumed early. A number of leading Californian producers make their wines to be drunk young. Their strength is their primary fruit, which fades over time. His only word of caution about such wines: "You have to be careful not to forget about them before they go south on you." It's true, I've made that mistake myself. In fact, I wish someone would invent a wine gadget called the Maturity Meter. It would chime softly as a bottle of wine in the cellar starts to approach its peak, then build to a full-scale house alarm when it's mature.

Bordeaux may have been McInerney's first love, but lately he's turned to burgundy. As he puts it, "Burgundy is more Watteau than Breughel, more Jaguar than Porsche." He orders a pinot noir from Burgundy, the Clos de la Bussiere 1997 Domaine Georges Roumier, a premier cru from Morey St. Denis. In his book, he describes drinking pinot as like "performing a sexual act that involves silk sheets, melted dark chocolate and black cherries, while the mingled scent of cinnamon, coffee and cola wafts through the air."

I feel more mystical about the wine once I taste the Roumier. (Then again, my thoughts that lie too deep for words may have more to do with the now vanished bubbly and Condrieu.) This wine searches through me, yet feels as though it's been there all along. I wonder if every wine we taste is really just a reaction to the previous one, which eventually chains back to our first experience. Like so many other things in life, do we spend our years trying to recapture the sensory wonder of that first taste?

McInerney observes, "Any idiot can buy expensive wines, but you need to know what you're doing to choose something delicious and reasonably priced."

"You mean like finding a designer suit in the department store bargain basement?" I ask.

"Exactly."

The main course arrives. McInerney has ordered the squab, which comes with spiced prunes, and braised eggplant with onions and parsley. I'm having the wagyu hangar steak, curried escarole with porcini, and sweet potato purée. The melting flavors of the food are divine with the burgundy. We've made a serious dent in the bottle and we're feeling quite festive.

Some wine lovers find bargains (or at least guaranteed prices and availability) by buying futures—wines not yet barreled. This is an especially good strategy for rare wines for which demand exceeds supply, such as Napa Valley cult cabernets, Super Tuscans, and first-growth Bordeaux châteaux. In France, futures are called *en primeur*. Since the wines are unavailable to taste, wine lovers buy them based on their enjoyment of previous vintages and the early reviews of critics.

Buy futures, though, only from reputable and long-established retailers or importers, since you need to pay a portion up front to secure your allocation. In Britain, a network of fake firms swindled millions of pounds from unwary consumers in what became known as the Claret Web. The fraud artists got hold of the shareholder lists of several public companies and then cold-called people, promising huge returns on wines for a small investment. The wines never materialized.

You can also get on some winery mailing lists to buy the wines. (This is more a New World phenomenon, as many wineries in France won't sell directly to consumers.)

However, this may take a while in some cases. Colgin Cellars in Napa Valley, for example, makes just a couple thousand cases of wine a year. According to owner Ann Colgin, it'll be three to five years before the twenty-five hundred people currently on her waiting list can buy the wine. It's not surprising that those who already have an allocation of the wine guard it fiercely. A few years ago, Colgin received a registered letter from a law firm in the Midwest. It was a copy of a divorce agreement from a couple on her mailing list, which declared that the wife would receive the Colgin allocation.

It's the rare and pricey bottles that also provoke the strangest behavior from collectors. I've heard about wine lovers naming their pets and even their children after the wine to curry favor with some vintners. Others have requests for their ashes to be scattered among the vines. Now McInerney tells me more tales of the lengths people will go to get onto the buying lists for rare wines. "One person told the winery he was only twenty and had cancer. It was his dying wish to drink the wine. It worked—but not when he tried it again the next year, still miraculously holding on to life and to his place on the list."

Nothing brings out the hunting instinct in a collector like a wine auction. These have been around for a while: In 1766, James Christie, in London, England, sold a large quantity of "Madeira and high flavour'd claret, late of the property of a noble personage deceas'd." Christie, of course, went on to found the eponymous auction house that's one of the world's largest, selling wine in the U.K., the United States, Canada, and several other countries.

Until recently, though, wine auctions (like wine drinking)

were the domain of rich, self-absorbed hedonists who could appreciate and afford expensive wines. Today, the popularity of wine auctions reflects the upswing in wine drinking across a broad social spectrum. In fact, auctions are now the frontal disturbances of the wine world, where vinous trends gain momentum like developing weather systems and popular bottles fetch stratospheric prices.

At auctions, most of the buzz is about record-shattering prices. In 2002, *Wine Spectator* reported on a Sotheby's auction: "Two collectors on the telephone battled over a lot of seven bottles of Domaine de la Romanée-Conti Montrachet 1978, estimated at $7,000–$10,000. The winning bid of $167,500 constituted the most expensive lot of 750 ml bottles ever sold at a commercial auction." Auctions for charity often attract even higher bids. At the annual Auction Napa Valley in 2000, in support of local causes, a six-liter bottle of the California cult cabernet Screaming Eagle sold for $500,000—that's $12,500 a glass.

McInerney has his own strategies for auctions. "You should look for the ugly ducklings: mixed cases of wines that don't interest serious collectors and restaurants, nor do unheralded vintages, lesser-known wines," he says. "Many American buyers tend to be sunshine patriots, buying only in great years." He also has some practical advice for auction newbies: the best time to attend is on a stormy night, "preferably when the phone lines are down so you don't have much competition bidding," he adds, smiling.

That aspect of rivalry is what thrills many wine fans. Auctions are about more than investing and collecting, or even fund-raising. Smelling and sipping wine may satisfy one's civilized nature, but only hunting and competing for a bottle can quiet those deeper atavistic urges. For them, the difference between buying wine and bidding for it is the same as the difference between picking up a frozen steak at the grocery store and tracking your kill on the Serengeti.

Besides, the tale of a successful acquisition results in a better story at dinner parties. The tale is even better if the bottle was previously owned by a celebrity. At a 1997 Sotheby's auction, Andrew Lloyd Webber's cellar of eighteen thousand bottles went for more than $6 million—an inflated price now known as the celebrity premium. (Of course, that doesn't guarantee the wines will taste good—just that its taste appeals to the man who gave us *Phantom of the Opera*.) In 2001, the remaining thirty-five cases of John F. Kennedy's cellar were sold for $95,335. The last lot in the collection on the block had seven bottles of 1963 Quinta do Noval port—from the year the president was assassinated.

Usually, McInerney is savvy enough to stay out of the bidding wars. Once, he remembers, he ignored his own advice, buying a 1970 Château Pétrus for $700. This was cheaper than its retail market price at the time, and more important, it was for a good cause: the Society for the Prevention of Cruelty to Children. In fact, wine auctions are usually efficient fund-raisers since appeasing the appetites of the elite is an excellent way to rally support for good causes. Unlike a check, a $100 bottle donated to the cause can raise more than its appraised value if bidders are willing to cooperate. Few people can afford a $450,000 impressionist painting, but many can spend $200 on a bottle of wine.

A word of caution, though: buying wine at auction isn't always a sound investment. Prices can swing wildly as fashions in taste change. A case of 1945 Mouton-Rothschild that sold for $81,700 in 1996 changed hands later the same year for only $51,750. Of course, if you buy the wines you like, you can always drink your liquid assets if the market collapses. That is, unless you end up with an expensive bottle of vinegar. Unlike other luxury goods, such as jewelry, fine art, and cars, wine is a fickle substance that needs careful handling. Auction organizers often don't guarantee the bottle's provenance, meaning who owned it and how it was kept before it goes on the block. Pristine provenance would mean that the bottle came straight from a winery, where it was kept in ideal cellar conditions. The next-best origin would be the private cellar of a meticulous owner whose wines were consigned to auction by uncultivated and dissolute heirs, who only wanted to cash in the estate and spend it all.

In reality, many mature wines have had several owners and have experienced varying storage conditions. These range from the merely bad (overheated kitchens, car trunks, attics) to the outrageous: I once saw an expensive bottle under hot bright lights in a store window, its label already peeling and discolored. So just as you might visit the stables before a horse race, check out auction bottles carefully at the preview. Look for "ullage," the air space between cork and wine. New bottles have gaps of less than an inch. After about fifteen years, some wine will evaporate through the cork, so a fill level to the bottle's top shoulder is acceptable. Below that could mean that enough air has seeped in to oxidize the wine and ruin it. A bottle or label that's stained with wine could also have been stored in conditions too hot, causing seepage.

Although McInerney himself doesn't buy wine as an investment, he knows people who do: some seek the thrill of trying to pick the winners, others speculate purely for profit. For instance, the prices of the top sixty-one Bordeaux châteaux have increased by some 12.3 percent a year, on average, ever since 1983, according to Mahesh Kumar, a finance professor at Mount Royal College in Calgary. That return is greater than for the bond market and most stocks. The professor goes so far as to say that fine wine should be part of a diversified investment portfolio. He's even created a Fine Wine 50 Index to highlight the wines with the strongest track records. But wine investing is far from a sure thing. Those occasional stratospheric prices may grab the headlines, but most wines don't command such gains. Those that do are rare or obscure, which makes them hard to buy in the first place. Besides, cyclical periods of overproduction can soften worldwide prices unpredictably.

To top it off, the resale market for wine is actually quite illiquid. For one thing, fine wines, such as bordeaux and port, can require from ten to twenty-five years of aging. And unlike other assets, they don't pay interest or dividends in the interim. The only way to realize any gain is to sell the wine, but the timing has to be right. Wine prices peak about six to eighteen months after release; then again at maturity, when the wine is ready to drink; and then one last time in old age, once the wine has become rare—if it's still drinkable.

In the meantime, storing, protecting, and tracking your wine doesn't necessarily come cheap. Some collectors go high-tech, with computerized alarm systems that page the owner in the event of a break-in or power failure. There's also a simple solution: use a thermometer that shows the existing temperature and records the daily maximum and minimum temperatures. Other collectors install computers in their cellar with high-speed Internet connections to pull up wine reviews from the Web, keep online logs of their cache, and send gloating e-mails to absent friends. Tracking your collection can also be simple in a notebook or a spreadsheet.

Whether you stock your cellar hoping for dazzling profit or

for having a good bottle on hand, you want to be sure it's good stuff. That means, particularly if you buy at auction, that you're wary of fraud. Wine is a natural target for fakery: it combines an aura of sophistication with a substantial price tag. (Substituted wine costs only a few bucks, giving counterfeiters a nice profit margin when they sell it as fine wine.) In 2002, a gang of counterfeiters in China relabeled $200 bottles of wine as 1982 Château Lafite-Rothschild, which sells for up to $5,700 a pop, and then sold them for $1,100. Customs agents eventually seized more than seven hundred bottles, but weren't sure how many more bottles had already been sold before the raid. Sometimes, the only method needed to spot a fake is a sound education in spelling. On several phony bottles of 1990 Penfold's Grange, the word *pour* was spelled as *poor.*

As McInerney and I finish off the Roumier, he sits back thoughtfully and says, "This is why I could never be a socialist: I enjoy the good life too much." His features have softened with the liquid relaxation of the evening. He compliments me on my ability to hold my liquor. I tell him that I'm not affluenced by incohol.

We leave the restaurant and walk out into the nudging shadows. The dark contours of the buildings on Fifth Avenue are haloed from the lights behind them. Drifting on the night air is the scent of freshly baked bread. I'm reminded of the end of *Bright Lights, Big City,* where the hero trades his flashy Ray•Ban sunglasses for a loaf of bread, symbolizing his new quest for the authentic. McInerney, and all of us who love alcoholic grape juice, are on a parallel search for wine that tells us where it's from, who made it, and even who we are in drinking it. Fortunately, finding these wines is a journey that lasts a lifetime.

A Finish That Begins Again

WRITING A BOOK about wine was something I'd always thought I'd tackle much later in my life, when I'd have enough experience to feel confident. But after launching my Web site, www.nataliemaclean.com, and e-newsletter, Nat Decants, I received such an unexpected level of interest from my readers that I decided to do so much earlier. I didn't want to leave their excellent questions unanswered for many years.

Once I was committed to the project, I faced several challenges. For one thing, I hadn't traveled to many of the world's great wine regions because I started writing while I was on maternity leave—I wanted to stay close to my son during his early years. In fact, before I began this book, I hadn't been to French wine regions at all. So my stories here from Burgundy and Champagne are based on my first experiences of those places. Some might say that a neophyte should wait for more layered experience before writing about it, but to my mind, first visits make the deepest impressions. Certainly, there was the excitement of seeing everything with new eyes—and the panic of getting lost on the busy highways (and of asking for directions with shaking hands and rusty French).

My other challenge was to write a wine book that didn't need updating every year. I wanted to be practical, but not specific. I hoped to give readers advice and insights they could use, but not to recommend wines that would be unavailable in stores the following year. Even though rare and expensive wines make great stories, with their long histories and attentive owners, I know that you (like me) probably won't be cracking open a bottle of Romanée-Conti with tonight's spaghetti.

I had no idea how many people were thirsting for delicious but affordable wines. Within a month of the launch of my newsletter, I had more than two hundred subscribers. (On the Internet, word of mouth spreads faster than vine disease.) Every two weeks, I sent out some wine picks, along with tips on enjoying wine and information about upcoming events. New people kept subscribing and asking for copies of past newsletters. After three months of this, I found I was spending most of my time on e-mail. So I decided to archive my articles and wine picks on the Web site I created. I've since posted more than a thousand links to cellar consultants, vintage charts, wine accessories, food-matching advice, wine-region tour guides, producers and retailers, clubs and courses, industry jobs, wine-related charities, and my favorite wine books and movies.

Today, more than fifty thousand wine lovers in thirty-six countries subscribe to *Nat Decants*. I plan to keep my newsletter free so that it'll continue to grow quickly and reach a broad audience. The diversity of the readership is proof that wine truly is for everyone. Among the readers who have written to me are a customs inspector in Paris, an emergency night nurse in Toronto, a storm-water reservoir manager in Tulsa, a florist in Dijon, an IRS auditor in Washington, and a teacher in London. One subscriber from Chicago is blind, but he listens to my newsletter on his specially equipped computer, which reads it aloud to him. He hopes to become a sommelier.

In 2003 and 2005, my newsletter was nominated as one of the

three best in North America by the James Beard Foundation. Those journalism awards are considered the Oscars of food and wine writing, so naturally I was thrilled, especially since *Nat Decants* was the first electronic newsletter ever to receive such recognition.

More important than the honor, though, is that my newsletter keeps me grounded with readers. I get a couple hundred e-mails every day, so I know immediately when I've struck a chord. (And when I've goofed: now I know without a doubt that not all wine regions in Australia are warm, after 236 readers corrected me on it.) Some days, I feel as though I have a fiber-optic cable attached to my nervous system. The Internet has formed me as a writer: it gives me a nanosecond appreciation of what makes wine lovers passionate.

That sense of connectedness with my readers was also one of the things that gave me the confidence to write this book. At least, I knew I was addressing some of the important questions. I'm happy with the effort, but even 274 pages later, I know I've barely grazed the subject. This book is like an evening breeze that ruffles the tops of the vine leaves but doesn't disturb the middle.

There's so much more I want to write about. I'd like to explore other parts of France, not to mention other countries such as Canada, Australia, New Zealand, Chile, Germany, and Italy. I'd like to expand on wine-and-food matching, look at the new approaches to marketing wine, and dive into the influences of popular culture. Above all, I want to continue searching for the words to describe the widening of this world through wine's beauty and pleasure.

I'd love to hear from you. Let me know what interests you, puzzles you, irks you, impassions you. I invite you to visit my Web site, e-mail me your thoughts, and join my newsletter group.

The journey continues. Join me.

ACKNOWLEDGMENTS

Writing these acknowledgments was actually the toughest part of this book. How could I make this text beat like my grateful heart? Listing names seems so inadequate, so I hope that we can all get together for some great glasses of wine—that's the only way I can convey my deepest thanks to the people to whom I owe so much.

I couldn't have written any of these stories without the help of the generous souls who invited me into their wineries, their stores, their restaurants, and their thoughts: Aubert de Villaine, Lalou Bize-Leroy, Anne-Claude Leflaive, Frédéric Drouhin, Randall Grahm, Camille Seghesio, Pete Seghesio, Frédéric Panaïotis, Delphine Cazals, Martine Lorson, Christian Dennis, Gérard Liger-Belair, Marianne Barbier, Thierry Gasco, Jancis Robinson MW, Robert Parker, Kermit Lynch, Chuck Hayward, Ellisa Cooper, Georg Riedel, Robyn Osgood, Shelley Page, Shirley McGregor-Ford, Natasha Thiessen, Debi Rosati, Debbie Trenholm, Lisa Courtney-Lloyd, Danielle Dupont, and Jay McInerney.

In a book about wine, especially your first one, there are thousands of facts that you can screw up. I'd like to thank everyone who saved me from embarrassment with their technical expertise and nuanced understanding of this subject. A toast to: Steve Beckta, Dave Brackett, James Chatto, Kent Currie, Evan Goldstein MS, Elspeth Murray, Véronique Rivest, Igor Ryjenkov MW, Brian Schmidt, Larry Stone MS, John Szabo MS, Debbie Trenholm, and Greg Tresner MS. Their comments and corrections made me realize how much more I still have to learn about wine. Any remaining errors are entirely my own.

I am also deeply indebted to all those who patiently answered round after round of my questions: Michael Aaron, Laurent Barbier, Eric Benn, Jacques Berthomeau, Michael Brajkovich MW, Brigitte Batonnet, Phil Bilodeau, Nathalie Bloch-Marlet, Robert Bohr, Donald Bull, Phillip Casella, Jean-Marie Chadronnier, Ann Colgin, Bill Deutsch, Dr. Curt Ellison, Marc Engel, Mario Evangelista, Cécile Fichet, Paul Freese, Kristin Gelder, John Gillespie, Charles Goemaere, Jamie Goode, Charles Grieco, Paige Granback, Frédéric Heidsieck, Gladys Horiuchi, Julie Ann Kodmur, Mahesh Kumar, Rémi Krug, Dr. Adrienne Lehrer, Dr. Larry Lockshin, Angela Lyons, Christian Maille, Tom Matthews, François Mauss, Elin McCoy, Dr. Carole Meredith, Dr. David Mills, Dr. Ann Noble, Renate Peer, Joel Peterson, Marie-Emmanuelle Peyronne, Dr. Serge Renaud, Mary Ellen Ryan, Delphine Rigall, Michel Rolland, Veronique Sanders, Floribeth Schumacher, Margaret Stern, Kristina Streeter, Jan Stuebing, Sean Thackrey, Mary Ann Vangrin, Dr. Andrew Waterhouse, and Dr. Paul White.

For their assistance with the daunting task of planning the logistics of my trips abroad, I would like to acknowledge the help of Nelly Blau Picard, Sam Heitner, Marie-Elaine Hvizdak, Paula Oreskovich, Florence Raffard, Margaret Shepard, Philippe Wibrotte, and Kim Wiss.

I would be a jellyfish without the backbone of my supportive assistants, Daisy Marcellana and Erin Bolling. Their incredible work ethic allowed me to focus on this book.

I'd like to thank the editors in my journalistic life who have given me a shot at this career: Rosa Harris-Adler, Arjun Basu, Selby Bateman, Iris Benaroia, Val Berenyi, Roger Bird, Ann Brocklehurst, Sarah Brown, Rosanna Caira, John Clark, Dré Dee, David Dehaas, Donna Dooher, Jody Dunn, Barbara Fairchild, Lianne George, Line Goguen-Hughes, Jim Gourlay, Pat Holtz, Jaimie Hubbard, Carol Jankowski, Randy Johnson, Carolyn Kennedy, Peggy McKee, Sheilagh McEvenue, Liz Mezaros, Linda Murphy, Liz Payne, Charlene Rooke, Rita Silvan, Trish Snyder, Tanya Steel, Andrea Stewart, Beth Tomkiw, Kylie Walker, and Heather White. They helped me to hone my craft and gave me the confidence to take on this project.

In a category of her own is Antonia Morton, whom I affectionately call my personal word trainer. Antonia has read everything I have ever written professionally—buffing and polishing it before the world saw it.

This book would never have been conceived without the enthusiastic support of my publishers Mary Davis, Rosemary Davidson, Colin Dickerman, Brad Martin, Maya Mavjee, Karen Rinaldi, and Jacqueline Smit. They were all remarkably visionary to see what could be created from the original proposal.

I owe an incalculable debt (and many great bottles) to my editors Kathy Belden and Lara Hinchberger, who prodded, praised, coaxed, and consoled me along with their impeccable good taste and judgment. I couldn't have asked for better guidance.

Steve Boldt and Greg Villepique did a masterful job of copy-editing the manuscript. Without the suggested title from Panio Gianopoulos, this book might have been called *A Book About Wine*. Once the book was finished, publicists Maya Baran, Stephanie Gowan, and Sara Mercurio breathed new life into it with their supreme media relations skills. Also making essential contributions to this project were Brian Ajhar, Randy Chan, Lisa Charters, Kristin Cochrane, Barb Dunn, Ron Eckel, Sabrina Farber, Marlene Fraser, Mike Fuhr, Val Gow, Amy King, and Annik Lafarge.

I am grateful to my agent, Jackie Kaiser, who believed in this book from the beginning, back when it was just a glint on a wineglass. Her delight in words is contagious. Jackie is, and always has been, steadfast and gracious.

On a personal note, I'd especially like to thank my mother, Ann MacLean, my husband, Andrew Waitman, and my son, Rian—all of whom have lived with this manuscript for so long that they have it memorized. I'm grateful to my mom for so many things (starting with my DNA). She voluntarily came out of retirement to be my full-time fact-checker when she wasn't moonlighting as my emotional counselor. When I grow up, I hope to be as dignified and decent as she is. Andrew has always believed in my career—at times, more than I did myself. He is the guardian angel of this book and of my dreams. And then there is Rian, whose name I cannot say without feeling hugged. Thank you, my precious son, for bringing such joy into my life and for spending so many hours playing quietly alone beside my desk because Mommy had to write *just one more page.*

I raise my glass to you all!

Natalie MacLean is an accredited sommelier and publishes her free e-newsletter, *Nat Decants,* at www.nataliemaclean.com. She has won numerous awards, among them four James Beard Journalism Awards, including the MFK Fisher Distinguished Writing Award; five IACP Bert Greene Awards; four Association of Food Journalists Awards; and four North America Travel Journalists Association Awards; and she was named the World's Best Drink Writer. Her work has appeared in *Best Food Writing,* and she has written for *Bon Appétit, Chatelaine, EnRoute, Food & Wine, Saltscapes, Wine Enthusiast,* and many others. A Rhodes Scholarship finalist and champion Scottish Highland dancer, Natalie lives with her husband and son outside of Ottawa.